Crisis, Movement, Management: Globalising Dynamics

Globalised neo-liberalism has produced multiple crises – social, ecological and political. In the past, crises of global order have generated large-scale social transformations, and the current crises likewise hold a transformative promise. Social movements become a crucial barometer, in signalling both the demise and rise of political formations and programs. Elite strategies, framed as crisis management, create their own disordering side-effects. Experiments in movement strategy gain greater significance, as do contending elite efforts at repressing, managing or displacing the fall-out. In this book we investigate both movements and management in the face of crisis, taking crisis and unanticipated consequences as a normal state-of-play. The book enquires into the winners and losers from crisis, and investigates the movement-management nexus as it unfolds in particular localities as well as in broader contexts.

The book deals with some of the most pressing conflicts of our time, and produces a range of theoretical insights: the ubiquity of crisis is seen as not only a hallmark of social life, but a way into a different kind of social analysis.

This book was published as a special issue of *Globalizations*.

James Goodman researches social movements and globalization with a focus on global justice and climate change. He lectures at the University of Technology, Sydney. He is co-author of *Justice Globalism: Ideology, Crises, Policy* (Sage 2013), and *Climate Upsurge: The Ethnography of Climate Movement Politics* (Routledge 2013), and *Disorder and the Disinformation Society* (Routledge 2014).

Jonathan Paul Marshall is an anthropologist who primarily focuses on issues of technology, society and disorder. He works as a Researcher at the University of Technology, Sydney. He is author of *Living on Cybermind: Categories, Communication and Control* (Peter Lang 2007), and co-author of *Disorder and the Disinformation Society* (Routledge 2014).

Rethinking Globalizations
Edited by Barry K. Gills, Newcastle University, UK

This series is designed to break new ground in the literature on globalization and its academic and popular understanding. Rather than perpetuating or simply reacting to the economic understanding of globalization, this series seeks to capture the term and broaden its meaning to encompass a wide range of issues and disciplines and convey a sense of alternative possibilities for the future.

1. Whither Globalization?
The vortex of knowledge and globalization
James H. Mittelman

2. Globalization and Global History
Edited by Barry K. Gills and William R. Thompson

3. Rethinking Civilization
Communication and terror in the global village
Majid Tehranian

4. Globalization and Contestation
The new great counter-movement
Ronaldo Munck

5. Global Activism
Ruth Reitan

6. Globalization, the City and Civil Society in Pacific Asia
Edited by Mike Douglass, K.C. Ho and Giok Ling Ooi

7. Challenging Euro-America's Politics of Identity
The return of the native
Jorge Luis Andrade Fernandes

8. The Global Politics of Globalization
"Empire" vs "Cosmopolis"
Edited by Barry K. Gills

9. The Globalization of Environmental Crisis
Edited by Jan Oosthoek and Barry K. Gills

10. Globalization as Evolutionary Process
Modeling global change
Edited by Geroge Modelski, Tessaleno Devezas and William R. Thompson

11. The Political Economy of Global Security
War, future crises and changes in global governance
Heikki Patomäki

12. Cultures of Globalization
Coherence, hybridity, contestation
Edited by Kevin Archer, M. Martin Bosman, M. Mark Amen and Ella Schmidt

13. **Globalization and the Global Politics of Justice**
Edited by Barry K. Gills

14. **Global Economy Contested**
Power and conflict across the international division of labor
Edited by Marcus Taylor

15. **Rethinking Insecurity, War and Violence**
Beyond savage globalization?
Edited by Damian Grenfell and Paul James

16. **Recognition and Redistribution**
Beyond international development
Edited by Heloise Weber and Mark T. Berger

17. **The Social Economy**
Working alternatives in a globalizing era
Edited by Hasmet M. Uluorta

18. **The Global Governance of Food**
Edited by Sara R. Curran, April Linton, Abigail Cooke and Andrew Schrank

19. **Global Poverty, Ethics and Human Rights**
The role of multilateral organisations
Desmond McNeill and Asunción Lera St. Clair

20. **Globalization and Popular Sovereignty**
Democracy's transnational dilemma
Adam Lupel

21. **Limits to Globalization**
North-South divergence
William R. Thompson and Rafael Reuveny

22. **Globalisation, Knowledge and Labour**
Education for solidarity within spaces of resistance
Edited by Mario Novelli and Anibel Ferus-Comelo

23. **Dying Empire**
U.S. imperialism and global resistance
Francis Shor

24. **Alternative Globalizations**
An integrative approach to studying dissident knowledge in the global justice movement
S. A. Hamed Hosseini

25. **Global Restructuring, Labour and the Challenges for Transnational Solidarity**
Edited by Andreas Bieler and Ingemar Lindberg

26. **Global South to the Rescue**
Emerging humanitarian superpowers and globalizing rescue industries
Edited by Paul Amar

27. **Global Ideologies and Urban Landscapes**
Edited by Manfred B. Steger and Anne McNevin

28. **Power and Transnational Activism**
Edited by Thomas Olesen

29. **Globalization and Crisis**
Edited by Barry K. Gills

30. **Andre Gunder Frank and Global Development**
Visions, remembrances and explorations
Edited by Patrick Manning and Barry K. Gills

31. **Global Social Justice**
Edited by Heather Widdows and Nicola J. Smith

32. **Globalization, Labor Export and Resistance**
A study of Filipino migrant domestic workers in global cities.
Ligaya Lindio-McGovern

33. **Situating Global Resistance**
Between Discipline and Dissent
Edited by Lara Montesinos Coleman and Karen Tucker

34. **A History of World Order and Resistance**
The Making and Unmaking of Global Subjects
André C. Drainville

35. **Migration, Work and Citizenship in the New Global Order**
Edited by Ronaldo Munck, Carl-Ulrik Schierup and Raúl Delgado Wise

36. **Edges of Global Justice**
The World Social Forum and Its 'Others'
Janet Conway

37. **Land Grabbing and Global Governance**
Edited by Matias E. Margulis, Nora McKeon and Saturnino Borras Jr.

38. **Dialectics in World Politics**
Edited by Shannon Brincat

39. **Crisis, Movement, Management: Globalising Dynamics**
Edited by James Goodman and Jonathan Paul Marshall

40. **China's Development**
Capitalism and Empire
Michel Aglietta and Guo Bai

41. **Global Governance and NGO Participation**
Charlotte Dany

42. **Arab Revolutions and World Transformations**
Edited by Anna M. Agathangelou and Nevzat Soguk

43. **Global Movement**
Edited by Ruth Reitan

44. **Free Trade and the Transnational Labour Movement**
Edited by Andreas Bieler, Bruno Ciccaglione, John Hilary and Ingemar Lindberg

45. **Counter-Globalization and Socialism in the 21st Century**
The Bolivarian Alliance for the Peoples of our America
Thomas Muhr

46. **Global Civil Society and Transversal Hegemony**
The Globalization-Contestation Nexus
Karen M. Buckley

47. **Contentious Agency and Natural Resource Politics**
Markus Kröger

48. **Social Movements, the Poor and the New Politics of the Americas**
Edited by Håvard Haarstad, Mark Amen and Asuncion Lera St Clair

49. **Development in an Era of Neoliberal Globalization**
Edited by Henry Veltmeyer

Crisis, Movement, Management: Globalising Dynamics

Edited by

James Goodman & Jonathan Paul Marshall

LONDON AND NEW YORK

First published 2014
by Routledge
2 Park Square, Milton Park, Abingdon, Oxfordshire OX14 4RN

and by Routledge
711 Third Avenue, New York, NY 10017

First issued in paperback 2015

Routledge is an imprint of the Taylor & Francis Group, an informa business

© 2014 Taylor & Francis

All rights reserved. No part of this book may be reprinted or reproduced or utilised in any form or by any electronic, mechanical, or other means, now known or hereafter invented, including photocopying and recording, or in any information storage or retrieval system, without permission in writing from the publishers.

Trademark notice: Product or corporate names may be trademarks or registered trademarks, and are used only for identification and explanation without intent to infringe.

British Library Cataloguing in Publication Data
A catalogue record for this book is available from the British Library

ISBN 13: 978-1-138-95115-0 (pbk)
ISBN 13: 978-0-415-62835-8 (hbk)

Typeset in Times New Roman
by Taylor & Francis Books

Publisher's Note
The publisher accepts responsibility for any inconsistencies that may have arisen during the conversion of this book from journal articles to book chapters, namely the possible inclusion of journal terminology.

Disclaimer
Every effort has been made to contact copyright holders for their permission to reprint material in this book. The publishers would be grateful to hear from any copyright holder who is not here acknowledged and will undertake to rectify any errors or omissions in future editions of this book.

Contents

Citation Information	ix
1. Introduction: Crisis, Movement and Management in Contemporary Globalisations *James Goodman & Jonathan Paul Marshall*	1

Section 1 - Management

2. The Hydra Paradox: Global Disaster Management in a World of Crises *Bob Hodge*	13
3. Communication Failure and the Financial Crisis *Jonathan Paul Marshall*	25
4. The Rigidity Trap in Global Resilience: Neoliberalisation Through Principles, Standards, and Benchmarks *Peter Rogers*	41
5. 'Who is Grace?': Affect, Work, and Gender in Bangalore Call Centres *Devleena Ghosh*	55
6. The 'Green Economy': Class Hegemony and Counter-Hegemony *James Goodman & Ariel Salleh*	69

Section 2 - Movement

7. Occupy Cosmopolitanism: Ideological Transversalization in the Age of Global Economic Uncertainties *S. A. Hamed Hosseini*	83
8. Crisis Is Where We Live: Environmental Justice for the Anthropocene *Donna Houston*	97
9. Global Justice Organising in Australia: Crisis and Realignment after 9/11 *Elizabeth Humphrys*	109
10. Reinscribing the City: Art, Occupation and Citizen Journalism in Hong Kong *Francesca da Rimini*	123
11. Religious Globalisms in the Post-Secular Age *Erin K. Wilson & Manfred B. Steger*	139
Index	155

Citation Information

The chapters in this book were originally published in *Globalizations*, volume 10, issue 3 (June 2013). When citing this material, please use the original page numbering for each article, as follows:

Chapter 1
Introduction: Crisis, Movement and Management in Contemporary Globalisations
James Goodman & Jonathan Paul Marshall
Globalizations, volume 10, issue 3 (June 2013) pp. 343-354

Chapter 2
The Hydra Paradox: Global Disaster Management in a World of Crises
Bob Hodge
Globalizations, volume 10, issue 3 (June 2013) pp. 355-366

Chapter 3
Communication Failure and the Financial Crisis
Jonathan Paul Marshall
Globalizations, volume 10, issue 3 (June 2013) pp. 367-382

Chapter 4
The Rigidity Trap in Global Resilience: Neoliberalisation Through Principles, Standards, and Benchmarks
Peter Rogers
Globalizations, volume 10, issue 3 (June 2013) pp. 383-396

Chapter 5
'Who is Grace?': Affect, Work, and Gender in Bangalore Call Centres
Devleena Ghosh
Globalizations, volume 10, issue 3 (June 2013) pp. 397-410

Chapter 6
The 'Green Economy': Class Hegemony and Counter-Hegemony
James Goodman & Ariel Salleh
Globalizations, volume 10, issue 3 (June 2013) pp. 411-424

CITATION INFORMATION

Chapter 7
Occupy Cosmopolitanism: Ideological Transversalization in the Age of Global Economic Uncertainties
S. A. Hamed Hosseini
Globalizations, volume 10, issue 3 (June 2013) pp. 425-438

Chapter 8
Crisis Is Where We Live: Environmental Justice for the Anthropocene
Donna Houston
Globalizations, volume 10, issue 3 (June 2013) pp. 439-450

Chapter 9
Global Justice Organising in Australia: Crisis and Realignment after 9/11
Elizabeth Humphrys
Globalizations, volume 10, issue 3 (June 2013) pp. 451-464

Chapter 10
Reinscribing the City: Art, Occupation and Citizen Journalism in Hong Kong
Francesca da Rimini
Globalizations, volume 10, issue 3 (June 2013) pp. 465-480

Chapter 11
Religious Globalisms in the Post-Secular Age
Erin K. Wilson & Manfred B. Steger
Globalizations, volume 10, issue 3 (June 2013) pp. 481-495

Please direct any queries you may have about the citations to
clsuk.permissions@cengage.com

INTRODUCTION

Crisis, Movement and Management in Contemporary Globalisations

JAMES GOODMAN & JONATHAN PAUL MARSHALL
University of Technology Sydney, Australia

ABSTRACT *Globalised neoliberalism has produced multiple crises, social, ecological, political. In the past, crises of global order have generated large-scale social transformations, and the current crises likewise hold a transformative promise. Elite strategies, framed as crisis management, seek to exploit crisis for deepened neoliberalism. The failure of elite policy to address the causes of crisis creates new forms of politicisation. Social movements become a crucial barometer, in signalling both the demise and rise of political formations and programs. Experiments in movement strategy gain greater significance, as do contending elite efforts at repressing, managing, or displacing the fall-out. In this Special Issue we investigate both management and movements in the face of crisis, taking crisis and unanticipated consequences as a normal state of play. The issue enquires into the winners and losers from crisis, and investigates the movement–management nexus as it unfolds in particular localities as well as in broader contexts. The Special Issue deals with pressing conflicts, and produces a range of theoretical insights: the ubiquity of crisis is seen as not only a hallmark of social life, but a way into a different kind of social analysis.*

Societies are today intimately drawn into the growing crisis-prone logic of the world system. Crisis arises from an internal malignancy, not from an external shock, and originates conceptually in the idea of a physiological turning point arising from disease. The globalisation of crisis, then, involves conflicts and contradictions at the heart of the global condition. Any attempts at addressing crisis raise the question of how to cure the 'disease' from which we are suffering. Moving from the analogy, to the social formation, crises are caused by internal structural conflicts and cannot be cured without structural change. The key question is how to characterise these conflicts, and what kind of political action can bring them to the fore, so they can be confronted and acted on (Goodman, 2011). Given that we live in capitalist society the conflicts that have most capacity to throw societies into crisis today are those that result from the process of capitalist accumulation. Capitalist accumulation relies upon the process of commodification, and it is in this process we find the most pervasive global crises coming into play. The global social crisis arising from inequality, for instance, has its origins in the appropriation of surplus from the production and sale of commodities and the relatively weak power of labour (Ghosh, 2013, this issue; Hosseini, 2013, this issue). Ecological crisis arises from the impacts of resource extraction and commodity production on nature: O'Connor's 'second contradiction of capitalism' (O'Connor, 1998; Goodman and Salleh, 2013, this issue; Houston, 2013, this issue). Financial crisis arises from conflicts and rivalries between contending centres of economic power, as Arrighi showed, it is no accident that financialisation follows hegemonic decline and transition (Arrighi, 1994; Marshall, 2013, this issue). Each of these types of conflict sees social forces brought into collision, and reflects deep contradictions within the fabric of society. Importantly, the process of capitalist accumulation produces these crises simultaneously—one or other may be more dominant, but it is the interaction between contradictions that generates the crisis of crises, the 'hydra' that we are faced with today (Hodge, 2013, this issue). A crisis of crises opens up broader existential questions, and can evoke civilisational challenges requiring a fundamental epistemological, or indeed, spiritual shift, perhaps as posed by indigenous or religious perspectives on future possibilities (Houston, 2013, this issue; Wilson and Steger, 2013, this issue).

If crisis is indeed understood as a manifestation of contradiction, then any action by the authorities to mitigate crisis or to 'crisis manage', will itself alter the terms of engagement and create new potential for politicisation. Responding to crisis, however framed, even as a non-response, alters the structural context, and is in this sense generative. In 2010 this journal published a Special Issue on 'Globalization and Crisis' that drew together a series of critiques addressing the multiplying logic of global crises, and how they relate with new 'alter-hegemonic' agendas. As such, the Issue took a broadly dialectical reading to understanding crisis, which looked to alternative possibilities that counter the dominant script. Whether understood as a crisis of neoliberalism, of capitalism or of civilisation, the process can be viewed as dialectical and potentially generative. As the Introduction to that Special Issue stated, 'we can remake this world, and it is the crisis(es) that compels us to do so' (Gills, 2010, p. 8). This Special Issue seeks to continue this discussion, defining the generative process as enabling new modes of capitalist managerialism, as well as solidaristic social movement challenges 'from below'.

Crisis Management and Movements

As reflected in the concept of 'disaster capitalism', crisis is in the first instance generative for capitalism (Klein, 2008). Implosions offer opportunities for accumulation and expansion. The 'barbarism' of capitalist competition, 'red in tooth and claw', is a key feature of our current global society. What may be rational self-seeking behaviour for a profit-maximising financier, for instance, can be barbarous for the system as a whole, rendering the whole process informationally flawed and 'irrational' (Marshall, 2013, this issue). Producing crises of social inequality and ecological degradation, and then profiting from them, is symptomatic. Colonial imperialism was an early model; financial securitisation is a more recent manifestation. Yet at the same time, the struggle to manage crisis for accumulation has become a central in-built dynamic of the world system.

Paradoxically (and ironically), crisis management is aimed at maintaining the conditions that generate crisis, hence the persistent 'fertility' of crisis tendencies (Hodge, 2013, this issue). These managerial efforts can never address internal contradictions, even if this was the hope or intent: as clearly demonstrated by global climate policy there is no agency able, or competent, to act in the interests of the system as a whole. Instead, as exemplified in the notion of a 'carbon credit', crisis managerialism serves more often to securitise and commodify the symptoms, and displace risks. Within the financial sector, the process of dispersing and profiting from risk has gained its own 'securitisation' terminology. More broadly from the 1990s flexibilisation became the dominant euphemism for displacing risk onto subordinates (see Fraser, 2003). Twenty years later the rhetoric of flexibilisation is now superseded by notions of resilience. Resilience—as against flexibility—betrays the permanency of disruption and normalcy of crisis, as a negative condition to be accommodated (Rogers, 2013, this issue). The demand for resilience is transnationalised as the increased globalisation of capitalist relations sets one set of social relations against another. At the macro level this accumulation-by-dispossession creates and exploits widening global divides (Harvey, 2003). At the micro level, super-exploitation is naturalised as a process of realising modern freedoms, and an idealised affective 'modernity', especially for instance, for women working in the call centres of Bangalore (Ghosh, 2013, this issue).

The crisis may create opportunities for managerialism, but it also creates possibilities for movements. In the context of crisis, social movements and political forces can find new traction, themselves imperilled by crisis and compelled into mobilisation. For movements, crises offer the possibility of delegitimising and upending a social order that has self-evidently failed. Movements seek to offer solutions that grapple with the causes of crisis, and in the process seek to unmask official responses as self-serving and counter-productive. As the official solutions fail, and the problems recur, crisis can undermine accumulation itself. Ironically, in these circumstances, the movement can come to indirectly assist the authorities in offering pathways for reform. Such reform is by definition within capitalism, but may at least be a type of 'non-reformist reform' that points in the direction of more transformative avenues, rather than closing them down (Bond, 2008). In these contexts of official disarray, for instance on climate change, movements can move to the centre of policy debate. The crucial component is the sense of rudderless confusion among those exercising power. When the ruling elites no longer know how to rule, movements can begin to gain leverage. To put the same point differently, it is only when the fundamental social contradictions become politically irresistible that we see movements realising their full potential.

In these movements political change can take on a new urgency. The political backwash from failed solutions is here felt as a crisis of system legitimacy. Amid the wreckage of global governance what was once consigned as impossible or utopian can quickly become possible and realistic. Given the character of crisis, though, the stakes can become very high, even existential. The failures of elite policy produce 'gravediggers', not just for the elites, but for all societies, and for the ecosystem as a whole (Goodman and Salleh, 2013, this issue). Nature's 'revenge' transmutes into the apprehension of an endgame, and not just for capitalism (Johnston et al., 2006). In the context of the Anthropocene especially, the world historical dialectic and with it the question of agency is dramatically reframed (Chakrabarty, 2009; Houston, 2013, this issue). In the Gramscian formulation, the pessimism of the intellect requires optimism of the will. As Mike Davis argues, pessimism about advancing climate change is unavoidable, but it also forces an 'optimism of the imagination' that creates sites for agency and capacity to address the crisis (Davis, 2010).

Agency, by definition, is an exercise in construction; it develops in action—it is 'willed' in the Gramscian sense and is never a given, whether 'from above' or 'from below'. Crises have a specific ideological logic that sets the frame for this process of construction, tilting it in favour of movements, which involve those who directly experience the crisis. Crisis creates new realities and possibilities by 'lifting the veil' and exposing the inner logic of the system: it is 'apocalyptic' in the sense of revealing the inner failings of the system. The perennial question, though, is what is to be done with that awareness, as exposure on its own does not produce collapse, or viable solutions. The 2008 financial crisis for instance, lifted the veil on the 'one per cent' who were able to misappropriate a fifth of global GDP through their bail-outs and stimulus packages (Harvard Business Review, 2009). The translation of that knowledge into mobilisation, through the 'Occupy' movement, popularised a new understanding of the global order (Hosseini, 2013, this issue). The movement though was after the event: the moment of vulnerability and the managerial tactical response 'from above' was already in place. It was the imposed austerity that sparked the movement, not the financial collapse, and in some respects the key moment of disarray (and possibility) had already passed (see Steger et al., 2013). Clearly the financial crisis is ongoing, and the managerial response has guaranteed it will return, likely with a vengeance. The experience of financial crisis, austerity, and mobilisation may now offer the foundation for future movement interventions. But political engagement is socially embedded and fluid, not a fixed stock that accumulates over time, and can melt away as fast as it agglomerates. There are, for instance, powerful political lessons to be learnt from a decade or more of global justice mobilisation, but these can become submerged over time (Humphrys, 2013, this issue). Other crises are more 'slow burning', and may enable longer-term development and mobilisation, yet also may be difficult to precipitate politically. Movements addressing the crisis of radioactive waste and the broader ecological crisis (Goodman and Salleh, 2013, this issue; Houston, 2013, this issue) seem to gain most traction in countering what passes for official policy.

In different ways, then, crisis is a field of opportunity. It is a moment of possibility both for the authorities and for subordinates. In Gramscian terms, crisis creates an opening for 'passive revolution', to establish a new ruling dispensation; it also creates the possibility for advancing counter-hegemonic projects, whether in ideological or revolutionary forms of contention (see Carroll, 2007; Munck, 2006). With crises we often witness a simultaneity of struggle: as the powers-that-be flounder and struggle to develop a means of maintaining their legitimacy, counter-movements can find new vitality in the broader social struggles. In this Special Issue we advance grounded analysis from both sides of the equation, seeking to analyse the different ways in which crisis is translated into opportunity. The Special Issue gathers a range of case studies that investigate how that process unfolds, drawing conclusions from different contexts of crisis.

From Crisis to Transformation?

Historically, crises of global order have generated large-scale social transformations and collapses, and there are similar impacts likely to arise from this current cascade of disordering dynamics. In the context of crisis, social forces may be dissolved or invigorated. Social movements can become a crucial barometer, in signalling both the demise and rise of political formations and programmes (Rupert, 2003). Movement cycles, which involve phases of mobilisation and institutionalisation, contribute to and closely correlate with the emerging salience of social conflicts and ideological contention. Likewise, crises elicit elite strategies, both reactive and anticipatory, framed as crisis management (Carroll, 2007).

As a result, governance structures become geared to the anticipation and pre-emption of crises and of the movements associated with them. In a period of cumulative and 'permanent' crisis, managerialist approaches become designed-in to the structures of rule. At one level, the globalisation of these dynamics simply involves a scaling-up and transnational transfer of techniques and strategies (Tarrow, 1998), as, for example, occurs in the making of international standards for dealing with disaster and emergency (Rogers, 2013, this issue). More fundamentally, the globalisation of crisis enables new forms of politicisation and problem-solving to emerge from beyond the elite, thereby creating the possibility for new forms of social engagement (Macdonald, 2006; Reitan, 2007). With diffusion of shared problems and approaches, new forms of mutual recognition and simultaneous action become available, and both the repressive and transformative potential of crisis is amplified (Hosseini, 2010).

From the contemporary confluence we may look to earlier periods of history, to explore present possibilities. The inter-war period saw a similarly globalising crisis, which likewise demonstrated the vulnerability of the capitalist social fabric and spawned new attempts at managing or addressing it. The crises produced a 'double movement', as Polanyi put it, where, in many different ways, people sought to create structures of 'self-protection' against the ravages of *laissez-faire* capitalism. The resulting modes of welfarist regulation, echoed today in the proposed 'Green New Deal' for instance, had the effect of accommodating tensions between capital and labour (Green New Deal Group, 2008). Along with a parallel post-colonial settlement, this welfarist 'historic compromise' was wrought principally at the national level. The resulting modes of developmentalism and welfarism were mechanisms of managing, not resolving, the underlying contradiction. This was borne out in the subsequent implosion of both the post-colonial and the welfarist models in the face of flexibilised neoliberalism, and the shift in power back to the corporate and financial sectors (as so amply described by, respectively, David Harvey, 2007, and Robert Biel, 2000).

As in the inter-war period, so the current crises generate a frantic search for new modes of regulation and management, with social movements and elites vying in a contest to shape the emergent structures of rule. As Van Der Pijl demonstrates, periods of crisis see 'cadres' marshalled both in defence of dominant interests to ensure the emergent settlement generates a new cycle of accumulation, and in opposition to those interests, through the mobilisation of movement intellectuals, especially through non-government advocacy organisations (Van Der Pijl, 1998). This current global confrontation between corporates and their consultants on the one hand, and NGO advocates on the other, allows Carroll for instance to define a set of global antimonies between hegemonic and counter-hegemonic organisations, such as between the World Economic Forum and the World Social Forum, that now set the frame for international policy-formation (Carroll, 2007).

The task as defined here for this Special Issue is driven by similar concerns. The context of multiple crises increases the significance of conflicts between movement and management. Clearly there is no single face of 'management groups', nor of 'movements', but we can speak of a distinction and an antagonism between the two on the basis of what they aim to achieve. We can also suggest that this antagonism is intensifying as, in the absence of a ready-made means of socialising conflicts through the state, conflicts have been bidded-up and displaced, and the impacts have escalated. With neoliberal precepts diffused across policy sites, the prospects for re-embedding and socialising what have become hugely destructive social forces have receded. As such, we see for instance, global food poverty exacerbated by the shift to biofuels, global insecurity intensified by resource-focused military interventions, financialisation bolstered by efforts to commodify greenhouse gas emissions, and control of greenhouse emissions destabilised by inherent financial volatility. The side-effects of management quickly become the main effect, overwhelming social relations as a whole. In these contexts, experiments in movement strategy gain greater significance, as do contending elite efforts at managing or repressing the fall-out. Often these experiments are localised, can be correlated and embedded in trans-local relations, and have proliferated, creating new interconnected network formations (see especially, Reitan, 2007).

In this issue of *Globalisations*, then, we investigate movements and management in the face of crisis, taking crisis as a normal state of play, deeply embedded within global trajectories and governance structures. The generative capacity of crisis is put to the fore, both in terms of driving movement responses and management reactions. We ask who wins from crisis, and who loses, and investigate the movement–management nexus as it unfolds in particular localities as well as in broader contexts. In understanding the process as a dynamic one, we question to what extent movement initiatives elicit and legitimise managerial responses, potentially taking us into the realm of 'reformist reform', namely one that perpetuates crises, albeit in a transmuted or displaced fashion (Bond, 2006). To what extent, by the same token, do managerial efforts at repression rechannel movement initiatives, creating new planes of resistance? It certainly can be observed that in the context of crisis modes of management come into greater proximity with movements. Managerialism, as a form of consent management, begins to accommodate itself to critics as its failures become self-evident. Management cadres here can become co-opted by movements, and dragged across the management–movement binary. The same, more commonly, happens in the reverse direction, as movement elites are co-opted into a managerialist strategy, drawn imperceptibly into the 'epistemic communities' and other modes of consensus-building efforts established by managerial agencies (Hirsch, 1995). The outcome of this engagement is of critical importance, in terms of determining whether responses to crises affirm and compound contradictions or, alternatively, open up new ways of addressing them and for securing wider transformations. What are the conditions for 'non-reformist reform', to open-up new agendas (Bond, 2006)? Beyond the immediate relevance of this question, there are a range of theoretical insights: the ubiquity of crisis is not only a hallmark of social life and a frame for social action, but also offers a way into a different kind of social analysis.

Crisis Responses, from 'Above' and 'Below'

Reflecting the general themes of this Special Issue, the articles are organised into two halves, 'management' and 'movement'. All in some way bear implications for both sides of the equation, and several explicitly bridge the two main themes, albeit with an emphasis on one of the other. The articles are discussed here each in turn, in order to reflect on how they approach the shared issues.

Management

Bob Hodge opens the section on Management with his article on the 'Hydra paradox' and its relation to global disaster management in a world of crises. Hodge's argument suggests that we can learn imaginatively from myth, although he implies we can also use a myth to simply reassert previous ways of action. For Hodge the story of Hercules and the Hydra allows us to think about the hyper-complexity and exponential growth of crises and the ways we try to manage them. Hercules' initial solution is linear; he tries to chop off the Hydra's heads, but another two heads grow back for each one he removes. The solution makes the problem worse. Hodge states the source of the problem is the Hydra's resilience: the source of threat is also a source of fertility and productivity. In the Hydra problem, positive and negative characteristics are completely intertwined; they are not separable. We cannot even agree on what the problem is or what the relevant data might be, never mind on what its causes or its linkages to other problems or social actions might be. Yet as Hodge points out, lack of action is also not an option. At a meta level, it is perhaps possible to agree that linear managerial solutions to the crises will not work, that we have to face paradox. Hodge, following Solnit (2009), points out that the social crises produced by Hurricane Katrina and the earlier San Francisco earthquake were compounded by managers fearing mobs. The ostensible aim of the authorities, to help mitigate the disaster, fed its most destructive aspects. While the people directly affected by the crisis seemed capable of a large degree of self-organisation, managers seemed to self-organise in panic and organise destructively. Furthermore, the reports written by the managers after the event failed to do more than suggest that the solution was better management. The problem then is perpetuated.

Co-editor Jonathan Marshall then looks at the management of finance, suggesting that ideas of rationality, control, and information in financial markets are continually undermined by the politics of working in finance, and by the increased computerisation of the industry. Participants in the market have incentives to lie about their products and cannot communicate with each other (even in the same firm) because of rivalries, departmental disjunctions, different interests, different understandings of the world, and the demands of hierarchy. Bad news, even if accurate, is not welcome and tends to be ignored. Computer programs are fed false data, constructed according to inaccurate models, used beyond their purpose as defined by programmers, and the whole system compounds in unexpected ways as everyone tries to second-guess how they think others, or wider systems, might respond. Staff are overstretched and unlikely to be able to respond to information which does not meet short term needs. In sum, the managerial techniques that ostensibly generate financial order and profit also generate the conditions for financial crisis and may eventually bury the industry under its own detritus. If financial management cannot solve its own problems, and causes the problems in the domains it is most associated with, how useful can it be elsewhere?

Peter Rogers examines the creeping 'neoliberalisation' of 'disaster resilience'. He argues that 'resilience' has become a key term in disaster management and underlies many of the forms of organisation and responses to disaster. Resilience has, in itself, become an institution through the imposition of standards. Here, the idea of resilience operates as an avoidance tool or acts as a way of distributing protection. While local organisations could be more resilient than national bodies, they can also be subject to neoliberal cost cutting, having already lost the war over resources unless they have a wealthy local population or donors. Rogers's important point is that neoliberal resilience and the formulaic standards it produces reduce the possibility of more flexible localised responses and local knowledge, and thus increase future vulnerability. This process Rogers calls a 'rigidity trap'. It is particularly destructive as the concept of resilience itself is hard to define. Standards, in contrast, are hard and fast, and appear irresistible. Organisations that reject standards are excluded from participation in disaster management projects and associated funding streams and are liable to blame. Rogers suggests that disorder is less the enemy than rigid ways of thinking, doing, and acting. Moreover, if resilience at the local level is exercised it may demonstrate a possibility of a counter-movement to neoliberal uniformity and managerialism.

From macro imperatives and standards we turn to localised managerial strategies with Devleena Ghosh's account of management and workers in a Bangalore call centre. In this globalised service centre, Ghosh finds management intimately tied to local ideology and affect. Rather than accept that call centre workers are just new 'coolies' being exploited by multinational call centres, Ghosh looks at how workers remake the context they find themselves in. Call centre work is positioned as offering a 'modern' life. Management sells a new lifestyle which subverts some local roles and behaviours while accentuating others. The workers encounter an imagined global society, through their work, and this has consequences for their personal and familial lives. New ways of living have to be negotiated, or people have to strike out without previously available support. In this case, the management produces new appearances of freedom as the workers respond to their situation. Yet the employers are by no means in control, as borne out by the constant need for micro-management of the labour process and also by high staff turnover. The experience is perhaps best summed up in the idea of *jugaar*, of making do with whatever is available in a highly contingent context. Responses to management are individualistic, and bounded by middle-class aspiration, but at the same time a new sociality may emerge among Indian workers, creating new tensions and possibilities.

The management–movement nexus is addressed at the level of the United Nations in the next article by James Goodman and Ariel Salleh. Here the focus is on the ecological crisis, which is seen as generating new neoliberal strategies 'from above'. Market-centred strategies for the 'Green Economy', which would legitimise the wholesale marketisation of ecologies, are seen as constituting a new attempted class hegemony. Countering this, a range of closely aligned movements, mobilised through the World Social Forum, have sought to produce an alternative model labelled 'bio-civilisation'. The conflict between the UN-led 'Green Economy' and the WSF-led 'bio-civilisation' models is mapped. The conflict is read as a reflection of underlying contradictions between transnational elites and a 'meta-industrial' class of people who are dispossessed and displaced by advancing market globalism. Goodman and Salleh find a deepening contest between these two blocs framed as a contest to define the future, as expressed in the scope of the UN programme 'The Future We Want' and the counter-programme 'Another Future is Possible'.

Movements

Hamed Hosseini points to the managerial techniques of neoliberalism as the starting point for his examination of movement 'transversalism'. The neoliberal state has become a provider of corporate welfare, not of social welfare, in almost every society affected by the crisis, and this has led to a revitalisation of justice movements that are increasingly correlated, on a transnational basis. Hosseini argues that the demands of cross-national organising have highlighted differences between the protestors and produced a new kind of 'transversal' cosmopolitanism. This mode of cosmopolitanism moves beyond an orderly narrative, where differences and disagreements are read as dysfunctional or secondary to a common purpose. In its place, he finds a strong cosmopolitan ethic of mutual comprehension and openness to the 'stranger'. This process of transversal cosmopolitanism is not in any sense smoothly plural, but rather is highly dialogic and contentious. He finds this ethic especially present in the logic of the Occupy movement, which has enabled locally embedded claims to be mutually recognised within an overarching

CRISIS, MOVEMENT, MANAGEMENT: GLOBALISING DYNAMICS

Occupy frame. Certainly the transversalism made the politics of Occupy confusing to those who wanted a straightforward ideology or political programme, but it also built local familiarity. These movements make, deliberately or not, a new attempt to solve the old problem of maintaining unity in diversity, against an enemy far better financed, and with far more control over communication.

Donna Houston focuses on movements that address environmental questions. Under the impact of neoliberal economic expansion, she notes we have entered the Anthropocene, an era in which human society becomes the key agent of ecological and geological change. In this era we are challenged to address the impacts of our 'failing modernisms' on the conditions of planetary existence. The challenge requires an exercise in the political imagination as the old stories of economic freedom and infinite expansion now actively work against us. Houston discusses environmental justice as a way of giving local concerns universal resonance. Here, 'not in my backyard' expands to not in anyone's backyard. In the context of advancing impacts, and the requirement for precaution, she argues for 'anticipatory histories'. Illustrating the power of the concept, she discusses the three-decade-long, and ultimately successful, struggle against the disposal of high-level radioactive waste at Yucca Mountain in Nevada. Here she finds histories interwoven in anticipation of ecological justice, connecting the geological and environmental history of the Great Basin and Mojave deserts with 500 years of colonisation of Native Americans and the social and industrial legacies of the Cold War. These 'uncovered stories' allowed people to begin to inhabit a new way of life as part of a diverse group of people with a troubled history, finding new means to work together though mutual recognition.

Crisis does not inevitably produce movements, and a key factor is how movement activists develop strategy. As revealed by Elizabeth Humphrys, much is revealed when movements fail to maintain momentum. Humphrys discusses the decline of the Global Justice Movement in Australia, partly as a result of the dramatically changed frame for global politics after the attacks on the twin towers in September 11, 2001. However, she argues that, despite the external challenges, such as the lack of interest in the media, the hijacking of respectable elements by global elites, and the portrayal of the Australian global justice movement as potentially terrorist, the main reasons for its apparent collapse were its internal problems. These centred on a failure to take a broader historical and strategic perspective on the development of the movement. Mobilisation did not build organisational capacity and tended to be episodic rather than sustained, and political campaigning had difficulty in addressing questions of state militarism and unilateralism as against corporate power. Organisational and ideological weakness magnified divisions in the movement, in particular between the more institutionalised parts of the movement and the extra- or anti-institutional sections. The failure to create movement spaces where these issues could be addressed is seen as symptomatic and generative of failure. This self-critical approach is especially useful in progressing an understanding of strategic capacity required of movements in responding to crisis.

Francesca da Rimini, in contrast, demonstrates the significance of non-institutionalised cultural protest in the context of authoritarian neoliberalism in the Hong Kong government. Neoliberalism in Hong Kong, that is the use of the state to support corporate enterprise at everyone else's expense, inspires a fluid protest movement, which behaves in many ways like the 'multitude' as described in Autonomist theory. For da Rimini, the movement creates 'Temporary Affective Spaces', using the tools of information capitalism to reclaim physical spaces of the city. In the events she recounts, protestors were able to step outside the boundaries of protest, as defined by official approval, to involve creative or artistic acts and engage a wider populace. Entertainment engaging with public memory becomes potentially radicalising. While the protests were not successful in their immediate aims of preventing the destruction of public spaces, they suggest the possibility of ongoing and widespread action against neoliberal ordering in Hong Kong. Like Houston and Hosseini, da Rimini points to the construction of movements, not governed by fixed or shared ideology, and able to act with generalised multiple aims and ideological positions. She suggests that the Occupy movement in the USA could learn something about continuation, and generally involving forms, from the Hong Kong protests, and in any case looks at a locale that is underrepresented in studies of social movements.

In the final article for this collection, Erin Wilson and Manfred Steger lift the gaze to discuss globalising religious movements. They argue that globalised neoliberal management has become widely identified with secularism. As such, its failings, its cultural specificity and violation of social norms, have led to the regrowth, or rebirth, of religious politics throughout the world. There is in that sense, now, a complex of post-post-secular movements. The aim of many of these religious movements is to replace market-centred managerialism with a spiritually centred authority or perspective. In the context of neoliberal management, religion can be an important source of meaning and identity that opens up alternative ways of being in and responding to the world, and which, as Wilson and Steger emphasise, may be more or less authoritarian. The article particularly looks at three kinds of movements—neoliberal religious globalisms, religious justice globalisms, and neo-traditional religious globalisms—although, as they remark, this list is by no means exhaustive. Neoliberal religious movements include the religions of prosperity, in which it is assumed that the invisible hand of the market is the providential hand of God. Religious justice globalisms, from across religious traditions, can gain traction as the state sheds social objectives and religious organisations take on advocacy roles. Neo-traditional religious movements tend to exclude non-believers and claim or invent traditions for a revived religious mobilisation, often in pursuit of political power. These three types of religious movement are, of course, ideal types, and shade into each other, but share a common rejection of neoliberal secularism and can offer challenging responses to it.

Across these articles we find contrasting imperatives. For management there is the dilemma of maintaining central control in a context of fluidity, where attempts at restoring market 'order' become radically destabilising. Distributed structures of rule offer little by way of flexibility as the required neoliberal prescriptions remain unchanged. Capacity to address the causes of crisis is contested and management lapses into a process of protective displacement and dispossession. The logic of movement mobilisation, in contrast, centres on re-embedding economic forces in socio-ecological relations, and on displacing the authorities through new forms of political participation. Whether defined in terms of social, cultural, or ecological justice, or indeed religious belonging, we find movements seeking to politicise power sources, to mobilise against them, and to produce alternatives. Central to their purpose is the capacity to construct collective identity that bridges and builds upon differing positions. As with management, such movements can be empowered by crisis, as disjunctures create possibilities for new interventions. Crisis, we may say, creates a fertile territory for global transformations.

Acknowledgements

This Special Issue arises from a project funded by the Australian Research Council entitled 'Chaos, Information Technology, Global Administration and Daily Life'. James Goodman and Jon Marshall wish to thank the ARC for funding this research.

References

Arrighi, G. (1994) *The Long Twentieth Century: Money, Power and the Origins of Our Times* (London: Verso).
Biel, R. (2000) *The New Imperialism: Crisis and Contradiction in North/South Relations* (London: Zed Books).
Bond, P. (2006) Civil society on global governance: Facing up to divergent analysis, strategy, and tactics, *Voluntas*, 17, pp. 359–371.
Bond, P. (2008) Reformist reforms, non-reformist reforms and global justice: Activist, NGO and intellectual challenges in the World Social Forum, *Societies Without Borders*, 3(1), pp. 4–19.
Carroll, W. (2007) Hegemony and counter-hegemony in the global field, *Studies in Social Justice*, 1(1), pp. 36–66.
Chakrabarty, D. (2009) The climate of history: Four theses, *Critical Inquiry*, 35, pp. 197–222.
Davis, M. (2010) Who will build the ark?, *New Left Review*, 61, pp. 29–46.
Fraser, N. (2003) From discipline to flexibilization? Rereading Foucault in the shadow of globalization, *Constellations*, 10(2), pp. 160–171.
Gills, B. (2010) The return of crisis in the era of globalization: One crisis or many? *Globalizations*, 7(1–2), pp. 3–9.
Goodman, J. (2011) The 'long frontier of insurgent action': Counter-globalism and climate justice, in B. Axford & R. Huggins (eds) *Cultures and/of Globalization* (Newcastle upon Tyne: Cambridge Scholars Publishing), pp. 64–84.
Green New Deal Group (2008) *Green New Deal: A New Initiative for Economic and Environmental Transformation* (London: New Economics Foundation).
Harvard Business Review (2010) A map to healthy—and ailing—markets, *Harvard Business Review*, 88(1–2), pp. 30–31.
Harvey, D. (2003) The 'new' imperialism: Accumulation by dispossession, *Socialist Register 2004: The Imperial Challenge*, 40, pp. 63–87.
Harvey, D. (2007) *A Brief History of Neoliberalism* (Oxford: Oxford University Press).
Held, D., Kaldor, M. & Quah, D. (2010) The Hydra-headed crisis, LSE Global Governance Working Paper (London: Centre for Global Governance).
Hirsch, J. (1995) Nation-state, international regulation and the question of democracy, *Review of International Political Economy*, 2(2), pp. 267–284.
Hosseini, S. A. H. (2010) *Alternative Globalizations: An Integrative Approach to Studying Dissident Knowledge in the Global Justice Movement* (London: Routledge).
Johnston, J., Gismondi, M. & Goodman, J. (eds) (2006) *Nature's Revenge: Reclaiming Sustainability in an Age of Corporate Globalism* (Peterborough, ON: Broadview Press).
Klein, N. (2008) *The Shock Doctrine: The Rise of Disaster Capitalism* (New York: Picador).
MacDonald, K. (2006) *Global Movements: Action and Culture* (Melbourne: Wiley-Blackwell).
Munck, R. (2006) Globalisation and contestation: A Polanyian problematic, *Globalizations*, 3(2), pp. 175–186.
O'Connor, J. (1998) *Natural Causes: Essays in Ecological Marxism* (New York: Guilford Press).
Reitan, R. (2007) *Global activism* (London: Routledge).
Rupert, M. (2003) Globalising common sense: a Marxian-Gramscian (re-)vision of the politics of governance/resistance, *Review of International Studies*, 29, pp. 181–198.
Solnit, R. (2009) *A Paradise Built in Hell* (New York: Viking).
Steger, M., Goodman, J. & Wilson, E. (2013) *Justice Globalism: Ideology, Crises, Policy* (London: Sage).
Tarrow, S. (1998) *Power in Movement* (Cambridge: Cambridge University Press).
Van Der Pijl, K. (1998) *Transnational Classes and International Relations* (London: Routledge).

James Goodman researches social movements and global politics at the University of Technology Sydney. He is co-author of *Justice Globalism: Ideology, Crises, Policy* (Sage, 2013) with Manfred Steger and Erin Wilson.

Jonathan Marshall is an honorary associate at the University of Technology Sydney. He is author of *Living on Cybermind: Categories, Communication and Control* (Peter Lang, 2007) and co-author of *Disorder and the Disinformation Society: The Social Dynamics of Networks and Software* (Routledge, 2013).

The Hydra Paradox: Global Disaster Management in a World of Crises

BOB HODGE
University of West Sydney, Australia

ABSTRACT *This article explores issues of disasters and their management, against a backdrop of multiple crises that are seen as defining the current condition of globalisation, driven by an ongoing dialectic between forces from 'above' and 'below'. The article draws on forms of chaos theory, treating disasters and their management as a key site in which to examine intersections of crisis and chaos in global processes, colliding with destructive natural events and forces which are still outside dominant systems of control. The exposition starts from a new look at the ancient myth of Hydra, still used to capture the intractability of global crises and problems. Hydra represented hyper-complexity and exponential growth, qualities that characterise global problems today. It also presented a fantasy solution to the problems of agency from below which dominant groups have found irresistibly seductive for millennia.*

'The Hydra-Headed Crisis'

In 2010, David Held, Mary Kaldor, and Danny Quah (hereinafter HKQ) published an influential article entitled 'The Hydra-Headed Crisis' (Held et al., 2010). The title phrase generated 12,800 Google hits from writers using or quoting the work. Yet after Hydra creates the dramatic title she disappears from the text, to re-emerge only as a flourish in the final sentence. We glimpse a head and tail, but no body.

These authors' use of Hydra was rhetorically successful, but in neglecting Hydra they wasted a rich image, through which I explore the intersection of their theme, problems of global governance, with my concern with the dialectic between 'management' and 'movement'. In the process, I show that this ancient monster has positive as well as negative messages for a world of crises and disasters.

HKQ begin by referring to six recent headline-grabbing events. Four of the six involve natural disasters, implying the innovative connection they make between 'crises' and 'disasters', in which the older conception of disasters as primarily 'natural' is overtaken by the new sense of disasters as never entirely 'natural' (Smith, 2006), always created or mitigated by social agents, always inserted into prevailing social systems. This underlies their key proposition, that the unprecedented crises of our times are products of deeply embedded systemic connections across global meta-systems. These produce successive crises, in 'an ever-deepening spiral of crisis' (Held et al., 2010, p. 2). They look at three 'overlapping categories of crisis: economic and financial, security and environmental'.

Many commentators share HKQ's sense of qualitatively new levels of chaos and complexity in a globalising world, requiring non-linear modes of thought (e.g. Urry, 2003). Many problems confronted by leaders and organisations today have the qualities of what Rittel and Webber (1973) called 'wicked problems'. 'Wicked problems' characteristically are not only intractable, they cannot even be formulated with the clarity that managers as problem-solvers expect and require. There is a problem in the nature of the problems. People cannot agree what the problem is, or what are its boundaries or structures or boundaries, with no beginning or end. The problem intertwines incompatible dimensions. Climate change is a 'wicked problem' of this kind (Hulme, 2009).

Global managers now see hyper-complexity as a crucial factor. A 2010 global survey of CEOs by IBM identified complexity as their top concern:

> We occupy a world that is connected on multiple dimensions, and a deeper level—a global system of systems. That means, among other things, that it is subject to systems-level failures which require systems-level thinking. (IBM, 2010, p. 3)

In this management discourse, complexity is both good and bad. It allows the global system to exist, superficially (in infinite, potentially unordered connections) and at 'deeper' unknown levels. It does not directly produce system-failure (chaos, crisis) but magnifies these effects. It may also show how to address problems of complexity, but this positive message is more in doubt. The IBM report recorded a sharp split in CEO opinions about complexity. Most recognised complexity as an escalating problem, but only 49% believed they could cope with it (2010, p. 19).

The Hydra myth is relevant to thinking about hyper-complexity. Hydra's many heads are an image for complexity created by dynamic multiplicity. Her myth also represents the unmanageable hyper-complexity that worried CEOs in the IBM survey. When the hero Hercules cuts one head off, two more grow in its place. That is, an obvious linear solution to control a Hydra-like problem may exponentially multiply problems. Inaction leaves serious problems untouched, but decisive action makes matters worse. I call this the Hydra paradox, where 'paradox' indicates intractable contradiction between expectations and outcomes.

HKQ also pose what they call a paradox:

> (T)he kind of global arrangements that are required have still not been constructed. This is the central paradox of our time: the collective issues we must grapple with are increasingly of global scope and reach and yet the means for addressing them are national, weak and incomplete. (2010, p. 1)

This is an important problem, but not a 'paradox' as I use the term. Paradoxes arise in complex analyses of hyper-complex situations, as with 'wicked problems'. The problem HKQ ask us to grapple with as described here is a big but linear problem, needing an expensive but linear solution.

To use the Hydra image to make the point, this solution would only need Hercules to have seven swords, and coordinate them. The resources may be hard to find or obtain, but that is a practical problem, not a paradox. The Hydra story carries the crucial distinction between problems which can be formulated and solved or not, and paradoxes or wicked problems, where it is not clear what the problem is, what would be needed to resolve it, and whether the cure might be worse than the disease.

The Hydra myth throws light on the way in which HKQ construct this problem of governance. They present a collective 'we' as primary agents who 'grapple' with this collective problem. But as they note, this 'we' is populated from many nations across the world who currently do not form a unity. 'We' are an unacknowledged Hydra.

The myth also dramatises another deeper division, between elites who currently manage the globe or parts of it and those managed by or resisting that management: Hercules and Hydra, management and movements, to use a binary for the moment. Even in a simple form, the Hydra paradox complicates the management fantasy that Hercules only needs more technology.

Myths to Think With

Political analysts usually ignore myths, and in contemporary English 'myth' often just means something untrue. However, as Gabriel (2000, 2004) shows, myths can play an important role in modern organisations. Even ancient myths can sustain profound reflections on dilemmas of modern organisations (Hodge et al., 2010). For Lévi-Strauss (1968) the major function of myth was to represent intractable problems in the logic of a society, 'wicked problems': not to solve them, because they are not strictly soluble, but to recognise their inconvenient existence.

The classical Hydra myth describes a task Hercules performed for Eurystheus, king of Argos, to kill Hydra, a many-headed water monster. Hercules tried to cut off her heads, but each time he did so two more grew in their place. He finally killed her, but after she died poison flowed from her body, polluting the environment.

This story is among other things a political allegory, for generic problems of rule from a ruler's perspective. In Renaissance iconography, Hydra was the mob, or heresy, with no division usually made between king and Hercules. But the classical myth represents power as a complex system, delegated from the king to Hercules. Only this mediated power could have prevailed, though the autocratic king does not recognise this.

The myth also encodes relations between humans and nature. Traditional myths of many peoples typically see the world in terms where animals and natural forces are represented as having human capacities. This has been seen as a mark of primitive thought processes (Lévi-Strauss, 1966). However, this quality makes it well suited to represent the interdependence that is now increasingly recognised between human (political, social, cultural, economic) and natural forces in constructing 'wicked problems'.

'Hydra' is related to Greek for water, and Lerne, Hydra's home, was a historically known swamp, 5 miles from Argos, Eurystheus' city. Lerne was Eurystheus' swamp, his piece of nature, a wild part of his kingdom. Hydra is water out of control. The story also implies association with pollution. Hydra was a many-headed myth. It encoded control problems over dangerous nature as well as rebellious populations, the spheres of environment and politics whose intersecting crises, for HKQ, produce a spiralling 'Hydra-headed' crisis.

This myth probably encoded a deeper level of meaning. Hydra is a female monster, descended from Gaia, Earth goddess. Over a thousand years after Heracles' supposed act, Greek author Pausanias (1971 [c.150]) reported that Lerne was the site of a major temple celebrating secret rites of Demeter the fertility goddess. When looked at from the point of view of adherents of the former religion, Hydra is positive. Respected and unmolested, she would be benign and essential. For Hercules, her trick of producing two heads to replace each one cut off is a problem, but from Hydra's perspective this is resilience. This is a corollary to the Hydra paradox: the source of threat is also the source of fertility and productivity.

The Hydra paradox, then, arises from a Hydra system. In Hydra systems, the system of control is seen by rulers as linear, distinct from and hostile to the rest of the system, which is organised in non-linear terms. Yet both parts of the Hydra system are interdependent non-linear parts of a single system, each affecting the other in a complex dialectic of complementarity and opposition. That is why Hercules cannot kill Hydra without huge cost to himself and the system. Conversely, Hydra does not need a brutal Hercules-manager, but her own dangerous powers do need limits. And paradoxically, without Hercules she would not have nearly so many heads.

Old Myths and New Disasters

Hydra and her myth are very ancient, so it is interesting to look at more recent manifestations of a similar body of myths. Mexican disaster researcher Virginia Garcia-Acosta reports responses to a 1982 eruption of the Chichonal volcano in south-east Mexico by the local Zoque Indians. Central in Zoque myths is Piowachue, Zoque for 'old woman who burns'.

> She is the 'mother earth' that warns, sanctions and attacks those who offend her or those who do not present her with religious offerings. In exchange, she offers water, richness, oil, and fertile lands. (Garcia-Acosta, 2002, p. 165)

Piowachue has structural similarities to Hydra, representing fire rather than water, but the two elements have the same oppositional relationship. This aspect also represents the second aspect of the Hydra paradox, the inseparability of creative and destructive forces. In the Zoque myth, Piowachue was rejected by Tunsawi, a potential lover, 'because of her extreme old age and dentated vagina'. She walks around the volcanic area, causing tremors which the Zoque associate with her footsteps. Three months before the eruption the Zoque reported her walking, but the authorities ignored these warnings, calling them 'an absurd myth' (Ibid., p. 166). The eruption killed 2,000 people, caused injuries to 3,500 families, and caused massive resettlement, turning the geological event into a human disaster.

As Garcia-Acosta emphasises, the myth had practical value, encoding a system of early warning signs which were fatally ignored. As important, the myth encodes complex social meanings which were equally ignored. Piowachue is an old woman angry that she is not respected, just as the colonised and dispossessed Zoque are not respected, no longer able to act in coordinated ways to preserve themselves and their culture. Garcia lists a Hydra-headed list of specific exacerbating factors proceeding from severe and chronic social inequality and marginalisation. Yet the Zoque are victims of this Hydra. This situation is a 'wicked problem', a Hydra paradox where factors interweave in what emerges as a poisonous cocktail.

My second example used 'myth' in a different sense, applied to a different situation. In September 2011, an earthquake in the Indian Ocean caused a massive tsunami, which hit a nuclear reactor at Fukushima, Japan. The Fukushima nuclear incident was a disaster within a disaster, a good illustration of how concatenating systems can produce unforeseen effects.

This accident created massive criticism in Japan. A special report commissioned by the Japanese government was released in July, an interim report on 5 July 2012, followed by the full report on 23 July. A press conference in English was reported under a headline in English: 'Fukushima crushed by "myth"' (*Australian*, 24 July 2012, p. 9).

The term 'myth' was not used in the report, and here it seems to be used in a superficial sense, to mean only 'false belief'. However, paradoxically the dismissive use of 'myth' in the text coexists with the deeper concept in the argument. The word 'myth' says that these beliefs are not true, but as the story unfolds it becomes clear that they are all too true. In the report itself the deep concept of myth is carried by 'culture', where Japanese culture is condemned for its key role in the disaster by no less a figure than Kurokawa, the committee chair:

> What must be admitted—very painfully—is that this was a disaster 'Made in Japan'. Its fundamental causes are to be found in the ingrained conventions of Japanese culture: our reflexive obedience; our reluctance to question authority; our devotion to 'sticking with the program'; our groupism; and our insularity. Had other Japanese been in the shoes of those who bear responsibility for this accident, the result may well have been the same. (National Diet of Japan, 2012, p. 9)

This culture is embedded in what is also called a 'mindset', containing five deeply entrenched beliefs. These are seen as what led to the disaster, and the Commission says it is therefore inappropriate to blame specific individuals. Because of the strength of this culture and its five heads, others in the same position would have acted in similar ways with similar effects. Kurokawa emphasises the unity of Japanese culture, but this unity, like Hydra's, is produced by the inextricable interconnections of its components.

There are two resonances with the Hydra paradox. The problem concerns a system so interconnected that simple punitive actions would miss the problem. Japanese culture is a Hydra. Additionally, positive and negative characteristics are completely intertwined. The qualities that made the disaster worse are not only 'made in Japan', they are what made Japan what it is today. These qualities have to be changed, and they cannot be changed.

The Hydra-problem here is not an external problem, a recalcitrant object of rule, but a problem of good governance, internal to the governing class itself. Indeed, this report can be seen to use the Hydra paradox to avoid blaming anyone in the ruling elite, so that problems of power and privilege, bribery and corruption are removed as targets. Yet this only brings out this dimension of the Hydra paradox, which comes from a sense of what is so inextricably enmeshed, in the situation of those who would address 'wicked problems' involving disasters in a chaotic world.

Chaos Theory and the Hydra Paradox

The growing awareness of intractable complexity in the contemporary global world has led to new interest in theories of chaos and complexity in the social sciences (see e.g. Hodge et al., 2010; Urry, 2003). This body of work is more like Hydra, with many heads, not a single theoretical fix able to explain chaos or show how to manage it in crises or disasters.

HKQ's key term—'crisis'—has different meanings and effects in frameworks which have a different take on chaos and complexity. HKQ do not define it specifically. It comes in two forms, an ordinary 'crisis', which is serious but manageable, and a 'spiralling crisis', which seems to escalate beyond limits and the possibility of control, like Hydra's multiplying heads. The word 'crisis' itself comes from the Greek *krisis*, turning point. It acquired its current sense in English as a dangerous situation from its use in medical discourse, where it referred to a turning point in a patient's condition, between sickness and health.

Chaos theorist Per Bak (1996) applies the term and concept to different states of systems more or less close to chaos. Such systems, he argues, can undergo rapid systemic changes, branches, or bifurcations, 'crises' in the Greek medical sense. As such systems become more chaotic they display a fluctuation of crises, an 'avalanche of bifurcations'. When this stage is reached, the system has entered a state of 'criticality'. This is roughly equivalent to HKQ's 'spiralling crises'.

For chaos theorists like Bak, many normal rules and logics no longer apply in such states. Systems become radically unpredictable and contradictory. There are still patterns and rules, but of a different kind. For instance, disasters like earthquakes are individually unpredictable, but a large set of disasters form a regular pattern, obeying a power law distribution of frequency and occurrence: that is, the distribution follows an exponential pattern. Most disasters have a power law distribution. For example, with earthquakes, this fact has become the basis for the Richter scale of classification, where huge new eruptions are not predicted but can be immediately classified.

A power law asserts the continuity of all such disasters. Massive earthquakes are rare and exceptional, but smaller earthquakes can be understood as homologous in structure. If small disasters can be used to understand and respond better to large ones, then the power law structure can be the basis for a research or action strategy.

The relationship between small and large disasters has been developed into a model for critical incident analysis (Hodge and Matthews, 2011). In these terms, an incident is described as 'critical' when a small effect ramifies through multiple interlocking systems, with chaotic and unpredictable consequences. Critical incidents have a diagnostic function of revealing where fault lines lie in a set of systems. Every disaster will contain a multiplicity of smaller disasters, ranged in a power law distribution from huge and exceptional to small and ordinary. With this principle it becomes possible to see crisis as both ordinary and extreme, a range of experiences that can be learnt from to build a well-prepared, resilient community.

The Hydra paradox signals a hyper-complex situation, beyond the normal limits of complexity. This principle is captured by the founder of fuzzy logic, Lotfi Zadeh:

> Stated informally, the essence of this principle is that as the complexity of a system increases, our ability to make precise and yet significant statements about its behaviour diminishes until a threshold is reached beyond which precision and significance (or relevance) become almost mutually exclusive characteristics. (1973, p. 28)

The notion of 'threshold' here implies a turning point, a crisis, on a boundary between two different kinds of system. One is a common-sense world where linear causality applies and applications of force will have predictable effects. The other is a world in which Hydras and their paradoxes flourish, where disasters and crises are understood and managed in many different ways.

The Upside of Down

The tantalising promise of chaos theories for analysing crises and disasters is to propose the possibility that there are some ways of responding to disaster which will not merely mitigate disasters, but may produce positive new outcomes. Or maybe not. The unpredictability predicted by forms of chaos theory can include outcomes worse than expected as well as better. Some disaster researchers (e.g. Bankoff et al., 2004) adapt a complexity framework to the field. Some have used the idea of self-organising systems to explain apparent miracles in some disasters, where communities left to themselves spontaneously produce better responses than the authorities could have done (Comfort et al., 2004). But self-organisation can happen everywhere. Adam Smith's famous image of the 'invisible hand' claims capitalism itself is a self-organising system, though capitalists as a class have always tried to twist its invisible arm for their benefit.

In his influential book *Upside of Down* (2008), Thomas Homer-Dixon begins by reflecting on two catastrophes, the San Francisco earthquake of 1906 and the fall of Rome. The fall of Rome he attributes to 'rising complexity, strangling the empire's ability to renew itself' (2008, p. 6), whereas with the earthquake 'a new and more resilient city rose from the ashes' (2008, p. 7). As in the Hydra myth, complexity was an enemy which strangled the empire, whereas the San Francisco responses created resilience.

In another popular book, Rebecca Solnit (2009) used the San Francisco example among other disasters to argue for a form of the Hydra paradox: that the disaster was the catalyst for an explosive and productive new sense of community, far more rapid and effective outcomes than were achieved by the authorities. In the case of San Francisco, Homer-Dixon saw long-term transformations, of the city itself and the US financial system.

New Orleans in the wake of Hurricane Katrina had a different version of this pattern. Community resilience was on display, but so also, here as in San Francisco, there was a punitive response by the authorities. Solnit points out that much of the carnage in San Francisco was produced by the authorities and the troops they sent in, an irrational overreaction produced by their fear of the 'mob', and the 'panic' that was assumed to be the only kind of response a mob could make. As in the Hydra paradox, the ostensible aim of the authorities, to help mitigate the disaster, fed its most destructive aspects.

A report commissioned by the US president on 'the lessons learned' from the Katrina disaster began by praising responses on the ground: 'the courage and fortitude (of government officials, business and community leaders and volunteers) in the face of tragedy was inspirational' (US Senate, 2006, p. i). But the authorities provoked 'disappointment and frustration at the seeming inability of "government"—local, State and Federal—to respond effectively to the crisis' (Ibid., p. 1).

Underlying this picture is a transformation of the Hydra myth. It has a binary division, between a heroic, united community, which is 'inspirational' but not part of the main game, and the authorities who alone could and should have acted, but did not. Yet this report is produced by and for the US managerial sector, and it produces a deceptively benign version of the Hydra myth, without the paradox. In its linear analysis, improvements will only come by reforming systems of control, and giving them more resources.

Adding Solnit's well-supported analysis, the Hurricane Katrina situation needs to be understood as the intersection of three forces in a system pushed into crisis by the natural event. The community responded creatively, as a self-organising system, but the local authorities also responded as a self-organising system, a Hydra affiliated to management not movements, responding to the imagined social threat more than to the natural disaster.

Solnit emphasises the effectiveness of power coming from below, while acknowledging that it is usually resisted and countered by official responses. Naomi Klein goes further, denouncing 'the rise of disaster capitalism' (2007). Klein assembles many instances of neoliberal or 'Neo-Con' entities using disasters to justify and legitimise many neoliberal measures that otherwise would have been politically hard to introduce, creating profitable new industries feeding off the opportunities opened up by these disasters and the apparatus created to deal with them. In the aftermath of Katrina, Smith (2006) claims the disaster provided many investment opportunities and chances for social engineering.

Klein's general case that capitalists and governments can seek to take advantage of crises needs no further proofs. President Bush went to war on Iraq and won a second term as president partly on the back of what he claimed was a response to September 11. However, he also lost credibility as that war turned increasingly sour, and he was judged a failure in the smaller-scale Katrina crisis. The stronger, more linear case Klein implies is less compelling, that capitalism is a single coherent agent that constructs disasters and profits from them: a Hydra myth in which Hercules is all-powerful but devious.

A more convincing argument is an extension of the Hydra paradox: that self-organisation happens from above as from below. Rulers can respond to the threat of a Hydra from below by unleashing their own Hydra, as Bush did with the 'war on terror'. However, that tactic and that Hydra are lateral, non-linear tactics. They may have short-term gains, but they risk unpredictable long-term outcomes. The Hydra paradox is a set of contradictory possibilities, not a single sure-fire recipe for successful governance. Or resistance.

Disaster Management Theory and Practice

Claims about revolutions need to be made tentatively, but there may be a revolution under way in disaster management, in the academic field, and in practices and policies. The claimed revolutions in these three domains at local and global levels are not entirely in step with each other, and doubts about the reality and scope of these revolutions pivot around lines of fissure constituted around the Hydra paradox. In this section I will give a brief overview of the main issues, as these impinge on the operations of the Hydra paradox.

Ingham's survey (Ingham et al., 2012) outlines the traditional premises and assumptions of the field. Disaster management is understood as a process with four phases, from prevention to preparation to response to recovery. But Ingham and others argue that tacitly a key distinction is made between the 'core' of disasters, especially focused around the dramatic event and immediate responses, including urgent preparations and relocation. Longer-term processes, including the rhythms of the disaster event, preparations or the lack thereof and the restoration of the affected communities, are relegated to the category of 'context', underfunded and ignored in the international media.

In this scheme of things, what happens in the 'core' has much higher priority, in practice and in research. Preparation is too long term to be fully taken account of in a disaster management framework, and recovery ought to be happening long after aid agencies have gone home and lost interest. So although what happens in the context is recognised as clearly relevant, it is the core that receives the most funding and attention. Reflecting this, older forms of disaster management took models from military and engineering sciences and practices (Shaw and Krishnamurty, 2009), what Hewitt (1983) called 'the technocratic approach'.

Relating this to the terms of the Hydra paradox, we can see that practices of the core are likely to be dominated by linear Hercules-control practices, whose more paradoxical causes and effects may be missed or underestimated by linear disciplines, for example, focusing on volumes of aid not the complex processes of uptake. But these limitations in research and policy are coming to be recognised. Ingham reports that more broadly framed policies have been promoted, and more socially oriented studies take account of a more complex picture and a richer set of hypotheses.

Research in this line includes work of the Latin American Disaster Resilience network, a group to which the present article is indebted. They insist that disasters are culturally constructed (Red Riesgo y Resilienca, 2010). In USA a similarly diverse social science approach is taken by Enrico Quanterelli and his group (1998). Researchers in this vein draw on Beck's influential work on risk (1992) to argue that 'risk is not simply a given; it is—at least in part—socially constructed' (Miller, 2009, p. 169). Beck's risk thesis can be seen as a form of the Hydra paradox, since it suggests that in the hyper-complex conditions of late modernity mechanisms intended to reduce risk may exacerbate concern: as a general proposition, he claims 'the crises of modernity follow closely the triumphs of modernity' (Beck, 2009, p. 212).

A seminal work in this counter-tradition was written by Charles Fritz in 1961 (1996). This extraordinary book influenced Solnit as well as Quantarelli's group, with claims that are startling and paradoxical premises for an anti-Hydra paradox.

Fritz (1996 [1961]) argued against a set of what he called 'myths' or mistaken beliefs. The central head in his analysis, the crucial head of his Hydra, was his premise that ordinary people mostly behave better in the crisis of the disaster, that disasters promoted individual and social health. 'Emergent "communities of sufferers"' were highly effective, with high levels of social solidarity, forming rapidly as forms of self-organised behaviour. The dominant beliefs, that crowds gave way to panic or primitive self-interest, were exactly opposite to what normally happened.

The other side to this coin was his critique of everyday life:

> No peace time or war time disaster in American history has ever produced the aggregate amount of death, dysfunction, pain and privation that is experienced in a single day of 'normal' life in the United States. (Fritz, 1996 [1961], p. 23)

The mindset that assumes that disasters produce antisocial behaviours and destroy social solidarity idealises everyday life, as it constructs the counter-myth of the helpless unhappiness of the 'community of sufferers'. This definitional unhappiness and dysfunctionality feeds a sense of superiority of those outside the disaster, and legitimates everything being done by the authorities.

Fritz's optimism and critique are limited. He notes that 'normality' usually returns, as the dominant structures resume their hold. That hold may even be tighter than before. No outcome is inevitable. He emphasises two factors that contribute to resilience: the capacity of members of the 'community of sufferers' to communicate with each other and be in control of their processes of adaptation. Lateral communication networks and relative autonomy allow self-organisation to occur locally. Both can be helped or hindered to some degree by actions of the authorities, but in general their effect is to transfer the locus of power and effectivity downwards, to the affected populace, to what is constructed in the dominant discourse as the problem (monster, Hydra, or victim).

Globalisation and Disaster

Fritz's perspective connects disaster studies with a strand in globalisation studies relevant to this special issue. In 1992, Robertson argued for a force he called 'globality', a sense of the globe as something that could be seen and defended, against the devastation being wrought by the political and economic forces more commonly called 'globalisation'. Sassen (2007) has developed a theory of globalisation in which global institutions operate in a complex network where activists and local interests play a global role. Others have seen hope in something like 'globality', arising in a form of self-organisation from below to produce positive new kinds of agent (e.g. Kaldor, 2003; Reitan, 2007). In terms of the Hydra myth, this trend is like the natural emergence of a benign Hydra, needing only a restraining order on Hercules for the world to be a far better, saner place.

In the broad area of disaster studies, Fassin has identified a new but ambiguous force he calls 'humanitarian reason', a world conscience created by the intersection of a 'global spectacle of suffering, and the global display of succour' (2012, p. ix). This produces billions of real dollars in aid, but always tied to a strategy of governing, in which Hercules remains in control. There is a similar problem with the increased concern for the vulnerability of the vulnerable, which Barbara Misztal (2012) sees as the potential basis for a new social contract, based on mutual trust. Trust indeed is what is most crucially lacking in the archetypal Hydra system. Yet that trust needs to recognise the creativity and power as well as the vulnerability of the 'vulnerable'.

The influential picture of globalisation painted by Marxists Hardt and Negri (2000) is less optimistic. They track the struggle between capital and labour into the late twentieth century, where both combatants have morphed into each other. 'Empire' has become a Hydra from above, absorbing her complexity into its ramifying, seemingly irresistible strategies of power. But in their scenario, Empire's eternal enemy has also morphed, into what they call 'multitude', as impossible to kill as the old Hydra. Or so they hope.

But disaster management has gone global only recently. In 1992, the 'Earth Summit' held in Rio de Janeiro brought together 172 governments and 2,400 representatives of NGOs to begin to translate 'globality' into a series of actions. Alongside it, a 'global forum' attended by 13,000 representatives of NGOs pursued its own version of this agenda. Movement towards a climate change agreement was a major outcome of this conference, but progress on this has been notoriously slow and vexed. Twenty years later, 'Rio + 20' has seemed a definitive defeat for the optimism of Rio, that the soft, dispersed power of globality could achieve real change.

But one consequence of the momentum created by Rio was another conference sponsored by the UN, held in Kobe, Japan, on 22 January 2005, on the theme of disaster reduction, building on a smaller conference in Yokohama in 1994. Kobe was a significant place for the conference, since it had suffered a major earthquake 10 years before, but 22 January was an even more potent date, less than a month after the Asian tsunami of 26 December 2004. The momentum gave force to the Hyogo Declaration and Framework for Action (HFA), a 10-year plan which over 130 states ultimately signed up to.

The title of the HFA declaration is: 'Building the resilience of nations and communities to disasters' (UNISDR, 2006). This signals the triumph of non-linear paradigms at the global policy levels. The key term is 'resilience', embedded in what they call 'a culture of disaster prevention and resilience, and associated pre-disaster strategies'. 'Resilience' here is associated with forces from below, in communities as well as nations. This paradigm has a definite place for a positive form of Hydra. We need of course to be sure that this triumph is not confined to discourse, appropriated as a new resource to sustain the old system.

A mid-term report issued in 2011 reviewed progress in the 5 years since the signing of the HFA (United Nations, 2011). The core problem they identified was one of governance. Disaster management was delegated downward to nation-states, as it had to be, given the framing structure of this UN organisation. The report is polite about the activities of these states, but it makes clear that this is where the problem lies.

They call for a 'new paradigm', a new culture of governance. This is precisely the problem of governance identified by HKQ: huge, complex global problems, and 'means which are national, weak and incomplete'. Yet it is also possible to use the Hydra myth to see this not as a problem but a paradox. This weak body still presides over and gives priority to a radical new line of research. Hercules still has the weapons and resources, but thanks to the Hydra paradox they are losing legitimacy.

Conclusion

I have used Hydra's myth as a device for representing and thinking about current intractable problems of global 'order', and potential realignments in relations between management and movements. For Lévi-Strauss, myths could represent insoluble problems of a culture. The Hydra paradox shows they are still productive strategies to think about 'wicked problems' of the Anthropocene, a hypothesised new geological stage of the planet, characterised by the decisive role of humans in shaping the geology and geography of the planet (Crutzen, 2002). In the Anthropocene, Hercules-humanity is damaging the planet, making his own heroism unsustainable.

The Hydra paradox poses problems, but makes no predictions. It points why a radical change is needed, but the form it needs to take, but that change is very far from certain. But the line of research pioneered by Fritz has gathered momentum over half a century, and finds hope where Fritz looked for it: not in massive schemes of disaster relief, not even in weak well-meaning bodies like the UN, but in grass-roots bodies, local and global, not fighting with Hercules but transforming him.

Like Piowachue the Mexican volcano goddess, the Hydra paradox may act as an early warning system, reminding humanity what is at stake in the current tsunami of interlocking crises. The healing message of the Hydra myth, freed from the dominance of the management perspective it enshrines, is that humans may organise themselves better without Hydra being slain.

Acknowledgements

I gratefully acknowledge the insightful commentaries of Jon Marshall and James Goodman for this and many other points in the article.

References

Bak, P. (1996) *How Nature Works* (New York: Springer).
Bankoff, G., Frerks, G. & Hilhorst, D. (2004) *Mapping Vulnerability* (London: Earthscan).
Beck, U. (1992) *Risk Society* (London: Sage).
Beck, U. (2009) *World at Risk* (London: Polity).
Comfort, L., Dunn, M., Johnson, D., Skertich, R. & Zagorecki, A. (2004) Co-ordination in complex systems, *Emergency Management*, 2(1–2), pp. 62–80.
Crutzen, P. (2002) Geology of mankind, *Nature*, 415(6867), p. 23.
Fassin, D. (2012) *Humanitarian Reason: A Moral History of the Present* (Berkeley: University of California Press).
Fritz, C. (1996 [1961]) *Disasters and Mental Health* (Delaware: Delaware Disaster Research Center).
Gabriel, Y. (2000) *Story-Telling in Organisations* (Oxford: Oxford University Press).
Gabriel, Y. (2004) *Myths, Organizations and Structure* (Oxford: Oxford University Press).
Garcia-Acosta, V. (2002) Conceptualization and experiences in Mexican disaster research, in C. Giordano & A. Boscoboinik (eds) *Constructing Risk, Threat, Catastrophe* (Fribourg, Switzerland: University Press Fribourg), pp. 161–166.
Hardt, M. & Negri, A. (2000) *Empire* (Cambridge, MA: Harvard University Press).
Held, D., Kaldor, M. & Quah, D. (2010) The Hydra-headed crisis, Global policy. LSE Global governance working papers.
Hewitt, K. (ed.) (1983) *Interpretations of Calamity* (Boston: Allen and Unwin).
Hodge, B. & Matthews, I. (2011) Complexity theory and engaged research, *Continuum*, 25(6), pp. 1–15.
Hodge, B., Coronado, G., Duarte, F. & Teal, G. (2010) *Chaos Theory and the Larrikin Principle* (Copenhagen: Liber).
Homer-Dixon, T. (2008) *Upside of Down* (Melbourne: Text Publishing Company).
Hulme, M. (2009) *Why We Disagree About Climate Change* (Cambridge: Cambridge University Press).
IBM Corporation (2010) *Capitalizing on Complexity* (Somers, NY: IBM Global Business Services).

Ingham, I., Hicks, J., Islam, R., Manock, I. & Sappey, R. (2012) An interdisciplinary approach to disaster management, incorporating economics and social psychology, *International Journal of Interdisciplinary Social Sciences*, 6(5), pp. 93–106.
Kaldor, M. (2003) *Global Civil Society: An Answer to War* (Cambridge: Polity).
Klein, N. (2007) *The Shock Doctrine: The Rise of Disaster Capitalism* (New York: Metropolitan Books).
Lévi-Strauss, C. (1966) *The Savage Mind* (London: Weidenfeld and Nicolson).
Lévi-Strauss, C. (1968) *Structural Anthropology* (Harmondsworth: Penguin).
Miller, K. (2009) Organizational risk after modernism, *Organization Studies*, 30(2–3), pp. 157–180.
Misztal, B. (2012) *The Challenges of Vulnerability* (London: Palgrave Macmillan).
National Diet of Japan (2012) *The Fukushima Nuclear Accident Independent Investigation Commission Official Report*.
Pausanias (1971 [c.150]) *Guide to Greece* (Harmondsworth: Penguin).
Quantarelli, E. (ed.) (1998) *What is a Disaster?* (London: Routledge).
Red Riesgo y Resiliencia (2010) http://redriesgoresilienca.ciesas.edu.mx.
Reitan, R. (2007) *Global Activism* (London: Taylor and Francis).
Rittel, H. & Webber, M. (1973) Dilemmas in a general theory of planning, *Policy Sciences*, 4, pp. 155–169.
Robertson, R. (1992) *Globalization* (Thousand Oaks, CA: Sage).
Sassen, S. (2007) *A Sociology of Globalization* (New York: Norton).
Shaw, R. & Krishnamurty, R. (eds) (2009) Disaster management: an overview, *Disaster Management—Global Challenges and Local Solutions* (Hyderabad: Universities Press).
Smith, N. (2006) There's nothing natural about a natural disaster, in *New Perspectives on Katrina*, SSRC, http://understandingkatrina.ssrc.org/Smith
Solnit, R. (2009) *A Paradise Built in Hell* (New York: Viking).
United Nations (2011) *Revealing Risk, Redefining Development* (Oxford: Information Press).
UNISDR/WCDR (2006) *Hyogo Framework for Action 2005–2015* (Geneva: UN Office for International Strategy for Disaster Reduction).
Urry, J. (2003) *Global Complexity* (London: Sage).
US Senate (2006) *Hurricane Katrina: A Nation Still Unprepared* (Washington, DC: US Government Printing Office).
Zadeh, L. (1973) Outline of a new approach to the analysis of complex systems and decision processes, *IEEE Transactions on Systems, Man, and Cybernetics*, 3(1), pp. 28–44.

Bob Hodge is Research Professor in Humanities at the Institute for Culture and Society, University of Western Sydney.

Communication Failure and the Financial Crisis

JONATHAN PAUL MARSHALL

University of Technology Sydney, Australia

ABSTRACT *The financial crisis is, among other things, a crisis in information. Bad information and bad models became the basis for toxic financial products, bought on faith. This article argues that the crisis in information begins in the networked corporate workplace, in the structures and drivers of management, and the building of workplace conformity through worker insecurity. This guarantees an environment in which information inaccuracy is normalised. The article primarily looks at a series of blog posts about people's experiences in work settings and the world of financial capital, during the financial crisis which began in 2008. The supposed rationality of capitalism, and capitalists' desire for control over markets, is undermined by its own uncontrolled and computerised extension. Disorder in information is shown to be a normal part of managerial dynamics. People can realise and be affected by these problems without necessarily seeming to be motivated to act against them.*

This article explores the power/ignorance nexus at the heart of managing and conducting work in the financial sector. It hypothesises that the environment created in this work is inimical to accurate information 'flow' and that this helps naturalise an experience in which financial crises, in particular the crisis of 2007 onwards, are generated. As most of the world's economic transactions involve speculative finance,[1] this implies that financial management and work is dangerous for world economy.

There are many explanations for the financial crisis. These include widespread criminal behaviour in the corporate sector (Ferguson, 2012; Hudson, 2010), the unintended consequences of designing an economy to benefit the rich and powerful (Bivens, 2011), the unintended consequences of attempting to benefit the poor through cheap loans (Sowell, 2010), falling rates of profit (Kliman, 2012), over-accumulation of capital with economic stagnation requiring a swollen financial sector to provide fictitious stimulus (Foster and Magdoff, 2009), failure to manage systemic risk (Williams, 2010), a run on financial organisations by other financial organisations freezing liquidity (Gorton, 2010), and the use of computer-based financial instruments such as derivatives and collateralised debt obligations (Dooling, 2008; Salmon, 2009), among others. Many of these authors draw attention to the rise of the financial sector, computer models, bad information, and unexpected or hidden linkages between trades arising through computer networks. This article does not criticise such explanations, but argues that confusion, communication failure, incoherence, inaccuracy, and panic are inherent in the management structures of financial workplaces and markets under information capitalism.

Managerialism is important to the dynamics of information society, with the solution for almost all problems being said to be more and better management, yet, outside of books written for by managers for managers, management seems largely ignored by information society theory. Recognising both the confusion and inherent inadequacy of contemporary management warns against uncritically embracing its perspective. Social movements, and on the ground workers, can be far better informed than the managerial elite.

This article briefly looks at the ways in which information and communication technology (ICT) increases disruption in the workplace and in information. Then it moves on to observe reader comments attached to a *New York Times* 'Business of Technology' (Bits) blog article by Saul Hansell (2008), entitled 'How Wall Street Lied to Its Computers'. These comments seem to come from a number of people who were either interested in finance or worked in finance. The comments, all posted in September to October 2008, reveal the chaos, exasperation, and pressures experienced by people at work, and imply that confusion and 'information mess' reside at the heart of the financial system.

The methodology could be criticised on the grounds that Internet posts do not reveal whether people are who they say they are. Detailed ethnographic observation of traders, programmers, quants, managers, risk officers, and so on would be preferable, but this is difficult; the ethnographic record is small, but can be used as a corrective (Ho, 2009). Autobiographies are useful (e.g. Derman, 2004; Knee, 2007; Michaelson, 2008), but can be accused of self-defence and bias. Interviews have the same problems. Given the open nature of Hansell's article and its blog, contributors likely reported their understanding of their general experience (whether it was precisely the experience they claimed or not), they could challenge reports of others (which was rare, implying that people accepted the possibility of such reports), and they could justify their position by retelling work experience and naming names, which would be open to challenge. There is no evidence of attempts to troll the blog or plant deliberate falsehoods. The comments usually seem knowledgeable, and given the conventional aim of authenticity, borne out in other sites, people are probably attempting to say something real to them. We can conclude that this source, *when used in conjunction with others*, provides useful information about people's experience of work and information, in information society. It is, however, probably correct that comments around a Fox news blog would have different orientations. This article does not claim total accuracy. It proposes a perspective and attempts to justify a set of hypotheses for further investigation.

Life in the Information Workplace

To understand the production of inaccurate information, we have to briefly summarise the conditions and context of information work. Modern workers (financial or otherwise) are generally insecure and unsure. Banker Jonathan Knee writes of an 'epidemic of professional distress'

(2007, p. xii). There are risks in standing up to management. Workers repeatedly deal with threats of outsourcing and/or dismissal (Hira and Hira, 2009). Furthermore, workers face constant restructurings and changes in management policy, as well as changes in the environment in which their company operates. New software changes work practices and disrupts work (often as part of restructuring), with added fears that this 'improvement' could lead to dismissal or downgrading. Software can be used to effect abstract management plans, with little relationship to reality or work that has to be done. Constant new ordering repeatedly disorders people's activities, so that the experience of disorder, confusion, and lack of understanding becomes part of the system rather than extraneous to it (Marshall, 2012).

ICT can collect and generate too much data for humans to process and faced with this information overload people may sort through the data by giving attention to what they already agree with (Shenk, 1998), or abrogate their decisions, taking the models in the software, and predictions based upon those models, as the complete reality rather than attending to reality itself (Derman, 2011; Triana, 2009). These factors all make inaccurate information flow more likely and, as we shall see, this is particularly true of finance work.

Moving into Financial Crisis

The instabilities people experience in information capitalism can be illustrated by summarising several news items written shortly after the beginning of the current financial crisis, then moving to the comments attached to the Hansell (2008) article. These 'popular' remarks display most of the approaches to the issues I have encountered so far; we cannot assume that academic analysis is somehow beyond, or outside, the popular.

Firstly, some terms need explanation. A 'subprime mortgage' is a mortgage initially issued to people with low credit ratings. The mortgage usually starts with low interest rates to attract the borrower, with interest rates increasing significantly after a contracted period of time. The aim is to charge the borrower refinancing fees, or to repossess the house and sell if the loan is not repaid, guaranteeing the lenders a profit when house prices increase faster than official interest rates rise (Gorton, 2010, pp. 68ff; Michaelson, 2008, pp. 2, 10ff, 86–9). A pool of mortgages can be divided into levels or 'tranches' of risk, and sold on to others. The highest tranches are supposed to be relatively safe and people investing in them get paid first; the lowest levels are risky and people investing in them get paid further down the queue. A collateralised debt obligation (CDO) is a cash flow from such a tranche. Some businesses further tranched CDOs, so that lower rated CDOs could be given a triple A credit rating (Soros, 2009, p. xviii; cf. Morris, 2008, p. 39ff). Complex tranching requires computers:

> In 1983 modelling the payout scenarios on . . . three-tranche [CDOs] took a mainframe computer a whole weekend. By the 1990s . . . [machines] gleefully spewed out phantasmagorical 125 tranche instruments that no one could possibly understand. (Morris, 2008, p. 41)

This lack of understanding is frequently mentioned. The tranched loans were sold to someone else who then marketed them elsewhere. Calculated risks could be lowered on the CDOs sold to others, to make them more attractive. Buyers had little knowledge of the original data, or risks, and depended on the instrument's credit rating to tell them how risky these schemes were. Credit ratings agencies were often paid by the companies whose products they rated. This conflict of interest generated distorted information. Capitalist theory insists people would normally avoid such bad information, but there is little evidence for that. Large parts of the system depended on cultivated ignorance.

Software, Quants, Models, Risks, and Inaccuracy

Dooling (2008) argues that, in making these financial tools, software created the financial problem by enabling unrestricted fictional wealth creation. Dooling essentially blames the 'quants' or quantitative analysts, who made the numerical models and sometimes sketched out the software. He writes:

> Somehow the genius quants — the best and brightest geeks Wall Street firms could buy — fed $1 trillion in subprime mortgage debt into their supercomputers, added some derivatives, massaged the arrangements with computer algorithms and — poof! — created $62 trillion in imaginary wealth . . .

He reiterates that the systems were complicated and:

> only computers can understand and derive a correlation structure from observed collateralized debt obligation tranche spreads.

With hindsight, many writers agree that the theories in the models made by quants were over-optimistic and underestimated risk. Hansell (2008) writes that the risk managers he discussed the issue with, said:

> most Wall Street computer models radically underestimated the risk of the complex mortgage securities. . . . That is partly because the level of financial distress is 'the equivalent of the 100-year flood,' in the words of Leslie Rahl, the president of Capital Market Risk Advisors, a consulting firm.

Models downplayed the possibilities of catastrophe and, according to these risk managers, overly buoyant assumptions were made. Subsequently, the models were fed with data which supported the expectation that markets were ordered and continued in an orderly manner. Rephrasing Gregg Berman of RiskMetrics, Hansell writes it was 'like a weather forecaster in Houston . . . talking about the onset of Hurricane Ike by giving the average wind speed for the previous month'. Posters to the Bits blog, also argued that modellers calculated future dangers by looking at past market behaviour, but if the market behaviour they used was stable then it was unlikely to predict future volatility. Other commentators pointed to common use of Bell curve models which assume the market is close to efficient, which, they wrote, can be demonstrated over the long term but tells you nothing about the short term (#39, #49).[2] Another person alleged the models did not contain proper feedback loops, and thus delivered the wanted 'right answer' (#150). Sometimes commentators thought that the models were not updated when they had been successful in the past, even if they no longer corresponded to current conditions (#102, #153). Many models simplified by assuming that liquidity was normal and that products could always be sold, which proved not to be true: liquidity dried up in the crisis so that debts and other items could not be sold as there were no buyers (#26, #141, #177). One person suggested that models should be reviewed by academics: 'People would be appalled at how intellectually poor those "models" are' (#103).

The commentators frequently discussed extreme risks in terms of Nassim Nicholas Taleb's (2007) work on improbable but highly disruptive 'black swan' events.[3] It was suggested that models ignored the possibility of such events (#8, #24, #39, #67, #105, #124, #172; cf. Salmon, 2009). As one person put it: 'It's kind of like thinking that there's no chance that your house will burn down because it hasn't burned down yet' (#27). Model makers either did not consider previous depressions or considered them unlikely to recur (#144). If such remarks are correct (and not everyone making them claims direct experience), then the common assumption in many models was that markets were generally smoothly ordered, rather than fluctuating and disordered. But even so, factoring in disruptions is difficult.

> If you use too long a time series, then models get unresponsive (i.e. market is collapsing and your model says it is not). If you use too short a time series then models over react (market is collapsing every other week). (#18)

More importantly, perhaps, if you tried to include disruptive events, the models might be ignored.

> I developed state-of-the-art Value-at-Risk models for Bloomberg in the mid-90's. Even then we knew that they underrepresented tail events and that Naseem Taleb's criticism was valid. We put skewness and kurtosis into the models in order to fatten the tails, which was better than what other places were doing (being an independent technology and information provider with no money in any part of the markets, we had no incentive to fudge things). However, we were still using historical data for volatilities and correlations, and therefore the outputs of these models needed to be interpreted very carefully. They were good at measuring relative risks, but not at predicting absolute probabilities of large events. I eventually got disillusioned with the abuse of mathematics — lots of PhD effort going into epicycles like 'GARCH' when it was obvious to me (a PhD mathematician myself) that the models had exceeded the limit of their usefulness. I eventually got tired of telling clients all about the range of validity and limitations of the models, because everyone wanted either to just get a number at the bottom of a printout they could blindly follow, or to tweak the assumptions until the output matched their hunch. I left Wall Street in 1998 and was completely unsurprised by LTCM[4] and all the later debacles . . .
>
> nobody had an incentive to update the models to reflect the fact that lending standards had been greatly relaxed. (#153)

Programmers and quants did not operate in a social, conceptual, or power vacuum, and the embedding networks did not favour accuracy. 'Peter' suggests that people knew the models were inadequate but it was hard to express effectively. Workers had to follow orders:

> Like some of the other people commenting here, I was one of the IT people that tried to model the work the quants were doing. On more than one occasion we were given computer code that the quants had already written to model the risk. The quants were already using the code, we were just supposed to put it in a production environment. Most of the time the code didn't really do what the quants thought it was doing. As smart as they were supposed to be, they wrote some of the worst computer code that I have ever seen . . . [They] would put people like us (IT people) under extraordinary pressure to try and do things that were impossible. We were never given the proper time to vet the work that they had done or to try to understand the nuances of what their models and trading strategies were. (#38)

Another commentator writes in another situation: 'I have personally seen CFOs stand late nights arguing with the risk analysts to make default ratio assumptions more optimistic just before loan is securitized and sold off' (#1). There was significant pressure to come up with useable and profitable results, approved by management. Accuracy could be secondary to satisfying managerial/corporate requirements.

Models Served Other Purposes than Modelling

Commentators almost overwhelmingly thought that managers liked the inaccurate models as they helped make money in the short term. It was not considered good to find high risk, as this might hinder sales. Hansell wrote that regulators required people to monitor risks and if:

a firm's risk has increased, the firm must either reduce its bets or set aside more capital as a cushion in case things go wrong.... Wall Street executives had lots of incentives to make sure their risk systems didn't see much risk.

In this case regulation made ignorance more strategically useful. Hansell quotes Gregg Berman, the co-head of the risk-management group at RiskMetrics, as saying that systems were *designed* not to pick up certain risks so that the firm's capital base could remain stable and 'the limits they imposed on their trading desks and portfolio managers would be stable'. Another person writes:

> They reduced the sensitivity of the systems to report extreme risk to allow them to prevent the system from restraining them . . . very much like the old practice of replacing blown fuses with copper pennies, so that the electricity would flow — and risk burning down the house. (#98)

Another person argued that quants had nothing to do with risk management, but:

> run investments or trading operations. While they need to handle risk their first focus is to improve the P + L [profit and loss ratio]. ie. they get paid when they reap the rewards of taking big risks . . . that doesn't jive with risk management at all. (#79)

However, a self-declared quant argued that it didn't matter how good his models were if he was given false data by others—in his case by another company (#61, cf. #65). The slogan of 'Garbage in, Garbage out' was frequently deployed as explanation (#16, #26, #63, #69, #167, #178). 'Computers produce faster and much more efficiently the errors that once took a lot of work' (#113). Explanations given for the provision of garbage information internally were similar to those given for the models being over-optimistic; the hierarchy of the firms, and the system of rewards and punishments, did not reinforce caution or the communication of pessimism.

Perils of Communication and Insecurity at Work

As well as not always being required, accuracy could be potentially damaging. 'Daniel' writes:

> Been in rooms where as an IT guy, where we had some portfolio manager explain their process, so we could automate it. After he left the room, there was dead silence, we looked at each other in shock and bewilderment, and not a word was said.... many knew that the assumptions were crazy.... the quant who keeps on arguing soon gets the label of being difficult, and 'not a team player', or worse 'does not understand the business', labels that are death knell to a career. Many people in positions of authority chose not to know. (#9)

Another commentator wrote: 'I've never seen a business or trade group pay for pure, disinterested research. They pay for purposeful research, specifically to support the business model they're committed to and to enhance its sale' (#47, cf. #54, #56).

Other writers implied that you would get fired or demoted if you did not give people the results they wanted even if those results were clearly false (#19, #168, #182), and this was not uncommon (#104, #182). One person stated that: 'Citigroup fired [the] entire lending brass in 2006 in CitiFinancial (people with actual lending experience) and replaced them with Citibank people to eliminate dual structures and save 1 billion in costs' (#90). 'The problem is that those with the gray hair or risk management savvy were all fired for questioning the business model' (#95, cf. #108). Employee experience and accuracy is not valued.

Information failure was standard. One person suggested that creative accounting was so ubiquitous it is considered normal, and thus people never react to their actual financial situation (#3). Similarly, if people make money out of inaccuracy there is no incentive for them to erect obstacles to the process (#23) and 'you can make any model tell you want you wish!!' (#16), so it's easy to be 'safe' in terms of job approval. Others thought the actions were deliberate and criminal; they 'played with their computer systems to conceal the risk of what they were doing' (#78). Banks were largely not interested in risk management as it does not directly make money and was seen 'only as a cost center and traders/bankers/PMs see it as a pain in the ass' (#79).

> It is apparent that the sophistication of risk management software is no match for the combined talents of aggressive traders, subjugated quants and incompetent risk managers who are respectively, determined to benefit from, happy to support and afraid to report the creation of transient profits from mis-pricing risk. (#145)

Risks had been pointed out 'but no one has been listening. The lure of the money was simply too strong and anyone that said otherwise was quickly silenced' (#50). It seems generally agreed among these commentators that there is little possibility of open communication in corporations, and that to communicate something which went against immediate profit would likely be seen by management as a failing in the communicator.

Models as Reality

Although the models were disrupted by failures of communication in a corporate hierarchy, commentators commonly thought that models were taken for reality (#177). People relied 'on what is basically just a tool as a replacement for human judgment' (#71, cf #6, #70). 'There was the sense that machine would save man from himself, substituting technical savvy for investment savvy' (#92). People found it difficult to understand what they were trading, due to its complexity, volume, and speed. It was suggested that perhaps people believed that they could make risky trades as the computers successfully calculated risks, and thus insured them from bad results (#126, #127). As such there was no need for them to try and understand the non-understandable risks involved. Taking models for reality also meant that ratings agency ratings were also easily taken as real, rather than fallible guesses (#67, #103, #146, #151). The hope was that someone, somewhere, understood things. Models distributed responsibility. When David Li, author of a widely used derivatives formula, warned that people did not understand his model, and that 'the most dangerous part is when people believe everything coming out of it', he was ignored (Salmon, 2009; Whitehouse, 2005).

Furthermore, problems with models could compound, as many companies traded their financial assets and obligations through networked computers at great speed, all using similar models (or trying to take advantage of known models), producing unexpected feedback effects, and making human judgement even harder:

> When the broad markets use roughly the same mathematical premises as the basis of their proprietary models, the behavior of the market participants becomes positively correlated, not diversified, as a result of which the markets move in unison; thus, when the sell lights go on, they go on in more or less every trading room, there's a rush to the exits, and eventually a big pile of bodies at the door. (#177)

Likewise Salmon quotes Kai Gilkes of the credit research firm CreditSights as saying:

> [David] Li can't be blamed. . . . After all, he just invented the model. Instead, we should blame the bankers who misinterpreted it. And even then, the real danger was created not because any given trader adopted it but because every trader did. In financial markets, everybody doing the same thing is the classic recipe for a bubble and inevitable bust.

Financial markets are mobs.

General Sources

Most of the above comes from one blog, so it is necessary to check whether the correlations written about are mentioned elsewhere. Although clearly not a disinterested account, Michaelson's autobiography of his time managing the marketing of home loans at Countrywide, conveys the sense he felt policy was decided above him (even though he was a major managerial figure) and that objections would not be listened to. When he objected that Countrywide could not assume that house prices would rise for ever, he was told that they have 'run the numbers' and that the 'risk is offset by opportunity for market share and revenue gain' and it's consistent with the company's 'mission' (2008, pp. 20–2). Corporate conformity (what he calls 'culture') produced obedience, and the only questions people could ask concerned how they might do what they were told (Ibid., pp. 2, 14). Jonathan Knee similarly reports on the difficulty of raising difficulties, the secrecy about internal organisation, and ongoing conflicts of interest (2007, pp. 52, 71, 198). Vicki Ward's journalistic account (2010) of life at Lehman Bros, shows an organisation riddled with secrecy and deceit at all levels and managed through fear, even in its supposed good and honest days. Karen Ho's ethnographic account of life on Wall Street draws attention to constant testing, 100-hour working weeks, segregation of different status people so that informal communication is unlikely, and the shock and disillusionment of realising that unless you came from the most elite universities or had contacts you were forever held back from the big money (2009, pp. 74–8, 80). Anything that is not high status, including technical support, is thought of as back office and a treated as a 'cost centre' (Ibid., p. 79), however vital the work. Back-office people are stigmatised (Ibid., p. 81). However, '[f]ront and back-office workers, however, do have a few things in common, namely job-insecurity and a sparse work environment' (Ibid., p. 80, cf. 11–12 for 'rampant insecurity'). Most finance workers live in a 'white-collar sweatshop' which is strongly hierarchical and values obedience rather than thought (Ibid., p. 83ff). Although primarily humorous, Rolfe and Troob's (2000) account of their lives on Wall Street similarly displays the fear, exhaustion, and conformity necessary for ambitious workers to succeed in these financial workplaces. 'As associates, nodding our heads in agreement was an involuntary reflex. We'd been taught to always concur. Conflict was confusing . . . Independent thought wasn't valued' (Ibid., p. 227–8).

One of the few serious inside sources on computer programming is Emanuel Derman's autobiography, *My Life as A Quant* (2004). While this describes events before the post 2007 financial crisis, it gives further insight into the way financial companies operate. For example, finance companies do have the endemic internal conflicts and status barriers we have just discussed, and these block communications. Derman mentions the pressure, bullying, and abuse although he claims to have enjoyed it (2004, p. 135). He argues that traders and quants have to work differently and the occupations favour different personality types; 'Traders and quants are genuinely different species' (Ibid., p. 11), and this makes 'professional cross-communication difficult' (Ibid., p. 12). Quants need time and coherent research but are constantly interrupted, with results demanded almost immediately (Ibid., pp. 8–9, 12). Traders played status games and put quants, as well as other types of traders, down (Ibid., pp. 10–13, 125). Management can intensify the barriers and sometimes the quants were overwhelmed by layers of management. In one case:

> Over time, the modeling and programming groups became inverted pyramids: one or two technically skilled people at the bottom, who could write programs or build models, supporting a larger number of human conduits above them who passed the results up to the trading desk and then passed the subsequent responses back down again. Having a PhD and being good at research or being able to program well was not an advantage in this structure. (Ibid., p. 137)

The passing of information up and down the hierarchy probably led to 'Chinese Whisper' effects. On one occasion Derman had proximity to the trading desks, but after six months they were moved away 'and lost our sense of community. From then on it became much harder to acquire the skill of communicating with traders, one of the more difficult tasks facing a new quant' (Ibid., p. 205). There are many barriers to communication and to delivering the right product in this kind of environment, so it is not surprising that people live in a haze of inaccuracy.

The models the quants deliver have different results. Derman writes:

> The best quantitative finance brings real insight into the relation between value and uncertainty, and it approaches the quality of real science; the worst is a pseudoscientific hodgepodge of complex mathematics used with obscure justification. (2004, p. 3)

He claims that most models are based upon the Black–Scholes options pricing model, which assumes market equilibrium and a Bell curve distribution of prices (2004, pp. 5, 145). This allows the manufacture of derivatives which supposedly allow clients (who usually buy the derivative from the inhouse trader, who has an incentive not to tell clients about conceptual problems) 'to tailor and fine-tune the risk they want to assume or avoid' (Ibid., p. 6). Although it is not the only model, 'the history of quants on Wall Street is the history of the ways in which practitioners and academics have refined and extended the Black-Scholes model' (Ibid., pp. 8, 10). Other quants work on divining future stock movements from past ones. However, 'probabilities are necessarily extracted from past events; they provide notoriously poor estimates of the likelihood of future catastrophes' (Ibid., p. 10). The models necessarily simplified reality by assuming market equilibrium, or by assuming past events mirror future events, and they furthermore had to be useable by traders.

> [S]electing a model becomes a question of finding one that is rich enough to represent most of the risks your product faces, efficient enough to run on a computer in a tolerable amount of time, and simple enough so that programming it is not too complex and burdensome a task. (Ibid., p. 161)

On other occasions, as with derivatives, not only was the terrain uncharted, with 'no commonly acknowledged best path through it', but there were structural communication problems: 'Every time we spoke with the traders, we faced such a flood of demands and choices that it was difficult to decide what to do first' (Ibid., p. 220). Finally there was the question of how the programs would be used.

> Watching traders occasionally put too much faith in the power of formalism and mathematics, I saw that if you listen to the models' siren song for too long, you may end up on the rocks or in the whirlpool. (2004, p. 261)

Using these other sources, it appears the kinds of disruptions discussed on the blog, were probably common throughout the finance, and other, knowledge work industries.

Critical Response Without a Movement

The perceptions that people expressed sometimes raised political responses. Some commentators pointed to crashes as a recurrent problem: 'I seem to recall 10 years ago when LTCM imploded that their Nobel principals were calling that a 100 year event too. Isn't it strange that these 100 year events seem to be occurring every 10 years' (#71).

> 100-year floods seem to happen every 3 or 4 years in the financial markets. We've had the S&L fiasco, the '87 crash, the junk bond debacle, the Latin American debt crisis, Long-Term Capital

Management's implosion, the Asian financial meltdown, the dot-com bomb, 9/11 and now this, all within the last two decades. (#100)

'Does the system of market economy have the built in feature of creating crisis in cycles and are we facing one of them now?' (#171).

> We saw this with the vastly inflated values of the technology bubble, the hunger for junk bonds in the ·80s, the promises of perpetual growth from the go-go stocks of the 60s. We are seeing it again in these esoteric securities. In each case, the form was different, but the results the same. The failure of a phantom economy that has unfortunately tangible effects for the real one. (#92)

One person further explained this as arising because 'we have decided to prioritize the symbolic aspect of money, thereby eliminating the need for real production to back up the creation of new value' (#143). 'The idea that you could ship jobs elsewhere and not worry about maintaining a manufacturing base only created idle minds and a pervasive need to create value out of nothing' (#179).

Surprisingly, few of the bloggers discussed the subprime mortgage market, which is widely held to be a driver for the crisis. However certain points were made. Subprime mortgages were explained as ways to 'bring new money into real estate once the market had been saturated' and artificially create a bubble (#17). Brokers made money on commissions even if the buyers defaulted (#114, #187). People were pushed into the increasing rate loans whether they were poor or not: 'The Federal Reserve estimated between 2003 & 2006 60% of the mortgages sold were of a non-traditional type' (#187). Some commentators were bemused at the lack of standards for loans where, for instance, companies issued loans based on the income the borrower stated they had without requiring any evidence (#41). Subprime mortgages further demonstrated to people that the financial economy was run on unreal principles, and inaccurate models. One person wrote of the financial economy generally: 'It was a multiplayer virtual reality version of the old pyramid scheme' (#123).

> when 'speculative bubbles' collapse—they always collapse relatively fast. All of them involve a phase transition—fantasy to reality. Every Ponzi scheme is a bubble and every bubble is a Ponzi scheme. None of them are sustainable because they become ever more unstable as the energy gets sucked out of them. (#179)

One commentator wrote 'no one asks the real question. Why aren't Americans able to own their own homes?' and answered greed (#86). Greed was a popular explanation (#5, #6, #15, #16, #29, #30, #40, #64, #72, #82, #123) which psychologises (and naturalises) capitalism and its crises. Greed was occasionally related to other moral issues, such as the loss of essential morals: 'Civics, Ethics, Values, mutual responsibility. Capitalism does not really work without them all' (#181; cf. #133). Yet there was little sign that capitalism helped sustain them.

Class

There was some expression of class sensibility. Fallout from the crash did not seem equally distributed. 'It is the guys in IT programming and managing the projects are the ones who get hurt from this' (#59). 'Don't blame the quants, they were doing the best they could with the tools they had. Blame the front office. The search for revenue or alpha always trumps the back office capabilities' (#185).

One person thought that the wealthy did not understand the conditions that most people lived in (#4). More commonly people argued that the wealthy had no incentive to be responsible, as they were protected from the consequences of their mistakes, or even benefited from mistakes (#20). There was no motivation for people at the top to worry about the continuance of their companies, as with a few years work they could leave with enough money to live extremely well for the rest of their lives, even if the company crashed as a result. They:

> have pocketed enough bonuses that they can retire quite comfortably, even at a very young age. All that taking the risk seriously would have done in the short run would have been to reduce earnings, and thus reduce bonuses. (#117)

'Problem is, the entire world economy is paying the price, and the top dogs are still walking away with their $20mil bonuses' (# 41, cf. #59, #102). There were some people who felt the crisis resulted from 'liberal' policies intended to close the housing gap, which led bankers to make stupid loans (#121, #138, #153), but they were surprisingly small in number given that theory's promotion by the political Right.

Remedies

Only occasionally was the crisis seen in wider political terms and that mainly focused on regulation. 'On the political side, there has been a systematic destruction of regulations preventing the rich from economically raping the rest of us' (#84). 'I'd be interested to know whether the reductions in constraints on leverage allegedly granted by the SEC in 2004 . . . were indeed a factor in this week's events' (#155). Solutions to ongoing crises could be implicated in causing further chaos: 'The solution to every financial hiccup has been to encourage even more debt though lower interest rates, and other mechanisms' (#127).

People did propose remedies more radical than the US government's: 'If a monster company must be bailed out with tax payers' money, then that company should be outright nationalized' (#127). It was suggested that commissions on mortgages should reflect repayments, not just the fact of people entering into the contract (#133), or that we should invest in communities rather than companies (#135). Occasionally the double standards were noticed.

> Why is it that with so much government money being given to the businesses where mistakes were made due to greed, no money is available for the individuals being foreclosed and losing their homes because they were lied to, intentionally confused, or just reaching for a dream beyond their grasp? (#160)

While recognising the unfairness and inadequacies of corporate financial capitalism, people commenting on this blog did not call for any radical political action or movement. There seemed to be a lack of hope about anything radically better, or of any sense of how to organise effectively. Finance was perhaps saved from active criticism by its unmanageable complexity.

Summary and Conclusions

The financial crisis was a crisis, which among other things, depended upon the normality of cultivated ignorance and bad communication, in markets that are generally theorised as requiring participants to uncover accurate information, or as generating accurate information. This failure of information resonates with the continual and necessary failure of information within the wider framework of the corporate workplace and its management.

This wider framework includes what we might call the 'networks of work'; that is the dynamic interconnections, ambience, conflicts, rewards, precarities, power relations, and communication conduits (or barriers) of the workplace. The attention of workers is directed as much towards this networked environment as to the 'business environment' in which the firm they work for operates in. In the network of work, most workers, including many managerial workers, are insecure, and repeatedly disrupted by restructurings and new software installations. Accuracy and worker's knowledge can count for little. Workers' positions are only as good as the next result, or their next agreement/argument with those above them. These factors promote widespread fear and exhaustion in the workplace. The expectation of insecurity about income and power, in lower echelon workers at least, means that information or criticism from these workers is blocked, even if they are the ones who know what they are doing. Cost cutting further lowers the experience levels of a corporation, especially in those areas that affect performance and checking. In the construction of financial software, structural communication barriers exist between quants, programmers, traders, risk analysts, and managers. All these features increase the prevalence of inaccurate information.

Similar pressures operate on the kinds of models that people use to make trades. People are not encouraged to communicate doubts or queries, and if they disagree with the demands of those superior to them, they can be subject to browbeatings, being seen as negative, or failing to understand their own work, and thus face dismissal. In an insecure network, people tend to go along with what is required of them. Hierarchy and potential punishment prevents the flow of information or corrective feedback. People worked under constant pressure to give the 'right' money making results, and the programs 'worked' in terms of what was demanded of them.

We can further conjecture that, as information affects prices, it can be profitable, especially when the risks are high, for sellers not to pass on all information about drawbacks to purchasers, as it could interrupt the sale. The market will be routinely full of misinformation, and inaccuracy tends to compound.

One result, of these inward and outward pressures, was that as risk could interrupt trade, then risks could be downplayed. Programs routinely underestimated the risk of catastrophic events, partly because these are difficult to describe, and partly because risk and accurate information is undervalued, and underreported, when profit is at stake. Programmers may also have avoided using, or not had time to use, more complex feedback loops, or factor in the effects of similar dealings happening simultaneously, for example, the foreclosure of so many mortgages at the same time that house prices would collapse and houses be unsellable. Social and managerial pressures increased the simplicity of models with respect to the world, and they did not, and possibly could not, include the effect of use of those models.

Furthermore, while risk maybe calculable for a stable system (such as with insurance for human death rates and weather patterns, with these patterns becoming particularly stable if acts of war, God, or self-harm are excised from the calculations), this may not be the case with financial markets, which are not stable, and where the risk calculations themselves change the risks people take. In finance, risk was tailored to expectations, depending on communications, power relations, and what is deemed practicable. As Derman writes:

> everyone who creates a useful model gets exposed to the truth that building a trading and risk management system around the model is a huge and often overwhelming software project that requires many more programmers than quants. Models, critical though they are, are only a small part of the story. (2004, p. 165)

Data the programs were tested with may have reinforced inaccuracy. Data could be supplied by people who did not understand the program, to make the results look better, or to sell the proposed behaviour and to continue short-term moneymaking. In any case, data (in itself) does not hold the future. The use of past data stripped the models of context. Economic events occur within a historical context, and that context changes the meaning of events which are by our measurements otherwise identical. People's reactions to events are affected by what they see going on around those events. Finally, when the programs where applied, they interacted with networks of other companies programs and the resulting numbers become less likely to reflect reality.

Software also allowed the set-up of trades and products that were so complex that humans could not understand them on their own, and so became separated from the reality the models were supposed to describe. This complexity means that faith was necessary and resonated with faith in stable, or flourishing, markets. Responsibility for accuracy was deferred elsewhere, and the distortions, which failure of human communication and understanding had introduced, were dismissed. The computerised models gave people a false sense of security, implying they actually understood the markets or were insured against bad happenings. Computerisation functioned as a form of magic, giving the appearance of control and safety, justifying the risk and further relieving the user of responsibility for taking the risk.

The networks of work also had an effect in that the reward structures did not significantly penalise those at the top who enforced mistaken actions, indeed they could receive huge rewards for failure, so they had no incentive to behave any differently. People who were fortunately placed in the business made huge amounts of money, and even if they were sacked they were still extremely well off in comparison to everyone else. There was little incentive for them to think of the long-term benefit of their company. It was mainly the more lowly placed workers who were punished by events. Reward structures can pay people to destroy the company if this gives a potential short-term reward that the person receiving it judges is good enough. Careers seem to depend on moving from company to company so there is no long-term loyalty. Loyalty depends on cash received now or potentially in the future. Going against the hierarchy is fairly strongly selected against, as loss of position is not easily recovered. Generally this is a network in which trickery, bad communication, and ruthlessness is rewarded. There is no particular benefit in being openly accurate or loyal.

Through this workplace network, corporate life gradually disconnects from other networks and other ecologies; productive, social, and natural. In this disconnection, it loses touch with the trust and relationships that stabilise it, and which are necessary for successful human social survival. It destroys the trust that allows money to function and, as money is its only basis and reward, it also destroys the internal bonds and accurate communication pathways that allow organisations to function and survive. All that is left is upheaval, shrouded in assumptions about order and the triumph of the will.

Bad information is not just an incidental part of capitalist finance which could be eliminated in a perfect world. It is inherent to the process of investment. Furthermore, we can suggest that the current economic crisis arises not from the failure of networks and software, but from their success both in extending the pathologies of capitalist management and the failure of information.

Notes

1   The Bank of International Settlements writes that the 'notional amount of outstanding over-the-counter (OTC) derivatives fell by 8%, to $648 trillion, in the second half of 2011' (BIS, 2012, p. 12). The world GDP is estimated by the CIA (2012) as a fraction of this figure, at $70 trillion.

2 (#n) refers to the numbered comment, 'n', in the blog.
3 Taleb, himself, is quoted as saying 'the financial crisis was not a black swan. It was perfectly predictable' (Wente, 2009).
4 Long-Term Capital Management. For a brief analysis of their fall, see Morris (2008, pp. 49–58).

References

BIS (2012) *BIS Quarterly Review*, June 2012, http://www.bis.org/publ/qtrpdf/r_qt1206.htm.
Bivens, J. (2011) *Failure by Design: The Story Behind America's Broken Economy* (Ithaca, NY: Cornell University Press).
CIA (2012) *World Fact Book*. Field Listing: GDP, https://www.cia.gov/library/publications/the-world-factbook/fields/2195.html.
Derman, E. (2004) *My Life as a Quant: Reflections on Physics and Finance* (Hoboken, NJ: John Wiley).
Derman, E. (2011) *Models Behaving Badly: Why Confusing Illusion with Reality Can Lead to Disaster, on Wall Street and in Life* (New York: Free Press).
Dooling, R. (2008) The rise of the machines, *New York Times*, 11 October, http://www.nytimes.com/2008/10/12/opinion/12dooling.html.
Ferguson, C. H. (2012) *Predator Nation: Corporate Criminals, Political Corruption and the Hijacking of America* (New York: Crown Business).
Foster, J. B. & Magdoff, F. (2009) *The Great Financial Crisis: Causes and Consequences* (New York: Monthly Review).
Gorton, G. B. (2010) *Slapped by the Invisible Hand: The Panic of 2007* (Oxford: Oxford University Press).
Hansell, S. (2008) How Wall Street lied to its computers, *New York Times, Bits*, 18 September, http://bits.blogs.nytimes.com/2008/09/18/how-wall-streets-quants-lied-to-their-computers/.
Hira, R. & Hira, A. (2009) *Outsourcing America: The True Cost of Shipping Jobs Overseas and What Can Be Done About It* (New York: AMACOM).
Ho, K. (2009) *Liquidated: An Ethnography of Wall St* (Durham, NC: Duke University Press).
Hudson, M. W. (2010) *The Monster: How a Gang of Predatory Lenders and Wall Street Bankers Fleeced America and Spawned a Global Crisis* (New York: Times Books).
Kliman, A. (2012) *The Failure of Capitalist Production: Underlying Causes of the Great Recession* (London: Pluto Press).
Knee, J. A. (2007) *The Accidental Investment Banker* (New York: Random House).
Marshall, J. P. (2012) Information technology and the experience of disorder, *Cultural Studies Review*, 18(3), pp. 281–309.
Michaelson, A. (2008) *The Foreclosure of America: The Inside Story of the Rise and Fall of Countrywide Home Loans, the Mortgage Crisis, and the Default of the American Dream* (New York: Berkley).
Morris, C. R. (2008) *The Trillion Dollar Meltdown: Easy Money, High Rollers, and the Great Credit Crash* (New York: Public Affairs).
Rolfe, J. & Troob, P. (2000) *Monkey Business: Swinging Through the Wall St Jungle* (New York: Warner Books).
Salmon, F. (2009) Recipe for disaster: The formula that killed Wall Street, *Wired Magazine*, 17 March, http://www.wired.com/techbiz/it/magazine/17-03/wp_quant.
Shenk, D. (1998) *Data Smog: Surviving the Information Glut* (San Francisco: HarperEdge).
Soros, G. (2009) *The Crash of 2008 and What it Means*, 2nd ed. (Melbourne: Scribe).
Sowell, T. (2010) *The Housing Boom and Bust*, revised ed. (New York: Basic Books).
Taleb, N. (2007) *The Black Swan: The Impact of the Highly Improbable* (New York: Random House).
Triana, P. (2009) *Lecturing Birds on Flying: Can Mathematical Theories Destroy the Financial Markets?* (New York: John Wiley).
Ward, V. (2010) *The Devil's Casino: Friendship, Betrayal, and the High-stakes Games Played Inside Lehman Brothers* (Hoboken, NJ: John Wiley).
Wente, E. (2009) Nassim Taleb on the economy: We still have the same disease, *Globe and Mail*, 13 September, http://www.theglobeandmail.com/report-on-business/economy/we-still-have-the-same-disease/article1202455/.
Whitehouse, M. (2005) Slices of risk: How a formula ignited market that burned some big investors, *Wall Street Journal*, 12 September, p. A1.
Williams Mark, T. (2010) *Uncontrolled Risk: Lessons of Lehman Brothers and how Systemic Risk Can Still Bring Down the World Financial System* (New York: McGraw Hill).

Jonathan Marshall is an honorary associate at the University of Technology Sydney. He has recently completed a project funded by the Australian Research Council entitled 'Chaos, Information Technology, Global Administration and Daily Life', from which this article originates. He has previously held a post-doctoral fellowship to investigate the use of Online Gender. He is author of *Living on Cybermind: Categories, Communication and Control* (Peter Lang, 2007) and co-author of *Disorder and the Disinformation Society: The Social Dynamics of Networks and Software* (Routledge, 2013).

The Rigidity Trap in Global Resilience: Neoliberalisation Through Principles, Standards, and Benchmarks

PETER ROGERS

Macquarie University, Sydney, Australia

ABSTRACT *This article offers a critical social science perspective on the globalisation of disaster resilience. It is argued that the regulatory experimentation, typical of neoliberalisation, has begun to increase standardisation of emergency and security practices. Examples of this can be seen in the growth of general principles, non-statutory guidance, and international standards designed to improve resilience to disasters. This represents the creeping 'neoliberalisation' of 'disaster resilience'. When this results in over-standardisation a 'rigidity trap' is created. Regulatory experimentation may enhance the resiliency of organisations and infrastructure, but when standards and benchmarks seek to create 'resilient subjects' and 'resilient communities' the positive potential is lost in bureaucratic inflexibility. The neoliberalisation of resilience, if unchecked, will undermine the very flexible capabilities and adaptive capacity it is claimed that a focus on resilience can create.*

Introduction

Over the last 50 years the concept of resilience has re-emerged from diverse research fields to become a key influence in disaster management. At the heart of neoliberal strategies for dealing with risk, uncertainty, and all forms of danger it can be argued that resilience has become a global institution. If 'institutions' are positioned as 'the rules of the game' and 'organisations' as coalitions of individuals with common purpose (North et al., 2010), then the concept of resilience has emerged as a key driver of reform in disaster management and now underpins how governments and key organisations understand risk, uncertainty, and disaster. This article elaborates a critical social science perspective on the globalisation of resilience by (a) outlining the transition of resilience from research metaphor to a policy-driven institution within global capitalism, and (b) offering a critical perspective on the implications of new international standards that seek to guide the implementation of resilience.

The continued rise of resilience in recent years demands a clear synthesis of the diverse definitions it has attracted, when aligned with the global pressures of potential disorderly crises and disaster events. I begin by presenting, in brief, the generation and application of the resilience research metaphor, then highlighting its contribution as a driver of increasingly variegated crisis and disaster management policies and tactics. Resilience re-emerges as, potentially, an institutional characteristic of governance. However, this reconceptualisation of resilience creates a two-edged blade, where not only does exposure to disaster increase resilience, but the danger remains of over-standardisation that reduces flexibility and increases future vulnerability, creating 'rigidity traps'. There is potential then for a positive or a negative outcome from an increased focus on resilience. The positive sees resilience as offering potential for dealing with danger that engages the public more directly in the cyclical process of disaster management. The negative shows resilience as another complex form of what has been identified as an ongoing and globalising process of neoliberalisation (Brenner et al., 2010), one that exacerbates rigidity, vulnerability and may distribute 'bad effects' even more unequally to those affected by disasters. The article concludes that standards and benchmarks are useful in so far that they offer tried and tested 'toolkits' to experts, but an adaptive and non-standardised process of learning sensitive to the ceaseless struggles for, and reorganisations of, power must remain at the heart of attempts to implement these tools in different contexts. Rigid or inflexible implementation of standards will undermine local adaptive capacities and capabilities and increase vulnerability to the disorderly nature of crises.

There may be potential here for resilience to act as a palliative to the excesses of a 'zombie neoliberalism'.[1] The tendential constraints on free-market alignment of governance in the 'push-back' of cross-scalar resiliency can be used to exemplify disarticulated counter-neoliberalisation. In such cases where national policy is negotiated through regional governance and distributed in locally managed projects more orchestrated forms of locally variegated action become possible[2] but often remain either poor coordinated or are curtailed by economic regulatory reform. The UK model of regional and local resilience forums (2002–2008) showed this in practice; first resisting the economy of scale imposed on emergency services (Rogers, 2009) before the regional tier of government was disbanded under the auspices of austerity measures imposed by the Conservative–Liberal coalition, again the potential of the macro-spatial resiliency rule-regime was dominated by market logic and thus undermined. In such examples the process-driven economy of scale was used to legitimise political co-option of resilience into post global financial crisis (GFC) economic austerity measures with little benefit to dealing with disasters. This *post hoc ergo propter hoc* could lead to resilience being used as an avoidance tool. Where resilience becomes the domain of charities and community interest companies (CiCs) governments become absolved of the costs for dealing with the cause of crises. Shared responsibility for dealing with danger between the government, the citizen, the charitable, and the private sectors may thus evolve into strategies of 'moralization' and 'responsibilization' (Shamir, 2008) at the expense of participatory and democratic routes forward.

Generating and Applying Resilience in Research

Resilience has re-emerged in recent years as a hot topic. The etymological Latin root *resiliens* and its derivatives *resilio* (Klien et al., 2003) and *resiliere* (Paton and Johnston, 2006) see resilience often evoked as 'recoil'. The earliest English usage emphasised the repercussive qualities of sound, namely 'resilience of echoes' (Bacon, 1659). Later in engineering resilience re-emerged as the obdurate qualities of materials, for example, calculating the mechanical stress resistance of wooden/steel beams in shipbuilding (Young, 1877). In the twentieth century modern ecology extended engineering resilience, incorporating time required for a return to a 'steady state' in ecosystems. *Engineering* resilience was contrasted with *ecological* resilience—defined as the buffer capacity of ecosystems to absorb externally caused perturbation, maintain robust functions, and survive systemic shock (Holling, 1973). Concurrent with the seminal work of Holling, a psychological approach framed resilience as an adaptive capacity of humans. Research assessed the capability of children to mitigate high-risk circumstances and negotiate adversity to maintain positive healthy development (Garmezy, 1973).

More recently a corporate business model in risk management has incorporated resilience as an organisational characteristic. Risk, resistance, and durability are embedded in corporate 'business continuity' (Sheffi, 2005). This can be aligned with the risk calculus model of trying to convert the unknown into calculable probabilities to reduce financial costs to the corporation in the face of disorder.

In carrying meanings forward from research into policy, there is a significant shift from the determinate properties of sound and materials to the nuanced interplay of ecological, economic, and human systems. The realignment of natural and social scientific interpretations derives from the etymological root; however, disaster resilience policy deploys metaphorical 'bouncing' and 'returning to a previous state' as 'transformative' and 'adaptive'. The contextual embedding results in different goals and outcomes within different disciplinary and organisational contexts, a bifurcation which feeds the contestation of disaster resilience (Coaffee et al., 2008; Comfort et al., 2010; Paton and Johnston, 2006).

From Cross-disciplinary Research to Applied Disaster Resilience

Each iteration of research offers subtle but important distinctions in how resilience is operationalised. Theorists, researchers, and practitioners invoke differing characteristics[3] thus the emphasis changes the goals when translated into policy and practice.

Disaster resilience is commonly used to explore how (a) uncertainty and (b) exposure to potentially disorderly conditions, require positive change to mitigate negative impacts. The description of change differs across sectors, resulting in different targets, goals, and outcomes in governance, for business continuity, in international relations, adapting to climate change, etc. Differences in definition, benchmarking, or measurement result. Perhaps most advanced in articulating the contestation are progressive socio-ecological and corporate risk management approaches. The policy metaphor of resilience emerging here implies the exposure to crisis or disorder creates 'conditions of possibility' for *adaptation* and *transformation*. On the one hand, this can result in either more *positive, flexible*, and *resilient conditions* or, on the other, a more *negative rigidity* which is *resistant to perturbation* but potentially also more brittle under extreme conditions.

Arguably the most influential research group in applying the former is Stockholm Resilience Centre emphasising the analysis of complex socio-ecological systems and bureaucratic governance in neoliberal interpretations of global capitalism (Walker and Cooper, 2011, p. 20). Here, the extent to which characteristics of resilience can be realised, as adaptation or transformation, may be bound by the 'embeddedness' of four components in a complex system. Walker et al. (2004) frame these as: *latitude*—the threshold of persistence before breakdown of the pre-existing form; *resistance*—the persistence of the original form in yielding to, or resisting change; *precariousness*—how close to the threshold the original form is at present; and *panarchy*—the unforeseen dynamics operating across all scales of influence. Such uncertainties may include oppressive political regimes, military invasions, global economic crisis, biological disaster, and global climate change—any, or all of which, can trigger uncertainty at local, regional, national, or international levels in real time (Ibid., pp. 6–7).

This research may be the most progressive in defining resilience critically but it fails to engage with the contextually embedded neoliberalisation of governance practice, overemphasising the 9/11 security drivers, thus obscuring dynamic 'associated regulatory landscapes'. For example, the UK civil contingencies agenda operationalised an institutional need for increased resilience to large-scale security threats, natural hazards, and anthropogenic risks. It embedded a neoliberalising restructuring of disasters, not as discreet events but as a cycle of human capabilities and organisational capacities that could be evaluated and improved by rational economies of scale (Rogers, 2011a). It also provided a point of departure for 'resilience' to seed three neoliberal dimensions of disaster: '(i) regulatory experimentation; (ii) inter-jurisdictional policy transfer; and (iii) the formation of transnational rule-regimes' (Brenner et al., 2010). Resilience re-emerges in contextually specific and variegated reformulations in different scalar contexts, but always underpinned as 'disaster management' *in situ* by the same rhetorical logic (to adapt and transform) with similar characteristics (to anticipate, assess, prepare for, prevent, respond to, and recover from threats, hazards, and risks).[4] Governance processes are often benchmarked in ways not inimical, but certainly not immediately compatible, with this socio-ecological model. As such resilience emulates the 'ecological dominance' of neoliberalisation (Jessop, 2000) in disaster management operating across scales as an embedded but variegated institutionalised discourse. There is a drive to quantify resilience as a measurable outcome of new policy initiatives, to evaluate the programmes that claim to create resilience using 'metrics' and to provide standards, benchmarks, and 'toolkits' to enable others to become more resilient. This needs to be addressed if the form of resilience implemented in governance of crises, disorder, and disasters is to be understood in applied, rather than abstract or purely theoretical, terms.

Disaster Resilience: Operationalising the Policy Context

Disaster resilience is a contested concept, particularly given the variations of resilience in the focus of research and policy. For example, *organisational* resilience can be defined as 'a management concept that describes the ability of organisations to cope in the face of adversity—to recover and return to normality after confronting abnormal, alarming and often unexpected threats' (McAslan, 2010, p. 2). On the other hand, *community* resilience is far less tangible. Communities can be defined in different ways, consequently there is no one agreed upon definition. As a result, rather than try to define it, practical engagements may instead offer case study exemplars. For example, the UK Cabinet Office provides a community resilience database of projects to exemplify best practice. This is also paired with a move towards a discourse of 'shared responsibility'—between civil government and the community of citizens. In different aspects of the disaster cycle (across the cycle of anticipation, assessment, prevention, preparation, response and recovery (AA-PP-RR)) this could be read as an example of what Brenner et al. (2011) identify as an inherent contradiction in neoliberalisation, which due to its dynamism cannot be sustained without collision with its alternatives:

> ... through this collision, neoliberalization processes rework inherited forms of regulatory and spatial organisation, including those of state institutions themselves, to produce new forms of geo-institutional differentiation. (p. 331)

CRISIS, MOVEMENT, MANAGEMENT: GLOBALISING DYNAMICS

The contestation, and at times logical or ethical contradiction, between the operationalised forms of resilience here become examples of geo-institutional differentiation; creatively destroyed in resilience-driven cycles of regulatory reform. In seeking to identify potential 'rigidity traps', the remainder of this article focuses on organisational resilience; examining principles, guidance, and standards for practitioners who deal with disasters. Note the phrase 'who deal with disasters' is intended to include cross-sectoral experts (e.g. in disaster risk reduction, risk assessment), emergency services (e.g. police, ambulance, fire), the 'third sector' (charitable or volunteer agencies), as well as civil government and all multi-stakeholder public–private partnerships (from utilities and transport to industrial production etc.). For these experts and professionals (in any organisation) the implementation of an integrated cycle of learning can be seen as mitigating the existential and material vulnerabilities or insecurities exposed by crisis (Coaffee et al., 2009). However, there remains a lack of integration between resilience in research and the applied resilience that stakeholders attempt to implement.

The reach of resilience is increasing as the stakes and consequence for poor levels of preparedness grow (Coaffee and Rogers, 2008, 2010; Rogers, 2009, 2012b) and appears set to continue to do so through disaster, organisational, community varieties as well as new, yet to emerge, regulatory experimentations emerging from professional networks, operational guidelines, general principles, and quality standards that feed both the inter-jurisdictional policy transfer and the formation of a transnational rule-regime that guides the variegated globalisation of resilience.

Professional Networks: Guidelines, Principles, and Standards

Professional networks, guidelines for practice, guidance principles, and international standards are examples of the vehicles for the emergence of inter-jurisdictional policy transfer and the formation of transnational rule-regimes of 'resilience'. Contextually embedding disaster resilience policy in networks of security and emergency professionals shows how 'learning from exposure' enhances cross-border exchanges of expertise in the resultant regulatory regimes.[5] Through consultation experiences are shared, carried forwards into standards as process specific 'toolkits' designed to improve and coordinate 'best practice'. The emergent form of resilience is embedded in regulatory experimentation, for example the proliferation of national strategies for resilience.[6] The emergent standards enhance inter-jurisdictional policy transfer and intra-organisational exchange of lessons learned from the experiences of those exposed to crisis events in diverse vocations. It also recognises the benefits of capacity building across specialisations that helps break down the silos of overly specialised organisations.

Resilience in practice exists in a range of policies and standards. At the global scale there is evidence for 'contextual embeddedness' in international relations through organisational guidance on the safety of staff in high-risk locations. International governance agencies (e.g. World Bank, United Nations) also offer principles and operational guidance on humanitarian aid (discussed further below). Another cross-regional example is the planning for major events such as the Olympic Games or major political conferences (G8, Rio + 20, etc.). These events bring together experienced professionals in risk management, private security, military intelligence, and emergency planning, widening the influence of resilient thinking into other governance sectors (e.g. tourism and regional development). In such contexts the economic and reputational resilience of global cities is placed at a premium (Coaffee and Rogers, 2008), further enhancing engagement with resilient 'ways of thinking' and 'doing' *in situ*. This opens the door to 'function creep' where resilience may enable 'legitimate' citizens but exclude others—for example, the rhetoric of broken Britain and '120,000' troubled families positioned at the root of social problems and civil unrest after the UK riots (Cameron, 2011). Private sector and business associations (e.g. American Society for Industrial Security [ASIS], International Standards Organisation [ISO]) are also colonising this marketplace. Increasingly, professional organisations offer consultancy to develop non-statutory minimum standards, procedural toolkits, and implementation guides for risk assessment and risk management. Risk-driven models tend to emphasise a 'what works' practicality among practitioners,[7] echoed in the development of community engagement toolkits and databases of successful projects in community resilience, broadening the influence of the metaphor into political participation, community development, and community safety. Australia provides a good example of how these developments bring together intelligence, security, emergency services, academic consultants, charitable organisations, and community groups. In summary, international collaborations have become the norm when developing standards, guidance, and benchmarks; but also for training programmes that embed shared expertise in networked, flexible (and resilient) workers. Such changes are driven by the shared experience of exposure, a common engagement with national or international standards and increased awareness of the organisational process-improvements achievable when engaged with both statutory and non-statutory guidelines, principles, and standards.

The key points emerging from the policy metaphor into operational practice are: (a) common recognition that learning from exposure to an event is both required and can be applied to positive outcomes, especially when failures or shortcomings are uncovered; (b) the concept of resilience may be conceptually clear in research but it is not clear in diverse organisational contexts what it is that should be implemented *in situ* or what the outcomes of being more resilient should look like; (c) hence the debate over what resilience means for different organisations is still ongoing. This debate over meaning is becoming secondary to producing meaningful change in organisations. As such, the policy metaphor offers a 'way of thinking' (in policy), the standards offer toolkits for enhancing 'way of doing' (best practice) and the implemented standards are intended to provide the guidance framework for 'ways of acting' before, during, and after a disaster (actions taken throughout the disaster cycle). Professional networks provide the communication channels for the distribution of the guidelines, principles, and standards and a means for contextually embedding them into working practice. The guidelines, principles, and standards plug into this process between the policy rhetoric and the experience of stakeholders on the ground. A more thorough analysis of how these toolkits are constructed can provide examples of how the concept of resilience is being operationalised, but also flags up the rigidity trap of over-standardisation.

International Standards, General Principles, and Benchmarks

Perhaps the most developed example of standardisation is the International Standards Organisation (ISO). In relation to disaster resilience ISO now offers standards for information security (ISO27000 series), risk management (ISO31000 series), and the development of standards for societal security (ISO22300 series). ISO standards are different from the broad operational principles and operational guidance from agencies like the UN. UN principles exemplify resilient thinking in a different context; used more commonly in humanitarian aid and the management of displaced persons. Establishing a standard requirement for intervention between genocide and the responsibility to protect (R2P) doctrine (see Pape, 2012) is very different from an industry standard. As such, many guidelines and general principles are often voluntary, ISO standards may be voluntary or require statutory compliance; this varies by jurisdiction depending on the standard, principle, or benchmark. ISO are often thus perceived as politically neutral, leading to higher potential for ISO recommendations to provide a benchmark developed from national bodies (e.g. Standards Australia).

International/national standards frame the institutionalisation of practices but do not create a legal obligation. Institutionalised standards frame broad idealised characteristics for improved 'ways of doing' on the ground; also providing measurable benchmarks to show that something is being done through the adoption of recognised protocols. This contextually embeds standards in organisational practice and workplace culture. However, change is specific to each organisation—in many cases appearing as 'old wine for new skin' to professionals entrenched in previous models/methods. Conformance may be recommended or demanded, but voluntary adoption shows willing engagement; rejection of a standard may lead to exclusion from the growing profits in lucrative industries (e.g. security as disaster capitalism). Potential economic benefits are not limited to tax breaks for utilities providers, cost-saving product development in partnership with government organisations (with a statutory obligation to conform not shared by the private sector), and rebuilding, repairing, or upgrading critical infrastructure and disaster defences (e.g. pipelines, cables, flood barriers, border security) may all affect change on best practices, of course:

> this increasingly occurs within a geo-regulatory context defined by systemic tendencies towards market-disciplinary institutional reform, the formation of transnational webs of market-oriented policy transfer, deepening patterns of crisis formation and accelerating cycles of crisis-driven policy experimentation. (Brenner et al., 2011)

The Risk Management Standard (ISO31000:2009) is perhaps the best example of a market-driven need translated into an cross-sectoral industry standard then becoming common practice and embedded in diverse organisational contexts. Components of the ISO31000 series are now commonly used in the financial sector (from commercial to investment banking), utilities, food services, occupational health and safety, postal delivery, emergency management, and more. This is an example of problems with over-standardisation, where the accepted discourse of 'risk' becomes obfuscatory and thus potentially divisive (Adams and Purdy, 2012). The ongoing development of 'societal security' standards is now extending beyond the principles of risk management to offer minimum standards for emergency planning and disaster responses in ways not previously seen. These range from, but are not limited to: the creation of a common vocabulary, the requirements for preparedness and continuity management systems, video surveillance system interoperability, business continuity management, emergency command and control, exercises/testing guidelines, and statutory public–private partnership arrangements (ISO, 2011). This formal regimentation of emergency and crisis management has taken root internationally, creating a common language, a common set of tools, and a commonly shared set of best practices. It is unclear at this stage to what extent international standards have engaged the diversity of expertise at local levels or if they create the danger of rigidity traps through over-standardisation. As such, the relevance and applicability of standards across scales requires further investigation.

Tripping the Rigidity Trap: Exposure, Learning, and Transformation

This article has shown how research began to critically map the characteristics and features of resilience but to date genealogies have not been fully developed (Coaffee et al., 2009; Walker and Cooper, 2011). A genealogical approach must tease out the features and characteristics carried forward in each (r)evolution of the concept through the distinct policy and organisational rearticulation, but must also do so critically to engage with the inertia of entrenched neoliberalising power relations. For this discussion then, disaster resilience must be *contextually embedded* as a concept first in research, then in policy rhetoric, and finally in processual relations of power. It has been suggested here that this final step can be achieved in deeper analysis of operational benchmarks and quality standards, thus better understanding the force relations at play in a 'resilient' form of governance. Only then can the implications of any move towards a standard of global resilience be clearly understood. Following this train of thought to its conclusion, previous discussions have omitted a key contradiction embedded in the concept of resilience. Underpinning this concept is the interplay of danger and opportunity; this creates the conditions of possibility within each potential catastrophe for a positive learning to result from exposure to the catastrophic.

Research conducted in the United Kingdom and Australia has shown that the changes implied by the adoption of resilience as a general principle of governance extend beyond the policy metaphor (Coaffee et al., 2009; Rogers, 2011a). This is particularly important with regard to (a) the continued implementation of international standards on 'risk' and the potential impact of emerging 'societal security' standards, and (b) understanding the awkward balance between positive learning from exposure (to disorder, crisis, and disaster) and the implementation of standardised processes for the mitigation of negative impacts. When combined, these trends allow us to trace the contextual embedding of resilience into the processes of neoliberalisation; as yet, however, the results of this change are uncertain. Only time will tell the extent to which resilience forms a sustainable trajectory for positive or negative change or simply another cycle of regulatory experimentation.

It is increasingly accepted that when dealing with disasters the most direct lessons emerge from exposure; as organisations are able to learn from what worked and what went wrong before, during, and after an event. However, increasingly there is interest in how to measure resilience (Cutter et al., 2010; Rose, 2004). Measurement fails to address the qualitative influence of industry benchmarks, quality standards, and process-improvement models in the implementation of regulatory experiments in transnational rule-regimes. The contextual variation in the interjurisdictional policy transfer process is thus lost. There is a clear link between the need for metrics and measures and the call for more statutory compliance to standards in disaster resilience. However, where general principles and quality standards are superior to metrics is in the flexibility they retain when applied across variegated local contexts. Research suggests that the variegation by scalar context (local, regional, international, global, etc.) as well as by organisational structure and workplace culture still significantly limit engagement with change.[8] Compliance is often measured through key performance indicators within professional organisations providing non-governmental skill-based legitimisation for policy transfer with little oversight. Such processes demonstrate the neoliberalisation of resilience in working practices (see Coaffee et al., 2009) and potentially could form a rigidity trap if flexibility is undermined as a result. This article has traced a policy evolution that increasingly reflects the second-order logic of adaptation and positive change brought out by Walker and Cooper,[9] but when contextually embedded in the 'all hazards' approach to the disaster cycle we see a more nuanced reflection of policy and practice than previously offered. The details of this evolution are contextually variegated (see Brenner et al., 2010) but the importance of the UK as a driver of the emergent global metaphor should not be overlooked, as we can see in the similarities of the trajectory of transformation in other jurisdictions. The current formulation of resilience encompasses 'all hazards' be they security threats (such as terror attacks), anthropogenic risks (be they public protest or industrial/technological dangers), or natural hazards (from fire to flood, storm to earthquake, etc.), where separation occurs between fields of action it is by degree rather than of type. The drive for a comprehensive approach to resilience has also combined the existing local expertise across diverse areas of action within a national policy and governance rhetoric, becoming embedded in diverse institutional contexts. The causal relationship, however, appears in this analysis less direct than supposed by Walker and Cooper. The adoption of resilience in the UK—which fed the wider dissemination of the research logic into policy globally—appears to be a function of political expedience within the rhetoric of process-improvement and the development of standards for practitioners, rather than being seeded by the economic logic of Hayek or the socio-ecological research of the Stockholm Resilience Institute. It is important to note that resilience has not replaced any previous 'ways of doing' in the broader field of dealing with disasters. What has emerged is a broad policy metaphor that operates as a generative focus for the integration of best practices, shared experiences, and common benchmarks or standards. Resilience can be analysed as a context-specific pathway which co-constitutes the global neoliberalisation project in its current phase of regulatory reorganisation. Where it is most successful it seems to incorporate elements of neoliberalisation but in an adaptive and flexible way. This opens the door to a disarticulated counter-neoliberalisation, in its community form, but also in the organisational form for the extension and rearticulation of zombie neoliberalisation (Brenner et al., 2011). Future research must engage with this contradictory bifurcation to trip the 'rigidity trap' of inflexible standardisation. Resilience has both positive and negative dimensions, depending on the prominent features and characteristics. Resilience can enhance the ordering of disaster by enhancing the embedded capacity for adaptation in all players. Who those players are is changing. Increasingly to deal with uncertainty power is being moved to the local level, however this comes with a responsibilisation of the community to look after its own safety, creating a 'Catch 22' in the regulatory reform of crisis governance for organisations. The contextual variegation of resiliency applied *in situ* to the everyday experiences of the general public must be balanced with the inequalities of access[10] and power inherent in neoliberal governance, a complexity that one might find it hard to reconcile through the free-market—it requires regulation. This potential for locally disaggregated counter liberalisation however is an area that is at present notably lacking in solid empirical evidence. Resilience may also enhance disorder when rigid. The alignment of individuals, institutions, and organisations across complex global networks is ever more central to understanding the link between globalisation, resilience, crisis, and disaster.

While resilience is perhaps one measure of societal security, it is not obviously measurable. It is a feature or characteristic of secure social orders rather than a measurable metric of performance. As a characteristic it is likely to be less influential than concepts of risk, which it realigns rather than replaces. The resilience metaphor helps bridge the interests of public sector, the private sector, and the public community with a common frame of reference less laden with fear. Resilience suggests that we have certain dangers to deal with. We can identify them, assess the extent of threat, identify vulnerabilities in our capabilities to mitigate the danger, and in collaboration we can engage those capabilities to become more adaptable to the risks and uncertainties of the world around us. No one is a passive recipient of aid; everyone is a responsible stakeholder in societal security and all learn from preparation, practice, and exposure. Thus exposure to danger should not be feared any more than it should be sought out. Disorder is not the enemy, rather rigid ways of thinking, doing, and acting are to be feared.

Resilience allows us to bring together the experience of disaster and the knowledge gained from exposure to harness the transformative potential of risk more proactively and optimistically.

In a global community of learning this reaches from international standards for mitigating crises, reducing vulnerabilities—as features of the top-down view of systemic interdependency—to the local experience on the front line of emergency, disaster, or catastrophe—as the bottom-up view of individual, organisational, and community capability and capacity. Resilience has great potential to bring together forward-looking and progressive work in dealing with danger and learning from disorder. More support is required across sectors and more research in the potential of this discourse to embed the lessons we learn into how we deal with future potential dangers. While resilience contains the potential to develop in this direction—as a 'bottom-up' enabling metaphor—it appears at present to be formulated in practice as a tool of management. This too requires further analysis.

The emergence of resilience in the global neoliberalisation debate offers some insight into how individuals, organisations, and communities might learn from disasters as constituents of ongoing regulatory reform, and opens avenues for the exploration of alternatives to the ecological dominance of neoliberalisation. In the light of potentially overoptimistic views of enhanced preparedness, more comprehensive research is needed on the real role and impact of resilience across policy and practice (Boin and McConnell, 2007). Resilience may appear unmeasurable; however, the components of resilience may be subject to more qualitative evaluation. Quality-based and process-driven yet qualitative toolkits might be the route to more effective for benchmarking principles and standards of best practice. The problem here is that process-improvement models may also create 'rigidity traps' and embed the feared zombie neoliberalisation by rendering working practices inflexible to changing geographical sites, disaster types, organisational structures, or workplace cultures. By reflecting on the evolution and implementation of guidelines, principles, and standards we can gain insight into 'rigidity traps' fuelled by negative forms and enhance the contextual embeddedness of positive forms in the disarticulated practicalities of cross-scalar disaster and crisis management. This is true also of the broadening of resilience in other areas of governance. Resilience as a characteristic of systems and feature of individual ways of working becomes a way of thinking and a form of learning that can result from the experience of exposure; however, if learning is not flexible then standardisation increases vulnerability. Resilience at its metaphorical best informs adaptability—as the capacity of individuals and organisations to better deal with crisis *in statu nascendi*—and transformability—as the capability *and* capacity to develop new ways of thinking, doing, and acting as a result of experience. Resilience is perhaps best thought of as a characteristic of materials (e.g. critical infrastructure), systems (governance networks), and individuals (e.g. planners, policymakers, emergency services, and citizens) rather than a measurable function of any given element within dynamic and disorderly systems.

Conclusion

This article has summarised some of the ongoing developments around resilience and societal security, and will conclude by both asking a question and making a suggestion. Is it possible that order can ever be assured through securing best practice and standards of resilience? I would suggest not, but we can learn how to articulate adaptation and transformation in positive ways as a means to open opportunities for forms of counter-neoliberalisation. If the lessons of the past are not learned, and zombie neoliberalisation colonises these positive potentialities, then there will be bigger impacts with more loss of life. Learning from bushfires and floods in Australia, biological disasters in the UK, and the war on terror shows that exposure to danger is not simply negative. Exposure can increase our reflexive awareness of vulnerability and increase through regulatory experimentation the accountability of those who implement, or fail to implement, the required mitigations to address systemic and infrastructural vulnerabilities. This requires more than financial investment or a new policy metaphor; it requires collective engagement in the perpetual review cycle across all players, to generate adaptive attitudes and flexible ways of working for the future. While organisational resilience continues to replicate the self-legitimisation of crisis and risk-averse governmentalities, there are seeds of counter-neoliberalisation in community-driven forms of resiliency; even if these are currently only tendential to the current reality. It may not be fashionable to suggest that there is a positive trajectory for neoliberalisation, but a counter-neoliberalisation potential does exist in resilience, even if at present it exists only as potential.

Notes

1. Here I am referring to 'Zombie neoliberalism' as discussed by Brenner et al. (2010) as a reaffirmation and continued reliance on freemarket governance strategies in the face of extended and persistent crises created by such approaches.
2. This follows and reflects the analysis of power as moving, reconsitutive and reorganising substrate of force relations, by virtue of their inequality these are most unstable at the local level and can be traced through governance and analysed where they rhizomatically reemerge in the governmentality of crisis.
3. For a more comprehensive examination of this genealogy see Rogers (2012a).
4. This again reflects the chaotic variegated local capacity to organise and act. More case studies to compare local variegation would be useful, especially internationally (e.g. developing/developing nations).
5. It is important to note that these rule-regimes structure the interplay of organisations across jurisdictions but also affect the agency of those individuals within organisations. This creates a governmentaility of crisis that conditions a set series of actions, where this is flexible resiliency is increased where the actions are limited by procedural regulations rigity is increased. Further anthropological research on the agency of those engaged in disaster and crisis management would help clarify this *in situ*.
6. See for example the national strategies for disaster resilience (Aus), the national strategy for climate change resilient infrastructure (UK)—and for increased international profile—records of the Rio+20 forum in June 2012.
7. 'What works' can mean different things to different audiences. For clarity in this case I am referring to what works in service delivery models of governance. For more detail on this approach, see McLoughlin and Batley (2012).
8. The cycle of actions, and stages of disaster management are still defined in different ways by different agencies three dominant characteristics commonly appear: (a) the severity of often unexpected threats, (b) a high degree of uncertainty, and (c) the need for urgency in decision-making (McConnell and Drennan, 2006, p. 60). These three are doorstep conditions for a high level of disorder if, for example, emergency decision-making is not embedded in collaborative work-place culture, with strong multi-agency networks and well-practised processes of command and control.
9. Academic research, thematic conferencing through professional networks, targeted government funding initiatives and the enhancement of professional training have all also contributed significantly to the shape and focus of how 'risk' can be managed, how 'resilience' can be increased and how 'societal security' can be enhanced. These considerations lead to a conceptualisation of resilience in policy circles that shifts the focus of emergency and security professionals from post-Cold War response and recovery models onto the development of all hazard and risk-based flexibility, problem-solving tool-kits, quality-driven process improvement and the implementation of national and international quality standards as a statutory obligation.
10. Limited organisation access and institutional access can be understood through North, Wallis and Weingast (2009), where organisations are coalitions of like-minded individuals often with formal membership structures and institutions are the rules of the game underpinning social relations and interactions.

References

Adams, J. & Purdy, G. (2012) 'The quarterly question: is ISO 31000 fit for purpose?', *Risk Management Professional*, uploaded 19 June, http://www.rmprofessional.com/rm/is_iso_31000_fit_for_purpose.php

Alexander, D. (2005) Towards the development of a standard in emergency planning, *Disaster Prevention and Management*, 14(2), pp. 158–175.
Bacon, F. (1659) *Sylva Sylvarum, or, a Natural History in Ten Centuries* (London: William Lee).
Berke, P. R., Kartez, J. & Wenger, D. (1993) Recovery after disaster: achieving sustainable development, mitigation and equity, *Disasters*, 17(2), pp. 93–109.
Blount, T. (1656) *Glossographia, or, A dictionary interpreting all such hard words of whatsoever language now used in our refined English tongue* (London: Thomas Newcomb).
Boin, A. & McConnell, A. (2007) Preparing for critical infrastructure breakdowns: The limits of crisis management and the need for resilience, *Journal of Contingencies and Crisis Management*, 15(1), pp. 50–59.
Brenner, N., Peck, J. & Theodore, N. (2010) Variegated neoliberalization: geogrpahies, modalities, pathways, *Global Networks*, 10(2), pp. 182–222.
Brenner, N., Peck, J. & Theodore, N. (2011) After neoliberalization?, *Globalizations*, 7(3), pp. 327–345.
Cabinet Office (1960) *Home Defence Review*, CAB134/2041 (London: Cabinet Office).
Cameron, D. (2011), PM's speech on the fightback after the riots, Monday 15 August 2011, http://www.number10.gov.uk/news/pms-speech-on-the-fightback-after-the-riots/.
Coaffee, J. & Rogers, P. (2008) Reputational risk and resiliency: The branding of security in place-making, *Place Branding and Public Diplomacy*, 4, pp. 205–217.
Coaffee, J. & Rogers, P. (2010) Rebordering the city for new security challenges: From counter terrorism to community resilience, in C. Rumford (ed.) *Citizens and Borderwork in Contemporary Europe* (London: Routledge), pp. 101–118.
Coaffee, J., Murakami-Wood, D. F. J. & Rogers, P. (2009) *The Everyday Resilience of the City: How Cities Respond to Terrorism and Disaster* (London: Palgrave Macmillan).
Comfort, L. K., Boin, A. & Demchak, C. C. (2010) *Designing Resilience: Preparing for Extreme Events* (Pittsburgh: University of Pittsburgh Press).
Cutter, S. L., Burton, C. G. & Emrich, C. T. (2010) Disaster resilience indicators for benchmarking baseline conditions, *Journal of Homeland Security and Emergency Management*, 7(1), pp. 1–22.
Emergency Management Australia (2011) *Natural Disaster Relief and Recovery Arrangements: Determination 2011 (Version 1)* (Canberra: Department of the Attorney General).
Garmezy, N. (1973) Competence and adaptation in adult schizophrenic patients and children at risk, in S. R. Dean (ed.) *Schizophrenia: The First Ten Dean Award Lectures* (New York: MSS Information Corp), pp. 163–204.
Holling, C. S. (1973) Resilience and stability of ecological systems, *Annual Review of Ecology and Systematics*, 4, pp. 1–23.
International Standards Organisation (2011) http://www.iso.org/.
Jessop, B. (2000) Fordism and post Fordism: A critical reformulation, in M. Storper & A. J. Scott (eds) *Pathways to Industrialization and Regional Development* (New York: Routledge), pp. 46–69.
Klien, R. J. T., Nicholls, R. J. & Thomalla, F. (2003) Resilience to natural hazards: How useful is this concept?, *Global Environmental Change: PART B: Environmental Hazards*, 5(1–2), pp. 35–45.
Martin, G. (2010) 'No worries? Yes worries! How New South Wales is creeping towards a police state, *Alternative Law Journal*, 35(3), pp. 163–167.
McAslan, A. (2010) *Organisational Resilience: Understanding the Concept* (Adelaide: Torrens Resilience Institute).
McConnell, A. (2003) Overview: Crisis management, influences, responses and evaluation, *Parliamentary Affairs*, 56, pp. 393–409.
McConnell, A. & Drennan, L. (2006) Mission Impossible? Planning and preparing for crisis, *Journal of Contingencies and Crisis Management*, 14(2), pp. 59–70.
Mclouglin, C. & Batley, R. (2012) The politics of what works in service delivery: An evidence based review, Effective States & Inclusive Development Working Paper 06, February 2012.
North, D. C., Wallis, J. J. & Weingast, B. D. (2009) *Violence and Social Orders: A Conceptual Framework for Interpreting Recorded Human History* (Cambridge: Cambridge University Press).
O'Brien, G. & Reid, P. (2005) The future of UK emergency management: New wine, old skin?, *Disaster Prevention and Management*, 14(3), pp. 353–361.
Pape, R. A. (2012) When duty calls: A pragmatic standard of humanitarian intervention, *International Security*, 37(1), pp. 41–80.
Paton, D. & Johnston, D. (eds) (2006) *Disaster Resilience: An Integrated Approach* (Springfield, IL: Charles C. Thomas).
Rogers, P. (2009) Contesting and preventing terrorism: On the development of UK strategic policy on radicalisation and community resilience, *Journal of Policing, Intelligence and Counter-Terrorism*, 3(2), pp. 38–61.

Rogers, P. (2011a) Resilience and civil contingencies: Tensions in northeast and northwest UK (2000–2008), *Journal of Policing, Intelligence and Counter Terrorism*, 6(2), pp. 91–107.
Rogers, P. (2011b) Development of resilient Australia: Enhancing the PPRR approach with anticipation, assessment and registration of risks, *Australian Journal of Emergency Management*, 26(1), pp. 54–59.
Rogers, P. (2012a) Resilience revisited: An etymology & genealogy of a contested concept, *Climate Futures Working Paper Series*, No. 4, August.
Rogers, P. (2012b) Rethinking resilience: Surveillance, community and the UK riots, *Surveillance and Everyday Life Research Group (1st Annual Conference)*, University of Sydney, 20–21 February.
Rose, A. (2004) Defining and measuring economic resilience to disasters, *Disaster Prevention and Management*, 13(4), pp. 307–314.
Shamir, R. (2008) The age of responsibilization: On market-embedded morality, *Economy and Society*, 37(1), pp. 1–19.
Sheffi, Y. (2005) *The Resilient Enterprise: Overcoming Vulnerability for Competitive Advantage* (Cambridge, MA: MIT Press).
Young, T. (1877) *A Course of Lectures on the Natural Philosophy and the Mechanical Arts* (London: Taylor and Walton).
United Nations (2011) International Strategy for Disaster Risk reduction, http://www.unisdr.org/.
Walker, C. & Broderick, J. (2006) *The Civil Contingencies Act 2004: Risk, Resilience and the Law in the United Kingdom* (London: Oxford University Press).
Walker, J. & Cooper, M. (2011) Genealogies of resilience from systems ecology to the political economy of crisis adaptation, *Security Dialogue*, 42(2), pp. 143–160.
Walker, B., Holling, C. S., Carpenter, S. R. & Kinzig, A. (2004) Resilience, adaptability and transformability in social–ecological systems, *Ecology and Society*, 9(2), article 5, http://www.ecologyandsociety.org/vol9/iss2/art5.

Peter Rogers is Co-Director of Climate Futures at Macquarie University. His cross-disciplinary research and publications often address the subject of resilience, security, and disasters, which is also the subject of his 2012 book, *Resilience and the City* (Ashgate).

'Who is Grace?': Affect, Work, and Gender in Bangalore Call Centres

DEVLEENA GHOSH
University of Technology Sydney, Australia

ABSTRACT *Call centre workers are expected to 'listen' and provide both practical assistance and emotional support to customers across the world. At the same time, they are supposed to subscribe to cultural and social traditions that ensure that they remain within family and societal control. This article discusses gender and work transformations of call centre workers in the context of the networks they create in their engagements, not only with their managers and co-workers but with their invisible clients and families and communities.*

Introduction

This article reflects on the transformation of work relations, gender roles, and affective identities of Indian call centre workers. The empowerment and agency of call centre workers through their negotiation of gender and work relations has implications for the perception of their work in wider Indian society. There are various ways in which freedoms are bound into labour, for instance, the night shift as both a site of super-exploitation and a site of self-realisation through the deliberate construction of 'modern' informality in the workplace. This constructed informality is encouraged by the management and actively embraced, constructed, and made more complex by the workers who usually inhabit traditional lived spaces at home. Similarly, gender relations are manipulated by both management and workers to construct the workplace as a lifestyle—work as sociality—reflected in the recruitment strategy, of drawing in a mix of young people of both sexes and a similar class background, so that the arena of work becomes an escape from wider gender norms while gender relations in the real world remain unchanged. Paradoxically, gender norms are mobilised in the in-built notion that women are suited to emotional work, especially in terms of deference to the needs of often hostile customers. There is a co-construction of meaning in the call centre, where the agency of the workers is complicit with the managerial objectives of sustaining morale in what is a highly Taylorised and hostile work environment.

The late Mark Poster (1995), in his discussion of the political impact of the Internet, focused on a number of issues, inter alia access, technological determinism, commodification, the public sphere, gender, and ethnicity. He asked how one should attempt to assess the full extent of what is at stake in the new communications technology at the cultural level of identity formation, and whether the potentials for new forms of social spaces and relations that might empower individuals in new ways are foreclosed in favour of preserving existing relations of power benefiting economic and political globalisation. He pointed out that the issue of commodification is often restricted to the question of profit rather than open to the social impacts involved in, for example, translating the act of shopping into an electronic form, or the ways in which virtual interactions institute new social functions and identifications.

The call centre functions in an environment that is postcolonial and postmodern within the contexts of society, history, and technology. As Mustafa Bayoumi points out, Kwame Anthony Appiah considered postcolonialism to be in an ambivalent relationship with postmodern commodification of selfhood, while Homi Bhabha located postcolonialism as a reconfiguration of postmodern contingency via a type of wily agency. Both scholars noted the importance of disestablishing the primacy of the Self–Other division in this equation and championed the circulations and hybridities of contemporary cultures. This shuttling back and forth between various worlds works, not in terms of opposition, but of epistemic complicity: 'we are all already contaminated by each other' (Appiah in Bayoumi, 2001, p. 146). Commodification, on the one hand, is depoliticised and endorsed as 'circulation'; on the other hand, it is constructed in terms of power relations, the power to exploit, alienate, and accumulate.

Reflecting this, managerial techniques constituting 'global service industries' imply that call centre workers bear the full brunt of the abuses built into the logic of transnational accumulation, while being simultaneously enabled to construct a new sociality that affirms a positive identification as a no longer naïve, but worldly 'modern Indian'. Thus the tensions between capitalist managerialism and those who are to be managed for profit are generative, in producing new workplace subjectivities, social practices, and norms in the context of labour that is largely emotional and service-based. How are these subjectivities, practices, and norms translated into the lived experiences of workers? Do they have to juggle multiple identities and experiences which they feel are false or deceitful, or are they able to negotiate an affective and intellectual space with some integrity?

The contention here is that information technology, even when mediated by a relatively old form, such as the telephone, fundamentally changes the very nature of work. The sociologist, Arlie Hochschild (1983), coined the concept of emotional labour to reflect on the kind of work that flight attendants and bill collectors had to do. Such work may be defined as 'the effort, planning, and control needed to express organizationally desired emotions during interpersonal transactions' (Morris and Feldman, 1997, p. 98). Lewig and Dollard (2003) quote Ashforth and Humphrey as saying that 'emotional labour is a double-edged sword' (1993, p. 96).

In its functional capacity, emotional labour can serve to facilitate task effectiveness by providing the service worker with a means to regulate what are often dynamic and emergent interactions and thus provide him/her with a sense of increased self-efficacy. Emotional labour makes interactions with customers more predictable, and allows the service worker to maintain emotional equilibrium by cognitively distancing him or herself from the implicated affect involved in their daily dealing with strangers. Emotional labour may also facilitate self-expression by enabling the service worker to 'project at least some of the "authentic self" into the enactment' (Ashforth and Humphrey, 1993, p. 94 quoted in Lewig and Dollard, 2003, p. 368). In this case, the 'authentic self' relates to those service skills that largely match traditional Indian virtues: respect for elders and strangers, modesty and politeness at all costs, rather than the subjectivities that the employees own and live.

These changes in labour conditions and expectations of workers are taking place in a rapidly transforming work environment. After economic liberalisation in 1991, there was a spurt of significant investment in Indian industry, which included Information Technology Enabled Services-Business Process Outsourcing (ITES-BPO). This sector was phenomenally successful for more than a decade and continues to make profits. *India Today* (2002) boasted that India was 'the electronic housekeeper to the world, taking care of a host of routine activities for multinational giants' such as credit card inquiries, invoices and payrolls, medical transcriptions, applications, billings, and collections. Though ITES-BPO consists of a small part of India's domestic market (about 1.5% of the domestic information technology/IT market), its growth has been spectacular. During 2003–2004, this segment was estimated to have achieved a 54% growth in revenues (US$3.6 billion), up from US$2.5 billion in 2002–2003 (NASSCOM, 2005). During the financial year ending 2012, IT-BPO industry-aggregate revenues crossed the US$100 billion mark, with exports at US$69 billion. The industry's share of total Indian exports (merchandise plus services) increased from less than 4 per cent in 1998 to about 25 per cent in 2012. As a proportion of national GDP, the sector revenues have grown from 1.2 per cent in 1998 to an estimated 7.5 per cent in 2012. The industry continues to be a net employment generator - expected to add 230,000 jobs in the 2012 financial year, thus providing direct employment to about 2.8 million, and indirectly employing 8.9 million (NASSCOM, FY12).

It is worth noting that formal employment accounts for a very small proportion of overall employment in India—and white collar workers, including those in call centres are in a highly privileged position, whatever their economic and social backgrounds. However, the latest World Development Report by the World Bank says India's youth unemployment—as a percentage of the youth work force—remains high: 9.9% for males and 11.3% for females in 2010 and virtually 50% more than the national average, or total unemployment rate (Kundu, 2012). Such a pool of unemployed labour is, simultaneously, in high demand as well as insecure. In the traditional societal and family structure, the unemployed middle class citizen was incorporated into the joint family structure or the informal labour pool. The increasing erosion of these traditional spaces creates a more transient labour culture.

Global linkages of this sort do not just open new potentialities for capitalist efficiencies and profit, they also open new potentials for labour management and exploitation. For example, transnational corporations doing business in India benefit from a strategic use of time or 'time arbitrage' which is the exploitation of time discrepancies between geographical labour markets to achieve a 24-hour business cycle for profit making purposes. Shahzad Nadeem concludes that, in the Indian case, time arbitrage has resulted in long work hours, an intense work pace, and temporal displacement manifested in both health problems and alienation from family and friends (Nadeem, 2009, p. 21). Kiran Mirchandani (2004), on the other hand, focuses on the 'gaps, cracks and ironies' that make call centres contested terrain. Although multinational and transnational corporations attempt to domesticate regions, workforces, and governments, there are 'cracks' and inconsistencies in global economic capitalism that enable sites for the 'hidden transcript' of critiques of power and opportunities for political resistance (Scott, 1990). Thus focusing on the gaps between the representation and experience of call centre work reveals the incomplete and contested nature of transnational corporations in India, referring to Appadurai's view that 'if a global cultural system is emerging, it is filled with ironies and resistances' (1996, p. 29). The shrinking of the globe by technology implies the telescoping of geography and history, though both re-emerge in altered contexts. Most call centre workers to whom I spoke had never been overseas, though most planned to visit, some to emigrate. Dealing with a world largely unknown and unseen except virtually while situated in a local workplace transformed their worldviews and selves.

This transformation of the self through acquisition and consumerism functions as a fable about young people's ability to negotiate the random processes of continual social and personal displacement. In India, such processes are sometimes called *jugaar*; making do with whatever is available in a context where randomness and chaos are the only dependable factors. Call centre labour builds on this make-do culture of work and gender transformation, in responding to the fragmented, dissonant demands of an increasingly atomised consumer public. New subjectivities, liberties, and surveillances emerge from the tensions between managerial control, worker responses, and changes to life and work conditions and the reification and transformation of gender and work relations in these rapidly changing, 'make-do', hybrid and articulated cultures and problematic spaces.

In this article, I discuss two major issues; gender and labour transformation among call centre workers based on my interactions in the period 2009–2011 with 50 employees (half male and half female) from two companies, PG and TWKS (pseudonyms for two large business process outsourcing companies in Bangalore). The two companies were chosen because one focused on sales and the other on services and because they were among the oldest BPOs in Bangalore. They were also willing, within certain time constraints, to allow participant observation in their venues. Interviewees were recruited through the snowball method via social media. The respondent pool was deliberately kept small to allow for in-depth interviews and other qualitative data. One of the call centres was housed in a state of the art, purpose-built campus complete with a gym, coffee shop, restaurants, and international currency exchange offices with tight security that prevented casual visitors. The other call centre was located in a suburb on the outskirts of Bangalore. While participant observation was carried out on site, interviews (individual and group) were conducted in the spaces (pubs and cafes) that these workers frequented after hours.

Work

Call centres have a local climate, a culture, an ecology. Their employees work within a knowledge web, managing information by deploying the fragmentary methods of *jugaar*: emailing, speaking on the phone, looking up websites, multi-tracking with amazing fluidity. Daily communication with foreign cultures integrates the local mind with the universal cognitive map, producing its own context and history, a personality between different topographies, challenging essentialist notions of identity based solely on genealogy and not on geography. Identity and location are locked in a complex symbiotic relationship which has the potential to resist national wills and narrowly nationalist identities.

Most call centre workers would not agree that their jobs are necessarily more exploitative than the salaried jobs of their parents. In spite of the high burn-out rate and turnover of staff, the stress and abuse, and the unfriendly shifts, the fact is that call centre companies are able to pay 30% of Northern wages to staff who usually have a standard Bachelor's degree in a country where unskilled middle class jobs are extremely scarce. There is some evidence to show that jobs in outsourcing firms are highly sought after, and often pay much more than those servicing the local economy (Bond, 2004). Demand for call centre workers outstrips supply, with attrition in call centres ranging from 30% to 50% due to poaching of staff by competitors, and there is evidence to show that the Indian educational system does not provide enough English language speaking graduates to fulfil the labour demands of BPOs (Anand, 2011). One Convergys job advertisement in the *Times of India* promised to make prospective call centre employees 'a prime target of all the dons of the industry. You will be hunted down, with almost a king's ransom on your head' (*Economist*, 2004). In fact, call centres across India are quietly arriving at 'no-poaching' agreements to stop one company from hiring employees of another, or making it mandatory for staff to serve at least one year before they can work for another company (Attrition in BPO industries, 2010; Prasad, 2004). This cartel aims to contain two factors: the shortage of good BPO workers and the potential spiralling of wage costs from competition for labour. However, conditions at most centres compare favourably to many other workplaces, with free transport to and from the workplace, a particularly important consideration where social, cultural, and religious objections to women working at night persist. In addition many employers provide subsidised meals, bonuses, social evenings, and so on.

Sociality at work also reflects a larger transformation within Indian society particularly in global cities like Bangalore. Both Indian and Western festivals are now celebrated with enthusiasm. This reification of culture is often presented as multiculturalism, though some of the young people that I interviewed confessed that they learnt of Valentine's Day only after moving to Bangalore for education, work, or training when their workplaces were decorated with red hearts and balloons, and prizes were awarded for the smartest couple and the most romantic pair. This is clearly a managerial strategy—invoking a Western (US) practice to instil an aura of the modern, while simultaneously invoking workplace freedoms in terms of gender relations. The strategy is designed to boost morale by making work fun, modern, and Western. The emotional labour of consumer relations on the phone is accompanied by an emotional managerialism intended to make work and the workplace attractive and desirable, when compared to the tradition-bound places of the family and home.

There has been trenchant criticism of call centre workers 'passing' as British or American, the adoption of pseudonyms, accent training, cultural indoctrination, the study of British/American tabloids and weather reports. The, often failed, concealment of national identity typifies the stage of marginality characteristic of a liminal or transitional condition, a virtual journey through space and across frontiers. One consequence of this 'in between' means that the worker must rethink his/her relations both to her workplace and the destination of her work. This narrative imagination and these, sometimes fraught, relationships with others contribute to the reconstitution of the self. However, it is by no means certain that this produces virtuous cosmopolitans: it can as easily produce xenophobia and fundamentalism—on both sides of the call. *The Observer* newspaper in 2005 cited a study that claimed that abuse from British and American customers was driving increasing numbers of Indian call centre workers from their jobs, defeated by the strain of handling persistent rudeness (Gentleman, 2005).

Arundhati Roy sees call centre work on a par with the hate-mongering by the fundamentalist Hindu RSS as a national disgrace, a 'complete abasement of an ancient civilization' (Roy, 2001, p. 83; 2004, pp. 89–90). When Susan Sontag wrote 'The World as India' (2003) celebrating the success of Indians in deploying their English-speaking skills in the global economy through ITES/BPO services, Harish Trivedi, from Delhi University, wrote a blistering rejoinder, characterising call centres as 'brutally exploitative' and their employees as 'cyber coolies of our global age, working not on sugar plantations but on flickering screens, and lashed into submission through vigilant and punitive monitoring, each slip in accent or lapse in pretence meaning a cut in wages' (Trivedi, 2003).

Most of the workers I interviewed were puzzled by these judgements. A young Muslim man pointed out that people of his community had often had to take Hindu pseudonyms to get jobs or accommodation:

> So it's ok for me to become Manoj rather than Mahmud? That is acceptable so I can get a flat in Bombay or a job in service? But if I turn into Michael, it is insulting Indian culture? And are these people going to find me a job that pays as much as a call centre?[1]

The necessity of adopting foreign accents has now been almost completely debunked. The CEOs of three major ITES companies, Progeon (Infosys), Manipal, and Transworks now concentrate on eliminating 'mother-tongue influence'—that is, neutralising strong local accents rather than passing as American or British. The CEO of Transworks, Prakash Gurbaxani, said that this was a big shift in the mindset of his company. Their employees no longer had to deny that they were located in India. He added that since neither the US nor the UK had a standard accent, accent training now emphasised speaking slowly and clearly to enhance comprehension.

> They still can't answer the call in their own names, or go out of our way and tell people the call is being picked up in India, but if someone asked they have no need to lie anymore. And it actually helps. I have actually seen people going a little slower in the way they speak when they realise the call is being taken in India because they don't want to embarrass the call taker. There is a sense of cooperation as well as antagonism and anger. But an average housewife calling couldn't give a damn whether the call is picked up in the US or the call is picked up in India as long as the problem is solved. So this big phobia for accents that we had is now on the wane. The emphasis is no longer on imitating pathetically English and American accents.[2]

Gender

State encouragement of foreign capital plays a small, albeit contradictory, role in reshaping gender relations. The state has encouraged women's participation in employment while pushing economic liberalisation during the past 25 years and, under pressure from NASSCOM and other business groups, relaxed the Factory Act of 1948, which prohibited women from working at night, in 2005.

The female educated Indian call centre workforce operates within a country where women have traditionally low employment participation rates in the formal economy. Women's work in India has historically been based in the agricultural and manufacturing sector but middle class and lower middle class women now increasingly migrate to urban centres for employment. As such, gender roles and ideologies inscribed in traditional Indian society and culture need to be analysed alongside call centre labour processes. Additionally, gendered assumptions about women's ability to empathise, also lead to (pre)assumptions about women's ability to endure repetitive and routine work (Belt, 2002, p. 138). Such gendered notions of social skills and competencies have been synonymous with call centre operations irrespective of location and socio-cultural factors. Though one may query whether call centre work leads to further skill development, within the Indian context it is important to acknowledge that it provides greater employment and economic opportunities for women than previously existed (Ganguly-Scrase, 2005), while magnifying some conflicts.

Further, when customer and service provider are not co-locational or culturally and linguistically compatible, the demands of emotional and aesthetic labour, or voice and social skills, become more acute. Proficiency in English diction, 'personality', 'attitude', and social skills, rather than formal or technical qualifications, are sought in call centre workers (Perinotto, 2003). The management of call centres are quick to point out that they are keen to hire women because of their natural abilities to remain calm and diplomatic during stressful conversations with customers. Women call centre workers echoed these judgements, saying that customers were more patient and nicer to them than to their male colleagues and the latter would often 'escalate' problem calls to women[3] because they believe that women had better 'people skills', that they were better at communication. Scholars like Mies (1980, 1982) have noted the role juggling and performance in balancing a woman's personal desires with social expectations, learning from their mothers how to suppress and exert certain emotions to help perform these roles. When performing in the time-space distanciation of call centre work, women create specific identities for specific tasks that negotiate the spaces between the customer and agent, the agent and their remote supervisor, and so on. Aural attributes, such as putting a 'smile into your voice', are reflected in tight employee scripting where workers follow set opening and closing prompts. Employees are taught both the need to perform and the techniques of how to perform emotional labour, using terminology such as 'management of self', 'maintaining a good mood', and 'handling yourself emotionally'. However, whereas management sees emotional labour as a way of providing good customer service, employees tend to use emotional labour more as a tool of coping with the nature of call centre work.

One of my interviewees said:

> Actually, in confidence, women are better at this job. We are used to finding out what people want, family, friends whatever, and then doing it. We have to be emotionally strong; when we get married we have to leave our home and go and live in someone else's house. We have to take care of the feelings of our own and our husband's family; make sure no one feels belittled or insulted.[4]

In other situations, such anonymity may be useful as well as being some kind of 'alienation'. For instance, one female worker felt that when she donned her call centre persona, she was able to ignore insults or sexual innuendo; her pseudonym allowed her to inhabit a different self that had nothing to do with who she really was.

> So if a client says something really rude, I think, he is not talking to me, he does not know me. He is talking to Grace [*her call centre name*]. Who is Grace? I think she is much more forward than I am, much more confidence [*sic*]. She wouldn't care if someone even came on to her. She would know how to deal with it. It has nothing to do with me. So I don't care. I think that Grace wants to be a successful agent who can turn an angry customer into a happy one when he puts the phone down.[5]

Another person likewise put the pretence into a wider perspective of work, 'Is pretending to be someone else so much worse than all those salesmen who stretch the truth to sell their products?'

Female interviewees describe a transformation of women's work experience in call centres. One woman who used to work in public relations had to spend many late nights and weekends at work. Once she had a baby, she decided to work in a call centre.

> In PC [*her previous company*] I was expected to work like the men, most of whom had families, wives or mothers to take care of the home. I had no flexibility, I just had to finish my tasks regardless. Even on weekends, overtime was compulsory. I had to go to work by auto which cost eighty Rupees each way. [*Bangalore is a city whose public transport and infrastructure are becoming increasingly dysfunctional.*] Now I get free transport, cheap meals and I don't have to worry about being late. Okay, I have to work some night shifts but I know when they are so I can be ready for them. It is not like overtime every weekend and getting home at 11 at night like my job before.[6]

Getting to work is normally seen as the personal responsibility of the female employee or her male relations, rather than that of her employer. The fact that call centres provide free transport to the workplace was seen as liberating by women like her (see also Basi, 2009) even though the illusion of safety provided by the provision of transport was severely diminished by the rape and murder of a female call centre worker by a driver of the transporting vehicle in 2007 (Buzzle.com).

Most Indian women's everyday experiences are monitored or under surveillance and negotiated through patriarchal controls, so the surveillance at work may not feel that different. The measures of safety taken by call centres for their women employees reinforce this feeling. There are guards at the centres at night who, since the rape and murder mentioned above, also accompany the women workers home. J. Tina Basi documents the way in which, despite the associated managerial monitoring, Indian call centre workers find ways of subverting the system, using the 'weapons of the weak' strategies, maximising performance scores by concentrating on one dimension of the scores while sacrificing another, sabotaging call-timings by blaming customers for lengthy chit chats about trivialities, as well as other forms of employee manipulation, which subvert or disorder the task performance (Basi, 2009, p. 74). When I asked my interlocutors in a group interview how they dealt with difficult customers, there was some amusement:

> Well we have signs that we make when a difficult one comes on the phone; then one of us will leave our work briefly and come over and say, escalate, escalate [*divert the call to the supervisor*]. We also tell each other which supervisor to complain to, who is sympathetic, who is not. Some [*supervisors*] watch to see how long we go to talk with others and some will not accept that we are just asking for information. If a customer is very hard, we have to give them old or incomplete answers just to get them off the phone.[7]

Such behaviour while solving an immediate problem may further aggravate overseas customers' reactions to call centre workers and make life harder for the workers in future calls. Surviving the system can disorder the system.

BB, like others, looked forward to a whole different world post BPO work but enabled by it. She didn't see this as a permanent career; rather she was hoping that she could save up enough money to send her daughter to an expensive and fashionable school outside of Bangalore. Another woman wanted to open a beauty parlour in her garage,[8] while others were accumulating money for study overseas, to help pay for their marriages and dowries, or to fund alternative careers.

Love and Marriage

NL (aged 25) came from Nagaland, a state riven by regional insurgencies. A devout Christian, educated in a convent, she spoke good, relatively unaccented English and had passed her high school certificate but had no tertiary qualifications. She was recruited on the basis of her English skills by a spotting team for a Bangalore call centre which serviced several global software companies. She first started in sales but within three months realised that such work was not for her. She felt the exaggerations and obfuscations, if not outright lies, involved in selling were against the tenets of her faith. However, when she offered to resign the company made a counter-offer: a promotion to trainer with work hours from 8 p.m. to 4 a.m.

NL received this offer because of her fluency in English and her willingness to work the worst shift in the call centre labour structure. She was aware that this decision was going to have a serious impact on her marriage. Within two years of her arrival in Bangalore, she had married a young man from a different religious and linguistic background and the adjustments and compromises in her domestic life were compounded by the disruption caused by night shifts that meant that she came home to sleep at the time her husband was getting up to go to work. NL was very adamant, in spite of this, that she was lucky to keep her job. It was highly paid and, with only a high school qualification, she would be unable to get equivalent remuneration outside the sector.

NL's family had encouraged her migration to Bangalore as the opportunities for work in Nagaland were limited. She herself attributed her exposure to the 'outside world', as she called it, as enabling her to enter an inter-religious, inter-regional marriage; her parents, though not adamantly opposed to the union, were unhappy about it. Ironically, she subscribed to all the gender stereotypes of emotional labour mentioned above; she connected her inability to work the phones not only to her religion but also to being female (not assertive enough to sell commodities) and her abilities as a trainer to her persuasive ways (as a woman).

> I think being a woman and a Christian means that I can do this trainer job well. I am sensitive and kind to the trainees and aware of all their problems. My religion says that I must be kind and understanding of everyone. When I was in Nagaland, I couldn't dream of marrying outside my faith. Coming to Bangalore I realised that you can love someone even if they believe something different. And people who are different, like my mother in law, have been so nice to me. She does everything for me. [*I asked her about her children's religion.*] I think, live and let live. G [*her husband*] respects my religion and my children can be brought up respecting both our faiths. There is no need to choose, one or the other, right or wrong. [*Laughs.*] My parents think I have been spoilt by my stay in Bangalore but I think my eyes are opened.[9]

Most women say that their families are ambivalent about their careers. 'There are still people who do not know what a call centre is and have the wrong impression', says RR's mother, KR.[10] In her day, women who worked at night were presumed to be call girls, not call centre workers. One call centre manager recounts how the father of a young female employee recently came to him with suspicions that she was secretly dating someone at the office. 'He said, "We brought her up with good Indian morals, piety, respect for elders and so on but she has completely changed, and I blame it on this work".' This manager added, 'Parents think they've brought up their children according to Indian culture and tradition—but the façade is very superficial, very very fragile.'[11] But most of the women found this independence crucial. 'For me other things haven't changed much but at least we get out at night. You now see women more than men working at night. When I was in Bangalore, my parents would not let me out after 10 at night but now I work after 10.'[12] This autonomy from parents and guardians was liberating for most of my interlocutors. They also felt empowered by the fact that many of their families depended on the money they sent back home. The call centre generation is the first one in modern India where women not only worked away from their family base but did so in relatively independent circumstances; i.e. they did not necessarily live with relatives or people in loco parentis but as autonomous workers, sharing flats with other people in similar circumstances or renting on their own. However, though call centre work means money and independence, family ties and respect have not disappeared. The conflicts between family demands and the siren calls of modernity can create emotional and practical crises.

TR was conservative in dress and attitude before he joined a call centre. He wouldn't watch Hollywood movies because of explicit sexual scenes and expected an arranged marriage to a traditional girl from his community. He joined a call centre after being unable to get into engineering college because the salary was more than double his wages at previous jobs. Once he started working there he was drawn to the company of colleagues his own age and their lifestyle.[13] TR, a Hindu Brahmin (the highest caste) is now engaged to a young Muslim woman from a different linguistic background whom he met at work. They face intense opposition from both their families.

> We still want to get married but with the agreement of our families. We are really serious with each other. We are like husband and wife. But we are both very confused. We love our parents and each other the same so how can we choose? HA [*his fiancée*] says we should have a registration [*a legal civil ceremony*] but how can I disrespect my parents like that? Sometimes I feel like committing suicide; whenever I talk to my mother she starts crying and saying that if I marry a Muslim it will kill her and kill their status in the community. But I am so happy with HA; how can I leave her? And her parents are just as bad.[14]

SB and his future wife found themselves fielding calls from people who wanted to buy pornography on DVD. Occasionally men called from Europe or the USA to buy erotica for their sons as eighteenth or twenty-first birthday presents, something SB could never imagine an Indian parent doing. Outside the office, it was a different world. When he and his wife announced to their families that they were getting married and setting up their own household, both of their families raised strenuous objections. When SB picked up his wife on his motorbike at the end of her shift, they were sometimes stopped by the police who asked what they were doing out so late.[15]

NV who has set up call centres in both the UK and India told me that the unmitigated freedom of association between the sexes within call centres is unprecedented.

> You are there side by side for 7 hours. You have gone for dinner, for a snack, coffee, tea. The typical tendency, considering that each one operates in a work station of 40 to 60 sq ft area, is there is a physical proximity, there is your team leader breathing down your neck, there is your supervisor to whom you escalated the call, who has his arm around you. There is a constant physical touch which is much more than in any other industry. It isn't that its sexual, it's just that . . . he's telling her what to say, 'Don't get angry, go to the next cursor'. He is doing it on her pressure points, on her shoulder. In no other industry do you sit next to each other for 7 hours without moving. There is a lot of physical contact that happens. It is something unheard of in India. No workplace encouraged physical contact. Suddenly you are all touching and talking the whole time. It's a new kind of revolution. From that kind of physical overtures, moving on to the next level is very, very simple.[16]

I asked if any or some of the women workers objected to this kind of physical behaviour. She answered by saying that working in call centres takes a toll on spousal relationships.

> Some women do not like it. In my call centre, some of the girls complained to me. I had a talk about it at the weekly meetings but I don't know whether it had an effect. Besides what are they [*the supervisors*] to do? They can't say anything loudly and writing down would take too long. I think it is part and parcel of working in that environment. It is having an impact on marriage also. . . . Earlier the guy used to come back home in a different industry and he didn't discuss work with the wife because she didn't understand it. It is the reverse now. She cannot go back home and talk about what happens in the call centre because she thinks he doesn't understand. In most people's minds, a call centre job is a phone operator's job. If he is not from the industry, he has a kind of contempt. A crazy job, she just answers the phone.[17]

Women who are earning good money and are successful at their job may find it difficult to communicate with a husband in a more traditional profession. A psychiatrist working on call centres pinpoints corporeality as a key marital issue saying that 'even if the spouse was of a physical type at the start, s/he can't compete with the kind of physicality that one acquires in call centres'.[18] Relationships are broken as well as made. Though most of these women to whom I spoke would really like to continue work after marriage, they reluctantly accept that the decision would be strongly influenced by their future husbands and husbands' families.

CRISIS, MOVEMENT, MANAGEMENT: GLOBALISING DYNAMICS

These conversations reveal the power struggle and the distress embedded in the cultural and symbolic representation of communities: the double consciousness involved in living simultaneously inside and outside. This double consciousness can be disruptive, but it also denotes a potential opening to opportunities for developing an alternative knowledge of—and vision for—society, an opportunity for a different perspective. A consistent and haunting figure in these exchanges is the single young woman or man as anomaly, as threat and as object of uneasy reflections about the nature of cultural boundaries. These counterpolitics and interventions take place around young Indians, the past reinterpreted, the present translated, and new cultural spaces framed in the context of their narratives and everyday lives.

Conclusion

Outsourcing is an incredibly complex economic and ethical issue, with winners and losers on both sides. Seeing these call centre workers as exploited or over-organised and alienated cyber-coolies seems to be increasingly irrelevant to the graduates working in the 'cyberparks' in Bangalore or Gurgaon. It seems rather a spectre haunting the middle aged and middle class that their children will, in the future, have less access to the traditional high-status professions of medicine, engineering, or accountancy and will have to resort to service industries which, in their time and world, were the preserve of the lower classes. The call centre replaces the 'space of places' with the 'space of flows' (Dicken, 2003, p. 20). Yet, 'the end of geography' and 'the death of distance' disturbs and makes complex senses of geography and distance.

Many writers, in critiquing Ohmae's (1995, p. 94) assertion that a company's 'country of origin does not matter', have demonstrated the importance of the home base (Hirst and Thompson, 1999; Ruigrok and van Tulder, 1995). For call centre companies, not least because customers are located in culturally specific and localised places and yet the nature of the industry is geographically mobile, place must be considered as a crucial social construct, 'constituted out of spatialised social relations—and narratives about them—which not only lay down ever-new regional geographies, but also work to reshape social and cultural identities and how they are represented' (Allen et al., 1998). Thus call centre migration to India is illustrative of the growing interconnectedness of economic activities in the global economy. It reminds us that globalisation is a set of partially disruptive tendencies undetermined in advance, not a single predetermined trajectory with inevitable outcomes (Dicken, 2003; Held et al., 1999). And with the transformation of young peoples' lives (everyday, romantic, consumerist), this global industry has very local specific cultural effects.

Global shifts in capital not only change the nature and location of work but also have major implications for social relations and worker identities. As call centres are drawn to countries like India, it is important to recognise that Indian call centre workers are not merely cheap and more intensely exploited units of capital, but rather active social and cultural participants who construct their own meanings on the basis of waged work. Turnover statistics indicate that both male and female call centre workers are not passive observers of the globalisation process but are dealing with new conflicts and possibilities as a consequence of their employment.

Culture is one of the major sites of struggle in which local populations and global corporations transact their unequal relations. Networks—global, virtual, local—have the capacity to undermine transnational and national order as much as tie it together. The always contingent, contested nature of subjectivity does not float aimlessly in a postmodern moment but is revealed in its grounded nature, a thousand plateaus, felt and experienced through the body, through workscapes and domestic spaces, through the realm of the imaginary, of the impact of ideals and the weight of history.

Notes

1. SA, interview, 10 January 2011. (Unless otherwise stated, all interviews were with call centre workers.)
2. Prabash Gurbaxani, CEO of Transworks, interview, 15 December 2008.
3. RA, IL, BM, group interview, 29 January 2009.
4. AJ, interview, 14 January 2010.
5. AK, interview (translations from Hindi by author), 26 January 2009.
6. BB, interview, 29 January 2011.
7. RA, IL, BM, group interview, 29 January 2009.
8. LS, interview, 15 January 2008.
9. NL, interview, 7 January 2010.
10. KR, interview, 1 February 2008.
11. MG, call centre manager, interview, 20 January 2008.
12. RR, interview, 3 February 2008.
13. TR, interview, 14 January 2008.
14. TR, interview, 14 January 2008.
15. SB, interview, 12 January 2008.
16. NV, CEO of PG call centre, interview, 29 January 2009.
17. NV, interview, 29 January 2009.
18. HG, psychiatrist, interview, 30 January 2009.

References

Allen, J., Massey, D., Cochrane, A. & Charlesworth, J. (1998) *Rethinking the Region* (London: Routledge).
Anand, G. (2011), India graduates millions, but too few are fit to hire, http://online.wsj.com/article/SB10001424052748703515504576142092863219826.html.
Appadurai, A. (1996) *Modernity at Large: Cultural Dimensions of Globalization* (Minneapolis: University Minnesota Press).
Ashforth, B. E. & Humphrey, R. H. (1993) Emotional labour in service roles: The influence of identity, *Academy of Management Review*, 18(1), pp. 88–115.
Attrition in Indian BPO industry (2010) http://www.bpoindia.org/research/attrition.shtml.
Basi, J. K. T. (2009) *Women, Identity and India's Call Centre Industry* (London & New York: Routledge).
Bayoumi, M. (2001) Review of *Islands and Exiles: The Creole Identities of Post/Colonial Literature* by Chris Bongie, *African American Review*, Spring, pp. 146–148.
Belt, V. (2002) Capitalising on femininity: Gender and the utilisation of social skills in telephone call centres, in U. Holtgrewe, C. Kerst & K. Shire (eds) *Re-Organising Service Work: Call Centres in Germany and Britain* (Burlington, VA: Ashgate), pp. 123–145.
Bond, R. (2004) Call centre is 'my dream job', BBC Look East Business Correspondent in Bangalore, India, http://news.bbc.co.uk/1/hi/england/norfolk/3623993.stm.
Buzzle.com (no date) http://www.buzzle.com/articles/call-center-crimes-a-desperate-call-for-help.html.
Dicken, P. (2003) *Global Shift: Reshaping the Global Economic Map in the 21st Century* (London & New Delhi: Sage).
Economist, The (2004) The place to be, 373(8401), 13 November, p. 10.
Ganguly-Scrase, R. (2005) Globalisation, liberalisation and transformation of women's work in India, Conference paper for the Australian Sociological Annual Conference, University of Tasmania, Hobart, December.
Gentleman, A. (2005) Indian call staff quit over abuse on the line, *The Observer*, UK, 29 May.
Held, D., NcGrew, A., Goldblatt, D. & Perraton, J. (1999) *Global Transformations: Politics, Economics and Culture* (Stanford, CA: Stanford University Press).
Hirst, P. & Thompson, G. (1999) *Globalization in Question: The International Economy and the Possibilities of Governance* (Cambridge: Polity Press).
Hochschild, A. R. (1983) *The Managed Heart: The Commercialization of Human Feeling* (Berkeley, CA: University of California Press).

India Today (2002) Untitled article, 18 November, p. 36.
Kundu, K. (2012) Young, jobless and Indian, *The Wall St Journal*, 23 November, http://blogs.wsj.com/indiarealtime/2012/11/23/young-jobless-and-indian/.
Lewig, K. A. & Dollard, M. F. (2003) Emotional dissonance, emotional exhaustion and job satisfaction in call centre workers, *European Journal of Work and Organizational Psychology*, 12(4), pp. 366–392.
Mies, M. (1980) *Indian Women and Patriarchy: Conflicts and Dilemmas of Students and Working Women* (New Delhi: Concept).
Mies, M. (1982) *Lace Makers of Narsapur: Indian Housewives Produce for the World Market* (London: Zed Books).
Mirchandani, K. (2004) Practices of global capital: Gaps, cracks and ironies in transnational call centres in India, *Global Networks*, 4(4), pp. 355–373.
Morris, J. A. & Feldman, D. C. (1997) Managing emotions in the workplace, *Journal of Managerial Issues*, 9(3), pp. 257–274.
Nadeem, S. (2009) The uses and abuses of time: globalization and time arbitrage in India's outsourcing industries, *Global Networks*, 9(1), pp. 20–40.
National Association of Software and Services Companies (NASSCOM) (2005) Executive summary, http://www.bpo.nasscom.org/artdisplay.aspx?cat_id=619.
National Association of Software and Services Companies (NASSCOM) (2012) Report, http://www.nasscom.org/indian-itbo-industry.
Ohmae, K. (1995) *The End of the Nation-State: the Rise of Regional Economies* (New York: Simon and Schuster).
Perinotto, T. (2003) Call centres head for India, *Australian Financial Review*, 16 October, p. 56.
Poster, M. (1995), CyberDemocracy: Internet and the public sphere, http://www.hnet.uci.edu/mposter/writings/democ.html.
Prasad, S. (2004) Call-centres cartelize against job-hoppers, *Hindustan Times*, 3 July, http://www.zoominfo.com/CachedPage/?archive_id=0&page_id=626889949&page_url=//www.hindustantimes.com/news/i81_602834,0008.htm&page_lastLupdated=2004-03-07T05:12:58&firstName=Asim&lastName=Handa.
Roy, A. (2001) *Power Politics* (Cambridge, MA: South End Press).
Roy, A. (2004) *The Checkbook and the Cruise Missile* (Cambridge, MA: South End Press).
Ruigrok, W. & van Tulder, R. (1995) *The Logic of International Restructuring* (London: Routledge).
Scott, J. C. (1990) *Domination and the Arts of Resistance: Hidden Transcripts* (New Haven, CT: Yale University Press).
Sontag, S. (2003) The world as India, *Times Literary Supplement*, 13 June, http://www.susansontag.com/prize/onTranslation.shtml.
Trivedi, H. (2003) Cyber-coolies, Hindi and English, *Times Literary Supplement*, 27 June, http://www.the-tls.co.uk/.

Devleena Ghosh coordinates the Indian Ocean and South Asia Research Network, UTS and has pioneered intercolonial studies in Australia. She has published widely on environment, technology and culture, the political and cultural experiences of South Asians, including Fijians, in Australia and on circulations of ideas, people, and objects in the Indian Ocean. She is the author (with Paul Gillen) of *Colonialism and Modernity* (UNSW Press, 2007), co-editor of *The Cultures of Trade: Indian Ocean Exchanges* (Cambridge Scholars Publishing, 2007), *Water, Sovereignty, and Borders in Asia and Oceania* (Routledge, 2008), and editor of *Shadowlines: Women and Borders in Contemporary Asia* (Cambridge Scholars Publishing, 2012).

The 'Green Economy': Class Hegemony and Counter-Hegemony

JAMES GOODMAN* & ARIEL SALLEH**

*University of Technology Sydney, Australia
**University of Sydney, Australia

ABSTRACT *The transnational capitalist class is using the global ecological crisis to revive its failing financial system. Whereas environmental degradation was once seen as imposing a limit on economic accumulation, in the new 'green economy', ecologism appears to become a rationale for extending market activity. The intensification of neoliberal extraction, and corresponding social and environmental debt, meets resistance from the global justice movement whose articulation of a counter position is increasingly sophisticated. This article examines this dialectic as played out at the UN Rio + 20 Summit and parallel People's Summit in June 2012. The hegemonic 'green economy' formulation of corporations, multilateral agencies, unions, and big NGOs is contained in a document known as* The Future We Want. *A counter-hegemonic document entitled* Another Future is Possible, *facilitated by the World Social Forum, spells out an alternative route to global justice and environmental sustainability—a 'bio-civilisation'. In neo-Gramscian terms, a war of position is occurring between two 'transnational historic blocs around divergent social visions (Carroll, 2007, p. 36).*

As early as 2008, there were signs that the twentieth anniversary of the United Nations Conference on Environment and Development (UNCED) in Rio de Janeiro would be designed to promote global consensus on a 'green economy'. The UN Rio + 20 draft 'outcomes document' named *The Future We Want*, encapsulated this socially ambitious and universalising goal (UN, 2012a). On the road to Rio the European Environment Commissioner marvelled at the progressive 'move from protecting the environment from business, to using business to protect the environment' (Potočnik, 2011). For many, however, this was little more than a new attempt at what Goldman (1998) identified as furthering geopolitical order by privileging markets in 'global resource management' ostensibly to protect the 'earth system'. For this reason, the 'green economy' idea was quickly countered by a configuration of grassroots political organisations, CSOs, and global networks, judging it to be a rhetorical cover for private business interests. As UNEP conference plans began to lay bare the new 'green economy' model, a counter-hegemonic force of environmentalists, socialists, feminists, peasants, and indigenous peoples formed an oppositional alliance, supported by a few Southern elites. At the edges of a highly staged intergovernmental and UN agency Rio + 20 process, a genuine dialogue opened up, culminating in a broad-based World Social Forum (WSF) mediated People's Summit where alternatives were correlated and the notion of a 'bio-civilisation' was consolidated. The capitalist commodification of nature in notions like 'climate smart' GMO agriculture was contested. Ecosystem pricing in financial initiatives like carbon trading was interrogated; and the very meaning of 'value' was questioned. Official negotiations over implementing 'green economy' measures proceeded despite persistent grassroots interventions. We contend that Rio + 20 brought to the fore a political struggle between two clearly delineated global forces, introducing a new chapter in the history of class conflict.

The interpretation of politics as a confrontation between institutionalised social forces owes much to the Gramscian tradition of international relations theory (Cox, 1987; Gill, 2002). Applying this lens to the present global conjuncture, Carroll (2007, p. 39) identifies four dimensions of the hegemonic process: the struggle between what Gramsci called 'fundamental classes'; the exercise of intellectual and/or ideological leadership; the ecological question; and the construction of 'public spheres for forming consensus'. This article demonstrates how contests over the 'green economy' were waged across these several dimensions, engaging both state and non-state actors. Beyond this, the article calls for deepening Gramscian understandings of class by focusing on new conflicts apposite to a time of ecological exhaustion. First we address the emerging class dynamic under ecological crisis. This is followed by an examination of bloc formation as the UN and WSF each convene policy networks vying for control of the public agenda. The ideological programme of each grouping is read in their respective documents *The Future We Want* and *Another Future is Possible*.

Our conclusion points to unresolved political areas and counter potentials. The 'green economy' notion is geared to a homogenising discourse of international governance, a shared set of social and material expectations across nations, classes, and bodies. Our argument is that global consensus on a totalisation like the 'green economy' will do little for sustainability or democracy.

Ecological Crisis and Class Antagonism

The 'green economy' is plainly a class stratagem and accounts of the transnational capitalist class, its consumerist ideology, governing elites, neoliberal think tanks, and consultancies are powerfully relevant here (Sklair, 2001; van der Pijl, 1998). But the 'green economy' as a form of crisis management is highly problematic and circular in that it deals with symptoms by bolstering causes (Johnston et al., 2006). It is embedded in a system whose *raison d'être* of profit results in multiple levels of material extraction and degradation. These are treated as economic 'externalities' and defined as financial debits to be offset by equivalent credits on the financial markets. The financialisation obscures continued social and environmental exhaustion. Yet already, since World War II, 60% of environmental 'services' have been destroyed by industrialisation (World Watch, 2009, p. 14). The neoliberal 'green economy' requires industrial growth, yet every technological advance depends on a further cradle-to-grave cycle of mining and manufacture. Claims to 'dematerialisation' notwithstanding, efficiency gains are soon eroded by increased throughput (Foster et al., 2010). In the social 'metabolism' with nature, there is no such thing as a 'free lunch' (Commoner, 1971); rather, progress is achieved by displacement. The displacement may be spatial—shifted on to the backs of less powerful sectors of society, or temporal—shifted on to the backs of future generations.

If today's dominant class is identified by its support for the 'green economy', can the opposing bloc be identified as a class? The historical logic of accumulation unfolds an ever-changing composition of classes—dominant and subordinate (Luxemburg, 1968 [1913]). Marx's *Manifesto* (1848 [1952]) promises that the bourgeoisie will create its own 'grave-diggers' in the working class. However today, this working class is in danger of digging its own grave in the toxic cities of the industrialised world (Waterman, 2009). Capital meanwhile is rejuvenated by its own crises.

Left thinkers seek new emancipatory potentials among social groupings whose labour is indispensable to accumulation and thus, who are likely to be empowered to supersede capital. Hardt and Negri (2001), for example, favour the historical agency of 'immaterial labour' in high tech societies. They argue that the skills of cognitive and affective workers in service economies of the North now hold the key to overturning capitalism. As they perceive the means of production to be embodied in the capacities of these service workers, they argue that this 'general intellect' of capital can be reappropriated for revolutionary ends. But, hypothesising a transformative agent from a 'leading' sector of 'lead' societies omits and overrides many global 'others'. The current global order is marked by the dispossession of 'combined and uneven development' (Harvey, 2003; Rosenberg, 2006). The Hardt and Negri version of Marxism thus rings hollow in a world where the majority of people across continents are sacrificed to the material development of the North. Communities in the Global South may never experience the same stages of social change as has furnished Eurocentric affluence.

Another Left interpretation of historical agency sees resistance to capital as a cross-class phenomenon encompassing a variety of worker and peasant groupings along with disaffected middle-class individuals (Bello, 2002). This approach to social agency centres class alliances on state, region, or locale in order to reject the mandatory integration of local economies into global free trade regimes. Such alliances are common in Southern contexts where they thrive on postcolonial nationalism. Local leaders can build legitimacy by 'de-linking' from 'global resource managers'. Broad political alliances of this kind have gained considerable traction against globalism among socialists in Latin America (Lebowitz, 2012), and have informed foreign policy responses from the Philippines to Canada. Nevertheless, as played out in *dependencia* debates, too much reliance on the agency of domestic classes can result in an underestimation of transnational capitalist power (James, 1997).

An alternative emancipatory vision, one that responds directly to the global ecological crisis, comes from a worldwide resurgence of people whose labour involves social and ecological reproduction. Reproductive labour is performed in the main by women, but also by peasants and indigenous peoples. For several decades, socialist ecofeminists influenced by Luxemburg (Mies, 1986) have argued that colonisation of the 'housewife' in the domestic periphery is critical to capitalist accumulation through its unpaid support of the 'productive' sector. While workers at the 'point of production' remain a social force, increasingly workers in the reproductive sphere are mobilising against global neoliberalism (Goodman, 2002, 2010). Neither the domestic periphery nor geographic periphery of capital is significantly industrialised. In fact, the labour of each sector can be described as 'meta-industrial', carried out by a class undertaking 'holding labour' (Salleh, 1997). Metaphorically, the term 'holding' conjures an imagery of human nurture and care, but holding labour is 'relational' in a far deeper sense as well, as it bridges, integrates, and maintains the society–nature metabolism. Meta-industrial skills are synergistically creative in both social and ecological contexts. These forms of reproductive work foster energetic exchanges in complex metabolic webs (Salleh, 2004, 2009). Conversely, the 'instrumental linear' character of mechanised labour cuts through living matter leaving entropy and disorganisation (Shiva, 1989).

As a response to global environmental breakdown, the 'green economy' is guided by the principle of business-as-usual. But capitalist commodification exhausts living ecosystems just as it exhausts and exploits human bodies. It performs a double alienation—of nature and of labour—and it leads to a 'metabolic rift' between rural resources and urban parasitism (Foster et al., 2010). The production process derives a surplus by means of material extraction from nature, leaving behind a social debt to exploited workers, an embodied debt to unpaid women for reproductive labour, a postcolonial debt to peasants and indigenes for appropriating their livelihood, an intergenerational debt to youth, and an ecological debt to ecosystemic nature at large (Salleh, 2010). Ruling class exploitation of the geographic and domestic peripheries of capital (Luxemburg 1968 [1913]) relies on a comprador class, groomed by the coloniser. This social relationship is the real meaning of 'development' and such power relations are enacted through the UN, the business world, government, universities, and neoliberal NGOs. In the lead-up to Rio + 20, high-level consultations were very effective in training this managerial class of scientists and bureaucrats, mainstreaming women among them.

The contemporary global crisis brings a new class configuration into view; the classic social tension between centre and periphery is now complemented by an ecological tension between the prioritisation of nature for commodity production versus prioritisation of nature for the reproduction of livelihood. Now meta-industrial workers claim wide geopolitical legitimacy. The majority of global food growers are women in the South. It is peasants, women, fishers, and gatherers, outside of capital and interacting hands-on with natural ecological cycles, who meet everyday life needs for the majority of people on earth. Peasant modes of provisioning and indigenous technologies integrate precaution and sustainability. In contrast to industrial contrivances of the 'green economy', these are real 'green jobs'. Moreover, local economic provisioning and care-giving exemplifies the ethical principles of commoning, cultural autonomy, and sustainability (Regenvanu, 2010; Serrano, 2011). The notion of a meta-industrial class is powerfully integrative (Salleh, 2012b). It broadens the definition of labour beyond the Marxist preoccupation with production workers. It transcends the divisive idealism of postmodern 'identity' politics like feminism or indigeneity. Meta-industrial labour is grounded in the reproduction of embodied and environmental processes (Mujeres Manifesto, 2009). In maintaining the humanity–nature metabolism, this activity is in principle trans-cultural and non-gendered. That said, for historical reasons, women remain a majority among those colonised by capitalist reproduction.

Carroll and Harvey write of the need to discover an 'organic link between reclaiming the commons and opposing capital's domination of labour' in order to connect 'the struggle to decommodify land, intellectual property, public utilities and the like with the struggle to decommodify labour' (Carroll, 2010, p. 180; Harvey, 2005, p. 203). We suggest that meta-industrial labour has emerged as the key historical agent in that counter-hegemonic process. The intellectual leadership of this nascent class takes form as a call for a 'bio-civilisation'—a theme that is elucidated below.

CRISIS, MOVEMENT, MANAGEMENT: GLOBALISING DYNAMICS

Forging the Hegemonic 'Green Economy'

Tracking back to Rio + 20 and the hegemonic search for intergovernmental consensus, the 'green economy' idea took shape during a 20-year debate. This reflected the rise of neoliberal ecologism, with 'ecological' sustainability translated first into 'economic' sustainability, and then into 'free markets'. The 1992 UNCED established three pillars of sustainability: economic development, social development, and environmental protection. After 1992 the concept of sustainable development was increasingly captured for economic growth (Paton, 2011; Sklair, 2001). The Johannesburg Rio + 10 Summit privileged what it called 'sustained economic growth', marking an interregnum between sustainability and the 'green economy' (UN, 2002: paras 89, 138).

The UNCED 2012 or Rio + 20 was to take this neoliberalisation several steps further. Two themes were established by the General Assembly in 2010: 'a "green economy" in the context of sustainable development and poverty eradication and the institutional framework for sustainable development' (UNGA, 2010, p. 6). The Preparatory Committee embarked on a consultation process from May 2010, leading to a *Synthesis Report* presented in January 2011. The report stated there was 'no consensus definition or model of a "green economy"', yet there was said to be strong support for embedding the 'green economy' (however defined) in the three pillars of sustainability (UN, 2011a: para 118). The report stated that a key 'challenge' for the UN was to develop a '"green economy" road map' with 'transitional steps' that would minimise the 'burden on business' and prevent 'the creation of new barriers to trade' (Ibid.: paras 69, 79). On this basis the UN proposed a range of questions to shape 'the way forward': the first question sought 'new growth drivers' in green sectors while others asked how to mobilise 'international investment' for 'green infrastructure', how 'to meet environmental and climate objectives while promoting development and trade' (Ibid.: para 119).

With the *Synthesis Report*, several international agencies took an opportunity to affirm the pro-growth agenda, and predictably, international finance institutions swayed the debate (Bond, 2012). In an ideologically 'moralising' move, the World Bank (2011) insisted on 'inclusive green growth' against the more contestable 'green economy' concept. It selected policies to 'unleash the power of the private sector', to self-consciously manage popular resistance to market reform and to extend the reach of markets to manage resource use. The World Bank argued for the importance of exclusive property rights over 'common property resources', pricing them on the market to ensure 'rents would accrue to the scarce natural resource' (Ibid., p. 125).

UNEP played a key role in framing the agenda. Particularly significant was its 2008 study on 'green jobs', which defined the environment as a key driver of economic growth (UNEP and ILO, 2008). In October 2008 it established a '"green economy" Initiative' to define a 'blueprint for a "green economy"', a 'global plan for a green industrial revolution' (UNEP, 2008). The Initiative culminated in *Towards a 'green economy': Pathways to Sustainable Development and Poverty Eradication* (UNEP, 2011a). Two years in the making and 631 pages long, the report covered 'natural capital' relating to agriculture, forests, fisheries and water, and aspects of 'energy and resource efficiency' in relation to renewable energy, manufacturing, waste, buildings, transport, tourism, and cities. The report stated that across the various sectors 'a common message emerges: unless people have clear rights over a resource, they will lack the incentive to manage it well' (Ibid., p. 565). The absence of clear, enforceable property rights governing access to 'ecosystem services' created the 'the classic tragedy of the commons problem, and can lead to degradation of the ecosystems which are the basis of much economic activity and well-being' (Ibid.). The solution was increased market access, with 'strengthening international governance', especially in trade and investment. The approach was promoted by the UNEP's lobby, the '"green economy" Coalition', which was composed of NGOs and private sector associations. In March 2011 the Coalition published its *Road to Rio* submission, which favoured a 'recapitalisation of our natural resource base' to 'incentivise investment' ('Green Economy' Coalition, 2011, p. 7).

A parallel business lobby was established for Rio + 20 by the World Business Council for Sustainable Development (WBCSD) and the International Chamber of Commerce (ICC). This was dubbed Business Action for Sustainable Development (BASD). Described as a 'constructive voice' for business, the BASD was specifically 'committed to providing the market-based solutions and practices that are essential to create a sustainable world' (BASD, 2011). The ICC and BASD engaged with UNEP through a UNEP-Business and Industry Global Dialogue co-convened in April 2011 (Hoedeman, 2012), and in September 2011 the ICC published its *Ten Conditions for a Transition toward a Green Economy* emphasising 'the importance of sustainable growth and access to open, well-functioning, and efficient markets' (ICC, 2011, p. 5). An OECD contribution, *Towards Green Growth*, also appeared in May 2011. Dating from 2009, their 'Green Growth Initiative' positioned repricing through markets, including through tradeable permits, as the most effective and efficient answer to the ecological crisis (OECD, 2011, p. 35). In December 2011, the attempt by UNESCO to inject a more human-centred perspective into the debate with its report, *From Green Economies to Green Societies*, figured as an anomaly in an official debate that remained resolutely market-centred and economistic.

The ongoing UN preparatory process involved a broad orchestration of intergovernmental, governmental, and nongovernmental spheres. In the governmental sector, state ministers or their stand-ins met under the UNEP Governing Council and the Global Ministerial Environment Forum. National representatives were deployed to spell out a mix of new 'green economy' models 'tailored to different local and national conditions'; at once pro-growth but based on a measurement of well-being beyond GDP. The nongovernmental sector was marshalled under a Global Major Groups and Stakeholders Forum. Here designated forums were arranged for Women's groups, Children and Youth, Indigenous Peoples, NGOs, Labour and Unions, Business and Industry, the Science and Technology community, and Local Authorities (IISD, 2012).

UNEP assumed that the views of these Major Groups and Stakeholders would readily converge on the global 'green economy' theme. Peak bodies channelled the input, reframing the 'green economy' to their own purposes. As mentioned, input from the corporate sector was interpreted through BASD. The International Trade Union Confederation (ITUC) channelled trade union perspectives, prioritising access, right principles, concrete targets, and accountability. Likewise, the International Council for Science (ICS) aimed for clearer definitions and measurable implementation. With the concerns of Major Groups bundled into the operational logic of Rio + 20, the UNEP 'green economy' programme would proceed relatively unscathed with the status quo maintained by a well honed 'civil society'.

In December 2011, UNEP presented a further synthesis of perspectives from UN agencies. Here the UNEP director stressed the role of the private sector in financing the 'green economy', including policy geared to 'establishing and enforcing well-defined property rights so as to ensure sustainable use' (UNEP 2011b, pp. 12, 17–18). The draft Rio + 20 outcomes document *The Future We Want*, was released in January 2012 with a central section devoted to the 'green economy', characterised as offering 'win-win opportunities to improve the integration of economic development with environmental sustainability' (UN, 2012a, paras 27–29). Four caveats were offered: no new trade barriers; no new aid or finance conditionalities; no increase in technological dependence; and no limitation on policy space for development (Ibid., para 31). The document outlined the need for 'toolkits' to implement the 'green economy', framed within the rubric of 'best practice' policy options and shared indicators. Within this, a new framework for development financing was proposed, linked to 'green economy' initiatives.

From April 2012, Brazil, the Rio + 20 host government, sought to deepen the 'multi-stakeholder' consensus with online dialogues on nine key themes from the UN's January draft document. These deliberations would culminate in face-to-face panel discussions in the week prior to the official intergovernmental Rio + 20 Summit. Again, demonstrating the UN partnership with business the corporate-led World Economic Forum was invited to nominate a list of its affiliated experts to provide 'framing documents' for the nine dialogues (WEF, 2012). Pre-framing for the Summit was even expressed in the conference logo. As the UN stated: 'The logo shows the three components of sustainable development—social equity, economic growth, and environmental protection—connected in the shape of a globe' (UN, 2012c, p. 1). Economic growth was signified as a set of blue steps, at the centre of sustainability, linking environmental protection in the form of a green leaf and social equity as a red figure. In comparison, the official 1992 UNCED logo, which was also used at the 2002 Rio + 10 conference in Johannesburg, was considerably less didactic, being an image of a green dove bearing the globe on its back (University of York, 2005).

Creating a Counter-Hegemonic 'Bio-civilisation'

The 2010 decision that Rio + 20 would be oriented to the UN's 'green economy' agenda sent a strong signal to people concerned about market globalism and capitalist ecologism. Citizens, grassroots NGOs, and movements opposed to the commodification of water, agriculture, carbon and forests, as well as its impacts on women and the poor, soon came together in a series of encounters with governments and UN authorities. By 2011 it was clear that the 'green economy' was something of a Trojan Horse, to be incorporated into the sustainable development agenda but then outgrow it. As noted above, the idea had morphed from government intervention to create 'green jobs' into a universal agenda for the financialisation of environmental crisis. In March 2011 the influential Action Group on Erosion, Technology and Concentration (ETC, 2011) called for people to mobilise against 'ongoing destruction-as-usual'; it was time, they argued, to mount a counter-offensive, 'to organize massive campaigns to get the Earth Summit back on course—not just for a "green economy", but for a green, equitable, and just future' (Thomas, 2011).

A major aspect of this political struggle was the ownership of organising spaces at Rio + 20. The UN had sought to control public engagement through a designated People's Summit hosted by a Brazilian Facilitating Committee. As the electronic portal for Rio + 20 indicates, this semi-official civil society gathering would 'not be a parallel summit nor a counter summit, but rather a fundamental actor for Rio + 20' (UN, 2011b). In the event, the portal became a site for organising against the 'green economy' and to develop an alternative agenda before the Summit itself in June 2012.

In October 2011 the Facilitating Committee released its 'global call' to the Summit, to 'reject the marketization of life and nature, the false solutions and the old and new technologies that deepen inequalities or hurt the precautionary principle' (UN, 2011b). The Committee asked a series of questions:

> How can we build a new economy based on social and environmental justice? . . . How to stop the commodification (marketization) of life, nature and the privatization of the commons? . . . How to

enhance the coordination and control of strategies and campaigns to bring about new and existing campaigns? (UN, 2011b)

The Facilitating Committee announced a timetable to develop the 'agenda of struggles, mobilizations and building alternatives' (UN, 2011b). This was linked to the WSF and an anticipated Thematic Social Forum to be held at Porto Alegre in January 2012 specifically to help 'overcome the fragmentation and atomization of the struggles, encouraging convergence and common agendas'.

The link to WSF reflected its growing focus on ecological issues and the civilisational challenges they pose (Smyth and Byrd, 2010). The WSF had been established in Porto Alegre in 2001, and remained a powerful instrument for drawing together workers', women's, indigenous, and ecological voices (Conway, 2012; Karides et al., 2007). People with meta-industrial skills and values were already active in WSF—as peasant food sovereignty and indigenous environment networks, as women anti-toxics campaigners and peace activists (La Via Campesina, 2012; Shiva, 2006). Furthermore, the Forum had recently shifted from a focus on political dialogue to direct political intervention (Kirk, 2009). The device of the politically focused 'thematic assembly', developed at the 2009 Belèm WSF, was now to be used to host the Rio + 20 preparation.

The open invitation to the Thematic Forum heralded recent mobilisations, from the Occupy Movement to the Arab Spring, and defined Rio + 20 as a 'unique moment for rescuing the original sense of alter-worldism and of the World Social Forum' (WSF, 2011a, p. 5). To achieve this, the Forum was conceptualised as a deliberative site. While expressing a diversity of positions, the Forum had to 'focus on the agenda to be disputed at Rio + 20' and develop 'specific proposals' and 'strategic analysis capable of setting a horizon of actions' (WSF, 2011b). At the Forum itself in January 2012 a draft response to the Rio + 10 proposals was compiled as a 'dialogue platform' under the title 'Another Future is Possible: Come to Reinvent the World at Rio + 20' (WSF, 2012). The draft was then circulated and finalised at the June 2012 Peoples Summit.

By May 2012, then, a range of NGOs and social movements had effectively appropriated the UN civil society summit. Symbolically they renamed it the 'People's Summit in Rio +20 for Social and Environmental Justice in defense of the commons, against the commodification of life' (International Coordination Group, 2012). The UN hegemonic orchestration was backfiring and the People's Summit had begun to overshadow the theatre of intergovernmental negotiations. A key source of leverage was the *Another Future is Possible* document.

In its final form *Another Future is Possible* offers something of a new template for the global justice movement (People's Summit, 2012a). Running to 40 pages, it consolidates many of the insights accumulated by the movement since the 1994 Zapatista uprising, and while directed at Rio + 20, it reaches well beyond it. The central organising theme is an alternative 'bio-civilisation', a symbiosis of humanity and nature. This rests on an ethic of connectedness, of 'being more', not 'having more' (Ibid., p. 10). The message is not one of quantitative limits, but of qualitative transformation. There is no limit to 'being more' in a 'sustainable economy . . . based on care and on use that neither destroys nor generates waste, but renews and regenerates' (Ibid., p. 10). Although this alternative is grounded in existing meta-industrial practices, it was modestly asserted as a 'possible utopia' (Ibid., p. 11).

In contrast to the 'totalising civilisation' of capitalism, 'bio-civilisation' re-embedded life needs in economic sufficiency and was defined as intrinsically democratic. 'Bio-civilisation' was founded on the commons as a social relation, where 'one's full unfolding depends on the unfolding of others and vice versa'. The commons is thus based on direct participation—it is 'a place we are creating . . . we do not find paths to the future, we make them' (People's Summit, 2012a, p. 27). Here, a politics of embodied ecological relations directly challenges the abstract managerial ecologism that took hold after Rio in 1992. This systemic challenge is most succinctly expressed in the concept of 'living well', or *buen vivir,* rough Spanish for *sumak kawsay,* an Ecuadorean Kichwa term. Along with the eco-centric recognition of the 'Rights of Mother Nature', the idea of 'living well' had been the foundation for the 2010 Cochabamba Climate Summit in Bolivia, and for the broader climate justice movement.

In *Another Future is Possible,* the living well concept was developed across multiple fields of bio-civilisation. The document has three sections: 'ethical, philosophical and cultural foundations', 'production, distribution and consumption', and 'rights and power'. It is organised around principles and priorities, and offers policy proposals and institutional pathways. 'Green economy' advocates are seen as driving a 'private confinement of the commons' that assumes a 'large proportion of the goods of the planet have no owner, hence no one to care for them' (People's Summit, 2012a, p. 7). The sheer audacity of official Rio + 20 proposals spurred a new unity of purpose in the People's Summit. This 'revolution of minds' embraced 'a new ethical responsibility of care [for the planet] as much as for future generations and for all life'.

Another Future is Possible argues that shared ownership and collective management of livelihood resources must apply to all forms of resource use. Resource use that has an impact on society and ecology is viewed as rightfully a commons, even if it is not recognised as such. The private benefits of resource exploitation thus need to be socially managed to account for the public costs they generate. This principle of the commons, extended 'to society as a whole', is joined conceptually with the requirement to recognise the inherent 'rights of Mother Earth' (People's Summit, 2012a, p. 27). Energy for instance is a commons as its climate impacts potentially constrain livelihood for present and future generations, requiring it to be put under 'democratic control'. Land and agriculture is to be socially managed and grounded in food sovereignty and the inherent rights of the earth. Currency is to be defined as a commons with finance socialised as part of a 'solidarity economy' to provide for human need and for zero growth (Ibid., p. 25). The material commons flows into an ideational commons, as 'scientific knowledge, like traditional knowledge, is also part of the Commons, freely accessible to each and every one' (Ibid., p. 13).

The document translates principles into concrete proposals, although some proposals are at odds with the overall intent. While the document exposes the contradictions of 'green growth', it draws uncritically on the Intergovernmental Panel on Climate Change (IPCC) proposal for 100 million 'climate jobs' in low-emissions renewable energy projects. While the commons is embraced as an alternative to freewheeling markets and 'top-down' decision-making, household property ownership for small-holding agriculturalists is endorsed. New business practices for economic democracy and sustainable consumption are promoted through regulatory initiatives for corporate responsibility. Proposals to deprivatise water and health care are conceived in terms of public ownership with democratic 'oversight'. Urban planning is conceptualised as a problem for sustainable 'management'; and migration is a problem of 'regional citizenship'. Civil society is addressed in terms of networks, public access, transparency, and freedom of expression, not in terms of social movements.

Another Future is Possible should not be seen as definitive, but rather as a provisional working document. The document will no doubt inspire many thoughtful transformative strategies. Already there are proposals for a citizens' audit of global debt, spaces for alternative currencies, minimum and maximum wage levels, bank socialisation, trade regulation, a financial transactions tax, and an end to land, water, and biodiversity privatisation. Radical activists will see some of these gestures as reformist, but in terms of 'learning to walk from here to there' they provide powerful educational tools (Salleh, 2012a).

In this, the deliberative process and the document itself, exemplify the broader politics of loose coordination and consensus-building in the global justice movement (Goodman, 2013). The key aim is to inspire broad-based engagement and mobilisation, as Reitan notes, 'to challenge, and for some, collectively wield power at the transnational level while drawing power *downwards* and pushing it *outwards* to local communities and daily struggles' (2012, p. 325). Something of this is reflected in the final declaration of the People's Summit, which defined Rio + 20 as a 'unique opportunity . . . to build a common understanding . . . pointing to the necessary task of "reinventing the world"' (2012, p. 9). People would carry forward this platform as they returned to their 'territories, regions and countries to build convergences, fighting, resisting and advancing . . .' (Ibid., p. 10).

Static Outcomes and Dynamic Potentials

The People's Summit closing statement condemned the 'green economy' objective as 'kidnapping the common property of mankind to save the financial-economic system' (People's Summit, 2012b). The Rio + 20 process certainly had this potential. In the event, its outcome document—*The Future We Want*—was a disappointment even to 'green economy' advocates. The UNEP's own Stakeholder Forum observed that 'Rio + 20 did not put us on the path to the "future we want"' (Dodds and Navar, 2012, p. 18).

The official outcome document stands in vivid contrast to the People's Summit outcomes. The first section of *The Future We Want*, 'Our common vision', focuses on poverty as 'the greatest challenge facing the world today'. It confuses and subsumes ecological sustainability under socio-economic sustainability through 'sustainable management' and privileges 'sustained, inclusive and equitable economic growth' as the means to achieve this erstwhile environmental goal (UN, 2012b, para 4). The second section, 'Renewing political commitment', reiterates existing international agreements finding 'insufficient integration' of sustainable development objectives (Ibid., para 20). The spiralling multiple crises of sustainability are acknowledged, but the failure of global neoliberal policy frameworks is not recognised. Indeed, there is a warning against adoption of 'unilateral economic, financial or trade measures' (Ibid., para 26). Participation by citizens and corporations is emphasised, ironically through 'public-private partnerships' (Ibid., para 46). The idea of recognising 'rights of nature' is diluted as a voluntary commitment to 'promote harmony with nature' (Ibid., para 39).

On this foundation, the third section of *The Future We Want* focuses on the 'green economy' as 'one of the important tools available for achieving sustainable development'. But the tool is dispensable—offering 'options for policymakers', not a 'rigid set of rules' (UN, 2012b, para 56). The four limiting conditions in the original draft are quadrupled to 16, and no template if offered beyond country-specific initiatives (Ibid., para 59). The UN is empowered to disseminate models and best practice initiatives and again governments are advised to develop public–private partnerships to leverage finance (Ibid., paras 66, 71).

The Future We Want endorsed the 'green economy' but signally failed to define a 'roadmap' or obligations beyond acknowledging 'options'. The Third World Network, which had lobbied negotiators throughout, stated that the 'green economy' 'had absorbed most of the time and energy of the summit's preparatory meetings', with the EU in particular . . . After a 'titanic fight', the postcolonial countries had prevailed, with no rules for implementation except the set of 16 principles limiting the application of the concept (TWN, 2012, p. 23). The conference as a result was inconclusive, producing little in terms of commitments. It was a profound defeat for the goal of a sustainable future, as the causes of ecological crisis were left untouched. But it was also a victory, because the 'green economy' concept was emptied-out. In the words off one forest campaigner:

> Rio + 20 might be a turning point . . . Southern countries have clearly demonstrated here that they no longer want . . . sustainable development policies to be dictated by a small corporate elite in the North that is promoting socially unjust and unreliable environmental services markets. (Lovera, 2012)

In 2008 UNEP had grasped the 'green economy' idea as a new environmental orthodoxy, a 'blueprint' for sustainable development. The 'green economy' would restore the capitalist promise of consumer cornucopia. It offered vast tracts for 'greenfield' investors by unlocking previously conserved habitat and vastly increased scope for arbitrage. However, grassroots mobilisation against the agenda successfully encouraged governments to water down the proposition into a series of optional possibilities leaving the crisis unabated.

Rio + 20 brought two social formations, hegemonic and counter-hegemonic, into a deeper political engagement than either might have expected. The marshalling of oppositional views and alternatives through a preliminary WSF Thematic Social Forum and later concurrent Rio + 20 forums, led to a remarkably coherent vision for an ecologically sensitive and socially just 'bio-civilisation' grounded in a range of concrete movement demands. It contains many lessons for mobilising the knowledge of peoples exploited and displaced by capitalism. In the process of contestation the meta-industrial class would become visible to itself, and to the wider global polity, which now begins to discover new forms of agency in 'a wider framework of dispossession'. Class is indeed, 'the structural principle allowing commonalities to be recognized and acted upon' (Burgmann, 2003, p. 290).

Without doubt, the global majority of meta-industrial workers—urban women carers, rural subsistence dwellers, and indigenes—are hit hard by the exploitation and dispossession of ecological exhaustion. They also share the experience of exclusion and diminishment by social stratification and cultural bias. That said, the insights and class consciousness of this grouping are not negatively constructed. Meta-industrials are victims only to hegemonic eyes. In a time of multiple crises, there is an urgent need for political decisions informed by ecologically embedded modes of existence. Women and men with 'holding skills' have a head start in constructing the parameters of a 'bio-civilisation'. This positive concept of labour and creative knowledge making at the humanity–nature interface challenges conventional sociological categories. By the Eurocentric model, class is defined by 'lack' in relation to the mode of production and reproductive labour is deemed non-productive. As the focus of counter-hegemonic politics shifts from production to reproduction, 'another labour class' comes forward with unique capacities for regenerative knowledge. The document *Another Future is Possible* demonstrates the leverage that meta-industrial logic can wield. The next question is: under what conditions will this socially diverse labour grouping 'in itself' become a class 'for itself'?

References

BASD (2011) Business Council for Sustainable Development: About us, http://basd2012.org.
Bello, W. (2002) *Deglobalization: Ideas for a New World Economy* (London: Zed Press).

Bond, P. (2012) Inclusive green growth or extractive greenwashed decay? The World Bank and the green economy, *Triple Crisis: Global Perspectives on Finance, Development and Environment*, 18 May, http://triplecrisis.com.
Burgmann, V. (2003) *Power, Profit and Protest: Australian Social Movements and Globalisation* (Sydney: Allen & Unwin).
Carroll, W. (2007) Hegemony and counter-hegemony in a global field, *Studies in Social Justice*, 1(1), pp. 36–66.
Carroll, W. (2010) Crisis, movements, counter-hegemony: In search of the new, *Interface—a journal for and about social movements*, 2(2), pp. 168–198.
Commoner, B. (1971) *The Closing Circle: Nature, Man, and Technology* (New York: Knopf).
Conway, J. (2012) *Edges of Global Justice: The World Social Forum and Its 'Others'* (New York: Routledge).
Cox, R. (1987) *Production, Power and World Order: Social Forces in the Making of History* (New York: Columbia University Press).
Dodds, F. & Nayar, A. (2012) Rio +20: A new beginning, *UNEP Perspectives*, Issue 8, pp. 1–20.
ETC (2011) Who will control the 'green economy'? Building the People's Summit Rio+20, Rio+20 Portal, 17 December, info@forums.rio20.net.
Foster, J., Clark, B. & York, R. (2010) *The Ecological Rift* (New York: Monthly Review Press).
Gill, S. (2002) *Power and Resistance in the New World Order* (Basingstoke: Palgrave Macmillan).
Goldman, M. (ed.) (1998) *Privatizing Nature Political Struggles For the Global Commons* (London: Pluto Press).
Goodman, J. (ed.) (2002) *Protest and Globalisation: Prospects for Transnational Solidarity* (Sydney: Pluto Press and Vancouver: Fernwood Press).
Goodman, J. (2010) Counter global movement and post-globalisms of the marginalised, in D. SinghaRoy (ed.) *Social Movements in Globalised World Contesting Perspectives and Emerging Issues* (New Delhi: Manohar Publishing), pp. 30–45.
Goodman, J. (2013) Anti-globalization movements, in D. Snow, D. della Porta, B. Klandermans & D. McAdam (eds) *The Blackwell Encyclopedia of Social and Political Movements* (New Jersey: Wiley-Blackwell), pp. 145–151.
Green Economy Coalition (2011) *The Road to Rio* (London: IIED).
Hardt, M. & Negri, A. (2001) *Empire* (Cambridge: Harvard University Press).
Harvey, D. (2003) *The New Imperialism* (Oxford: Oxford University Press).
Harvey, D. (2005) *A Brief History of Neoliberalism* (Oxford: Oxford University Press).
Hoedeman, O. (2012) RIO+20 and the greenwashing of the global economy, *The Transnational Institute*, 13 January, http://www.tni.org.
IISD Reporting Service (2012) Briefing note on the Thirteenth Major Groups and Stakeholders Forum, 20 February, http://www.iisd.ca/unepgc/unepss12/gmgsf13.
International Chamber of Commerce (2011) *Ten Conditions for a Transition Toward a Green Economy* (Paris: ICC).
International Coordination Group (2012) What is at stake at Rio+20?, Statement of the International Coordination Group of the People's Summit for Social and Environmental Justice, 12 May, http://rio20.net.
James, P. (1997) 'Post-dependency? The Third World in an era of globalism and late-capitalism, *Alternatives*, 22(2), pp. 205–226.
Johnston, J., Gismondi, M. & Goodman, J. (eds) (2006) *Nature's Revenge: Reclaiming Sustainability in an Age of Corporate Globalism* (Toronto: Broadview Press).
Karides, M., Smith, J. & Becker, M. (eds) (2007) *Global Democracy and the World Social Forum* (Boulder, CO: Paradigm).
Kirk, A. (2009) World Social Forum: Resolution and a plan of action, *Inter-Press New Service*, 1 February, http://www.ipsnews.net.
La Via Campesina (2012) Call to action: Reclaiming our future: Rio+20 and Beyond, 16 February, via-info-en@googlegroups.com.
Lebowitz, M. (2012) *The Contradictions of Real Socialism* (New York: Monthly Review Press).
Lovera, S. (2012) Forest campaigners welcome opposition to REDD+ and other market-based approaches at RIO+20, Media Release 21 June 2012, Global Forest Coalition, Asunción, Paraguay, http://globalforestcoalition.org/.
Luxemburg, R. (1968 [1913]) *The Accumulation of Capital* (New York: Monthly Review Press).
Marx, K. (1952 [1848]) *Manifesto of the Communist Party* (Moscow: Progress Publishers).
Mies, M. (1986) *Patriarchy and Accumulation on a World Scale* (London: Zed Books).
Mujeres Manifesto (2009) First Continental Summit of Indigenous Women, *Lucha Indigena*, No. 34.
OECD (2011) *Towards Green Growth* (Paris: OECD).
Paton, J. (2011) *Seeking Sustainability: On the Prospect of an Ecological Liberalism* (London: Routledge).
People's Summit (2012a) *Another Future is Possible* (Rio de Janiero: People's Summit).

People's Summit (2012b) Final declaration, Peoples' Summit in Rio +20 for Social and Environmental Justice in defense of the commons, against the commodification of life, 22 June, http://rio20.net.

Potočnik, J. (2011) Towards the 'green economy', Speech to the 26th UNEP Governing Council—Global Ministerial Environment Forum in Nairobi (Kenya), European Commissioner for Environment, 22 February, http://europa.eu.

Regenvanu, R. (2010) The traditional economy as source of resilience in Vanuatu, in T. Anderson & G. Lee (eds) *In Defence of Melanesian Customary Land* (Sydney: AidWatch), pp. 30–34.

Reitan, R. (2012) Theorizing and engaging the global movement: From anti-globalization to global democratization, *Globalizations*, 9(3), pp. 323–335.

Rosenberg, J. (2006) Why is there no international historical sociology?, *European Journal of International Relations*, 12(3), pp. 307–340.

Salleh, A. (1997) *Ecofeminism as Politics: Nature, Marx and the Postmodern* (London: Zed Books).

Salleh, A. (2004) Global alternatives and the meta-industrial class, in R. Albritton, J. Bell, S. Bell, & R. Westra (eds) *New Socialisms: Futures Beyond Globalization* (London: Routledge), pp. 201–211.

Salleh, A. (2009) *Eco-Sufficiency & Global Justice: Women Write Political Ecology* (London: Pluto Press).

Salleh, A. (2010) From metabolic rift to metabolic value: Reflections on environmental sociology and the alternative globalization movement, *Organization & Environment*, 23(2), pp. 205–219.

Salleh, A. (2012a) Rio+20 and the green economy: Technocrats, meta-industrials, WSF and Occupy, *Z Net*, 31 March, http://www.zcommunications.org.

Salleh, A. (2012b) Green economy or green utopia? Rio+20 and the reproductive labor class, *Journal of World Systems Research*, 18(2), pp. 141–145.

Serrano, I. (2011) What sustainable development? (Manila: Philippine Rural Reconstruction Movement).

Shiva, V. (1989) *Staying Alive: Women, Development and Ecology* (London: Zed Books).

Shiva, V. (2006) *Earth Democracy* (London: Zed Books).

Sklair, S. (2001) *The Transnational Capitalist Class* (Oxford: Blackwell).

Smyth, E. & Byrd, S. (2010) World Social Forum activities in Belem and beyond, *Journal of World Systems Research*, 16(1), pp. 94–105.

Thomas, J. (2011) Rio+20: Toward a new 'green economy'—or a green-washed old economy? *Grist*, 25 March, http://grist.org/climate-policy.

TWN (2012) *Third World Network Newsletter*, 25 June, p. 23.

UN (2002) *Report of the World Summit on Sustainable Development* (New York: WSSD).

UN (2011) *Synthesis Report on Best Practices and Lessons Learned on the Objective and Themes of the United Nations Conference on Sustainable Development* (New York: UN).

UN (2012a) *The Future We Want: Draft Zero Document* (UN: New York).

UN (2012b) *Rio+20 Outcomes: The Future We Want* (UN: New York).

UN (2012c) *Logo Use Guidelines and Waiver of Liability Form* (New York: UN).

UN (2012d) *Rio+20 Portal: Building the People's Summit*, http://rio20.net/en/.

UNEP (2008) Crafting a blue-print for a green global economy, Press Release, Green Economy Initiative, 2 December.

UNEP (2011a) *Towards a Green Economy: Pathways to Sustainable Development and Poverty Eradication* (Nairobi: UNEP).

UNEP (2011b) *Working towards a Balanced and Inclusive Green Economy: A UN System-Wide Perspective* (New York: UN Environment Management Group).

UNEP & ILO (2008) *Green Jobs: Towards Decent Work in a Sustainable, Low-Carbon World* (Nairobi: UNEP).

UNGA (2010) Implementation of Agenda 21, General Assembly Resolution 64/236, 31 March.

University of York (2005) Sustainability-ed: Important milestones in sustainable development, http://www.sustainability-ed.org.uk.

Van der Pijl, K. (1998) *Transnational Classes and International Relations* (London: Routledge).

Waterman, P. (2009) Labour at the 2009 Belem World Social Forum: Between an ambiguous past and an uncertain future, www.netzwerkit.de/projekte/waterman/belem209.

World Bank (2011) *Inclusive Green Growth: The Pathway to Sustainable Development* (Washington: World Bank).

World Economic Forum (2012) *The Rio+20 Multi-stakeholder Dialogues: First Reactions from WEF Global Agenda Council Experts* (Geneva: WEF).

World Social Forum (2011a) Let's Reinvent the World: Group of Reflection and Support to the WSF Process (GRAPFSM), October, http://rio20.net.

World Social Forum (2011b) Thematic Social Forum Porto Alegre 2012: Capitalist Crisis, Social and Environmental Justice, Towards the People's Summit of Rio+20, 21 September, http://www.forumsocialmundial.org.br.

World Social Forum (2012) Dialogue Platform of the Thematic Social Forum, 'Another Future is Possible', 24 January, http://www.rio20.net.

World Watch Institute (2009) *Toward a Transatlantic Green New Deal: Tackling the Climate and Economic* (Brussels: Heinrich-Boell-Stiftung).

James Goodman researches social movements and global politics at the University of Technology Sydney. He is co-author of *Justice Globalism: Ideology, Crises, Policy* (Sage, 2013) with Manfred Steger and Erin Wilson.

Ariel Salleh is senior research fellow 2013 at the Institute for Sociology, Friedrich Schiller University, Jena and honorary associate professor at the Department of Political Economy, University of Sydney. She is a founding editor of the journal *Capitalism Nature Socialism* and editor of *Eco-Sufficiency and Global Justice: Women Write Political Ecology* (Pluto Press/Palgrave, 2009).

Occupy Cosmopolitanism: Ideological Transversalization in the Age of Global Economic Uncertainties

S. A. HAMED HOSSEINI

University of Newcastle, Callaghan, NSW, Australia

ABSTRACT *A new cycle of ideological clashes underpins the economic policy reforms in the aftermath of the 2008 global financial crisis and its continuing uncertainties. This article argues that the evolving complexity of the global economic system, especially after the crisis, has been associated with not only the growth of ideological fragmentations but also with the* transversalization *of ideas, identities, and solidarities among grassroots movements. Rooted in the transnational movements for justice of the 1990s–2000s, a more practically inclusive mode of 'cosmopolitanism', i.e.* transversalism, *has now evolved, significantly, into a growing number of consolidated demands and multi-issue agendas, in response to the post-crisis social injustices. By focusing on the 2011–2012 Occupy movements as its exemplary case study, the article delineates the features of such an ideological advancement and its implications for social theory.*

Introduction: The Post-Crisis Ideological Landscape

The collapse of confidence in the world's financial system with the 2008 global financial crisis (GFC) led to a new wave of government and intergovernmental intervention, including bailouts and stimulus expenditure. This has turned the neoliberal state into a state for corporate welfare in almost every society affected by the crisis (Johnston et al., 2010). The following recession, exacerbated by sharpening austerity in the face of rising government indebtedness—though followed by some weak signs of possibly unsustainable recovery—has increased hardship for many underprivileged groups. From private bailouts to public austerity, the management of crisis has become a battleground for contesting powers and stakeholders. While neoliberal and post-welfare mentalities still underpin policy reforms, divisive measures are taken by governments to stimulate demand for consumption, save big business (as the so-called engines of growth), and secure financial stability (Patomäki, 2013).

In the context of these top-down interventionist policies, there has been a wave of responses from Right and Left. Mobilizations have surfaced with the exposure of dishonesty and corruption in the leading political and economic powerhouses through Wikileaks, generating a massive escalation of cyber-activism across the world, and with the 2011 political turmoil and revolutions in the Middle East and the anti-austerity protests in Greece, Spain, Ireland, and France. From the Right, mobilizations have seen the rise of Tea Party in the USA, campaigning against the expansion of government's regulatory role, and the augmentation of anti-immigrant, far-right Islamophobic movements in Europe. Latterly, opposition to bank bailouts has seen the revitalization of global justice networks and an international proliferation of grassroots forums and general assemblies in the Occupy movements. All these aspects point to the re-formation of a global ideological landscape with new players in the post-GFC era. A new battleground is emerging where all types of forces—old and new, local and global, political and financial, public and private, economic and ecological—seek to control the redistribution of risks, consequences, and burdens. In this context, where tensions are heightened and the crisis is manifold, ideologies start to play more colorful roles.

One of the major ideological transitions attributed to the post-Cold War globalization era is the 'cosmopolitanization of visions' (Held, 2010). Such a perception of ideational change may not convincingly correspond to what the so-called 'Global Justice Movement' (GJM) or the global Left has experienced in the last decade. The 'chaotic processes of capitalist creative construction', according to Harvey (2012, p. 126), 'have reduced the collective left to a state of energetic but fragmented incoherence.' If metanarratives and ideologies like socialism or communism are no longer capable of matching the ever-growing complexities of capitalism, can meta-ideological and ethical frameworks like 'cosmopolitanism' provide the Left with the necessary capacity to go beyond periodic eruptions of mass protests, and create broadly agreed concrete proposals? Can the movement actors benefit from the virtues of 'cosmopolitanism' as a general framework for shaping solidarity and consistency, both within and across populations, against the sources of injustice? What ideological features must such a cosmopolitanist vision have, particularly in the post-crisis era?

To answer these questions, this article focuses particularly on the latest developments in the global justice activism, i.e. the Occupy Wall Street movement (OWS) and its associated transnational activist networks ('Occupy movements') across the Global North, as the most significant response to the recent economic reformations. To set up the theoretical framework necessary for this case study, I will start my argument with a brief discussion of 'cosmopolitanism' as both a metanarrative employed by the mainstream ideologues within the global field of resistance (especially in the North) and a theoretical notion adopted by mainstream social theory to describe the ideological landscape of the global Left. It will be explained how such conventional notions of 'cosmopolitanism' in both theory and practice have evolved in the last decade and what roles the progressive forces of the GJM like OWS have played in these shifts.

Though acknowledged by many observers and intellectuals (Hayduk, 2012), the historicity of the new movements in the context of evolving global resistance has remained undertheorized. To have a perceptive discussion of the future of post-crisis movements, we certainly need to examine the trajectory of changes in the broader field of global resistance. I will argue that the transitions in the GJM, alongside the post-crisis structural changes, have determined the ideational features of the recent uprisings. I will then delineate the features of a newly evolving mode of cosmopolitanist vision, coined here *transversal cosmopolitanism* (or *transversalism*) by this author, as a meta-ideological framework underpinning a diverse range of oppositional and reformist discourses in these movements. It will be explained how particularly the (delayed) resurrection and, at the same time, the transformation of the so-called GJM in response to the post-GFC reforms, have been associated with 'further materialization' of this new cosmopolitanist vision. It is worth mentioning again that the contrasts made here between the pre- and post-crisis activism are in fact ideal-typically constructed to highlight this evolving ideational process and to avoid far-reaching claims about the reality.

Occupy Cosmopolitanism: From Globalism to Transversalism

Mainstream notions of cosmopolitanism stress the duality of the *national* vs. the *cosmopolitan*. Today, however, both the literature on this issue and many activist conceptions of global justice have started to come of age and move beyond such dualistic assumptions. Although there is no consent on how to define and study cosmopolitanization processes, the rising debates around this issue bear witness to its importance and reality. Many of the academic debates imply that cosmopolitanization is a progressive move forward despite its limitations. They see it as a viable alternative to current international systems of governance, which have failed to provide us with democratically decided solutions to our complex supra-national problems (Held, 2010, pp. 143–83).

Cosmopolitan views, due to their anti-essentialist and pluralist values appear to be the most appropriate means to deal with the complexity of globalizing risks. However, challenges to cosmopolitanism are not all external. Arguably, the toughest threats come from those insider interpretations that fail to be reasonably integrated in terms of their own basic assumptions. Class-biased, Eurocentric, Orientalist, dualist, and determinist conceptions of cosmopolitanism, as well as the pragmatist approaches that reduce cosmopolitanism to ideological metanarratives and emancipatory political agendas, all arguably contradict the very basic cosmopolitan principle of obligations to mutual comprehension or openness to the 'stranger'.

Conventional cosmopolitanism is transcendental in its nature, meaning that it encourages openness to difference through transcending divisions and creating universal spaces where widely held ideals or shared attributes across cultures or groups can be practiced. Such a trend of cosmopolitanization has been associated with grand projects for seeking new translocal principles for self-rule; the reformation of current international institutions and regimes of global governance, according to universal rights and liberal or social democratic models; and the construction of transnational solidarity across imagined communities such as women, workers, Muslims, etc. (Brassett, 2010). This mode of cosmopolitanization can be very liable to see differences and disagreements as secondary and sometimes dysfunctional in terms of the prospect of growing 'global ethics', 'a global public sphere', 'global belonging', or 'global concerns about human future' (Germain and Kenny, 2005).

In contrast, a growing number of studies have recently pointed to these facts in recognition that 'there are multiple cosmopolitanisms' (Holton, 2009, p. 209). Cosmopolitanist values are not merely rooted in the history of Western Enlightenment and modern intellectual traditions; they cannot be reduced to universalistic and/or relativist ideals. Cosmopolitan projects may not be primarily epistemic; they are not essentially opposite to nationalist or localist values; nor are their perspectives always philosophically abstracted and ideologically formulated or exclusively limited to the concerns of well-educated globalist elite, frequent travelers, traders, artists, and middle-class consumers (Giri, 2006).

Conventional cosmopolitanism is fed by globalist imaginations. In reality, however, the ways in which ideational transformations can happen—as the result of inter-contextual transmissions—are so diverse that we can hardly theorize them under standardizing notions such as globalization. Transversalization, in contrast, refers to the ways in which this plurality is evolved out of interactions between conflicting grand processes such as liberalization, globalization, localization, Americanization, Balkanization, polarizations. Whereas some of these social changes and processes at the global level may lead to hybridization in some local contexts, others can cause fragmentation, conflict, marginalization, homogenization, or a mixture of these results in other contexts. Therefore, *transversality* must be defined as a quality produced through the interaction between such grand processes. Understanding transversality, according to new theoretical developments, requires the employment of dialectical imagination, acknowledgment of complexities, and the adoption of accommodative approaches (Hosseini, 2006).

Globalism is defined by R. T. Robertson (2003, p. 4) as a conscious process of globalization. Similarly, we may define transversalism as a conscious effort to lessen disparities, achieve equity, avoid violence, and enhance autonomy and democracy by creatively crossing (or redrawing) boundaries that mark politicized divisions (Cockburn and Hunter, 1999). Transversalism, both in theory and practice, aims to realize the necessary condition for all parties involved in transversalization processes to benefit mutually, receive equal recognition and representation, and finally become able to determine their destinies in their new conditions.

It is no longer difficult to see that cosmopolitanist assumptions underlying the GJM have also undergone the same path of transformation. Somewhere else (Hosseini, 2009, 2010), by drawing on a collection of discursive and experiential facts from global justice activism, and through the examination of theoretical controversies over the nature of these post-Cold War progressive movements, I have attempted to analytically map their changing ideological landscape. I argued that many of the ideologies and identities in the movement have experienced shifts that can be conceptualized under the title of 'cosmopolitanization'. However, the process of cosmopolitanization, contrary to many scholars' speculations (Held, 2010) is not only multidimensional but also plural and even contentious. The contribution of these rival ideological visions to the GJM has opened spaces of confusion and ambiguity for both scholarly theorizations and activist conceptions of the movement. However, paradoxically, this has also inspired the rise of 'transversal cosmopolitanism' in productive ways, alongside the persisting (justice) globalist agendas (see Hosseini, 2006).

'Transversal cosmopolitanism' (or 'transversalism') in this particular context refers to an underlying ideological vision within the current global resistance oriented towards redefining and redirecting global processes in alternative ways that cannot be simply identified with either radical particularism of localist visions and identity politics (Starr and Adams, 2003) on one hand, or the universalism of institutional cosmopolitanism on the other hand (Murray, 2010). Transversalism attempts to rebuild global governance and transnational relations not just through institutional reforms but also predominantly through the plural participation of grassroots from below in both local and trans-local solidarity networks and autonomous public spheres.

'Transversalism' acknowledges the differences between the national contexts of resistance and the diversity of roles played by different states. However, what makes this vision relatively unique is its commitment and openness for exchanging experiences and ideas across a variety of local fields of resistance. Both the practical and intellectual elements of this vision can be clearly traced back to adaptive and innovative initiatives used by some feminist networks (originally developed in Italy in the 1990s and later theorized by Yuval-Davis) to push for a politics of 'dialogue across differences' (Goodman, 2007, p. 190; Yuval-Davis and Stoetzler, 2002, p. 109). This so-called 'transversal politics' was later extended by trans/feminists further into other semi-peripheral societies in Europe to create shared empowering projects and to oppose intersectional inequalities beyond 'the imposition of a single universal' without retreating 'into those differences as tightly-bound, exclusivist and essentialist identities' (Massey, 1999, p. 7). Ideologically articulated elements of transversal cosmopolitanism can also be found in adaptive voices such as eco-feminists, autonomist Marxists, post-anarchists, horizontalist, and affinity groups, who tend to accommodate new perceptions from other visions (Hosseini, 2006).

With respect to the major elements of a social movement—such as strategies, organizational structure, challenges, and internal tensions—parallels between the GJM and OWS are unmistakable. The OWS was predominantly built on the legacy of the GJM, shown in its adoption of such distinctive concepts as 'direct action', 'participatory democracy', and 'horizontalism'; its social base, 'diverse rhetorical repertoire', deep engagement in reclaiming public spaces, creating forums and general assemblies; as well as the extensive use of social media, 'diversity of tactics', 'convergence centers', and 'spokescouncils' (Jones, 2012; Juris and Pleyers, 2009). The multiplicity of the post-GFC grassroots responses and anti-austerity protests across many countries in 2011–2012 reveals that the dynamics of global resistance are more complex than what has been conventionally conceptualized under the title of 'cosmopolitanization'.

The (justice) globalist views in the movement faced serious challenges due to the changing focus in the global field of resistance, deepening frustrations with the forums and their incapacity to create global alternatives, the shifting roles of global players in the context of unilateralist interventions in the Middle East, and the widening gaps in the post-Cancun WTO negotiations. Staggenborg (2011, pp. 153–4) argues that transnational activism continued targeting global institutions and policies throughout the 2000s, but it also experienced significant changes alongside the shifting global context. This shift consisted of the further decentralization of organizations, localization of protests and demands, as well as growing emphasis on issue-oriented campaigns. This movement later faced a new dilemma of how to respond to the GFC and post-GFC policy controversies.

The post-GFC struggles for justice like the Occupy movements appear now to be even more decentralized. Connection to local activist networks and unions have proved pivotal for the sustainability of these movements and their messages (Uitermark and Nicholls, 2012). Neoliberalism is still contested, as the number one enemy with a strong transnational dimension, but more closely and pragmatically within the structurally delimited contexts of state sponsored corporate welfare (Buell, 2011). The Occupy movements in the North remained focused on their national policy processes, domestic inequalities, and institutions (Shepard, 2012a). This can be interpreted as a significant shift from the movement's preexisting globalist cosmopolitanization process when we apply a conventional notion of cosmopolitanism. However, when considering less conventional concepts of cosmopolitanism (Holton, 2009), we realize that with the further advancement of multiple, competitive but still interdependent units of core–periphery relationships in the post-crisis world, many in the GJM are in fact becoming engaged in more balanced, transversal exchanges of experiences and values across the global rifts of inequality.

The emergence of this new trend is associated with a broader structural change that can be theorized under the title of *ideological transversalization*. As previously defined in this section, transversalization is about dynamic interplays and negotiations between multiple sources of attachment, engagement, belonging, suffering, and identification in the course of collective/networked actions. It is a proactive pluralism in function 'attuned to the realities of human co-existence' that needs to be experienced and explored (Lawson, 2011, p. 39).

Transcendental cosmopolitanism is based on interdependence, and while the counter-cosmopolitanism of localist agendas is oriented towards communal autonomy, transversalism adopts a non-dualistic logic of autonomy and interdependence. For instance, in the case of Zuccotti encampment, the hybridity of a 'privately' owned 'public space' symbolizes the transversality of the movement (Schrader and Wachsmuth, 2012).

Local oppositions to the post-crisis policy responses are still quite significantly attuned to broader globalist or regionalist agendas; i.e. the transnational pressures made by international (e.g. IMF) and regional (e.g. EU) institutions and powerful players (e.g. Germany, the USA, Britain) for further domestic bailouts, undemocratic regulations, austerity measures, foreign and environmental policy changes at the national level to maintain the neoliberal order and integrity at the global/regional level (Patomäki, 2013). Social inequalities, class conflicts, and unfair taxation systems inside each national context are brought to the forefront of struggles while, at the same time, many demands are framed using foreign symbols and tactics (e.g. embracing success of Tahrir encampments in Egypt, CLASSE in Québec, SYRIZA in Greece, or using social networking sites).

Within the global field of resistance, these shifts may not highlight a totally new or unprecedented format of solidarity. These trends in fact can be traced back easily to cases like the Zapatista uprising in the 1990s or the Landless People's Movement in Brazil. Even in cases like ATTAC (Association for the Taxation of financial Transactions and Aid to Citizens) that are seen as groups holding globalist values, the transversalization process appears to be the case, albeit as a more pragmatic issue than conscious. As shown by Uggla (2006), ATTAC has become highly centered at national level through their choices of alliances and objectives; an issue that can explain the ability of this organization to collaborate with the European Occupy movements and anti-austerity activism. However, the post-GFC civil society and grassroots resistance in the North manifest the transversalization trends more consciously than in cases like the Zapatista. Pamela McDonald (2011), a citizen journalist, observes how the Occupy Oakland clearly reflects the accommodation of local and national concerns into the internationally expanding movement against the dominance of finance sector priorities. Occupiers appeared to be very well aware of the practical dilemmas associated with the adoption of *transversal cosmopolitanism (transversalism)*. As one participant argued (McDonald, 2011):

> This movement is about creating a broad tent that everyone's issues can fit into. It's still early. Things will iron out as we continue day after day. But yes, it is challenging. . . . We localized this international movement by introducing local issues, such as Oscar Grant, solidarity with the Pelican Bay.

Associated with the transversalization of ideas is a transversalization of solidarities among justice activists. Transversalism in Cook's (2012, p. 15) words is a 'tangible set of attachments at play in everyday life, rather than some abstract engagement with a world of difference'. In practice, 'elements of self-doubt, reflexive self-distanciation and irony [would] enable . . . [the transversalist actors] to search for commonalities and connections without disregarding disparate and inequitable histories' (Ibid., p. 14).

This mode of solidarity traverses (not transcends) identities and ideologies by urging subjects to reinterpret their identities based on a more accommodative orientation towards other participants and actors in the field of resistance. In a transversal solidarity, the matter of community is not relinquished in favor of networks but, rather, it has gained a new fluid structure in practice, redefined in relation to commons. Such conceptions imply the *coexistence* of a broad range of desires from the expression of (post-)anarchist values and practices (http://occupywallst.org), to growing aspirations for collective autonomy as against privatization and reclaiming the public spaces (http://ourworldisnotforsale.org), to proposals for the implementation of Keynesian regulatory policies (Smith and Glidden, 2012; see also http://robinhoodtax.org, http://globalgovernancewatch.org, http://taxjustice.net, http://makingfinancework.org, http://neweconomyworkinggroup.org). These latter values are consciously articulated to reject exclusionist, communitarian, and conservative orientations.

Of course, the earlier movements for global justice had to deal with the issue of internal racial and communal divisions and suffered from internal struggles for symbolic dominance, especially between interfering traditional leftist ideologies (Ibrahim, 2013). It is also true that color- and gender-blindness are still important challenges for the new movements like OWS. 'It's time to realize that the concept of race operates in protestors' psyche when they choose to assemble', an Occupy blogger colorfully states (cited in thinking sociology, 2011). However, due to their further indigenized organizational structures and attachments to local physical spaces and local activist groups, these new movements appeared to be in a far better position to address their internal power relationships and their normally institutionalized intersectional inequalities. From the very early stages of the uprisings, there were reports of tensions and negotiations between actors in the movements. The white, middle-class activists were reported to show a greater tendency towards the personalization of politics and the universalization of ideals, whereas non-white, migrant, and lower class participants had more inclinations towards communitarian autonomy and solidarity (see Juris et al., 2012).

As the Occupy movements started to spread nationally and internationally, the composition of participants began to diversify demographically and minorities found opportunities to create blocks of resistance within the resistance. Facilitated by horizontalism and consensus techniques, deliberations on internal differences and disparities had a better chance of being translated into cross-sectional consciousness (see for instance, bruddaone, 2011; thinking sociology, 2011; Todd, 2011). Events like *Lil' Bobby Hutton Day Hoodie & Hijab March* in solidarity with Travon Martin (a black teenager) and Shaima Al Awadhi (a Muslim Iraqi female) both victims of racist violence, for instance, were organized by occupiers to oppose systematized racism in America's post-9/11 security apparatus.

Critical reflections on the representation of the so-called 99% (a 'majoritarianist' concept that is blind to color, gender, and class) appeared to become an essential element and product of deliberative democratic practices in many of these open spaces created in the Occupy movement (Ashraf, 2011; Beeman, 2012; Juris et al., 2012). There are good examples of how transversalization can advance through the employment of reflexive rationality in dealing with contradictions between ideals and facts. Smith et al. (2012) report how the initial tensions between the El Paso occupiers and the homeless evolved into the incorporation of the latter into the movement and the formation of more accommodative identities on both sides.

This advancement is the product of critical self-reflexive deliberations around the inconsistencies between ideals and facts (see Hosseini, 2010, Ch. 6). Transversalist orientations in the recent post-GFC movements may have not been able to overcome the very dire historical dilemmas their preceding movements had to face, but elements within these movements have grown reflective awareness about the limitations of micro-political techniques such as consensus building, horizontalism, and non-hierarchy (see Marcus, 2012). Voices from within and without have criticized the 'fetishization' of 'structurelessness', 'leaderlessness', and consensus-mania which can lead to the marginalization of the movement in mainstream politics on the one hand and the exclusion of the most marginalized within the movement on the other hand (see Smith and Glidden, 2012).

This ideological shift points to the expansion of a grassroots mode of cosmopolitanism that will have significant implications for our theoretical revisions of cosmopolitanism. We may ask how realistic (or normative) such an interpretation of ideological shifts is, especially when it is made about a highly diverse and inconsistent range of cases and claims such as the ones made by the Occupy movements in their rather short lifespan. Are the inconsistencies not strong enough to rule out such generalizations, no matter how abstract or 'ideal-typical' they are? This counter-argument might be valid to the extent that we still use the mainstream notions of cosmopolitanism. A significant part of the movement is nonetheless aware of the inconsistencies in the ways the GFC has been experienced by different societies. Such a reflexive consciousness would prevent many activists from developing an overarching ideological alternative to global capitalism and thereby resist the diversion of the new movements into formal politics.

The Occupy movements are not just about the occupation of ideological landscapes and de-legitimization of hegemonic systems. There is also an ongoing occupation of universalistic narratives within the broader field of resistance; this would determine the future of the movement and its social impacts: As *The Occupied Wall Street Journal* (West, 2011) states 'Our movement is a precious, sublime, messy, and funky form of incubation. Again like jazz, we must embody and enact a loving embrace of the art of our collaborative creations.' Reflecting on and resolving the inconsistencies between ideals and facts by occupiers have been a central element of this reflexive rationality. As observed by Chris Maisano and the Jacobin editorial board (2012), 'One of the chief ironies . . . was that their effectiveness was often attributed to their putative horizontalism, when in reality they demonstrated the absolute need for . . . some sort of *centralized, institutional* space to tie together its disparate currents and tendencies.' Attempts to institutionalize the reflexive rationality of the movement were manifested in the establishment of popular research projects, databases, and educational social media networks by many developers, librarians, occupiers, researchers, and artists (see http://www.occupyresearch.net/ and http://occupyarchive.org/ for instance).

Acknowledging diversity and difference is, however, not adequate for establishing sustainable solidarity and proactive consensus around alternatives. 'To agree to disagree' can itself become a deadlock on furthering interactions and pursuing goals. Open spaces of resistance today have been used by inter-activism to practice the possibilities for developing means of resolving disagreements; 'differences can be subjected to reflective criticism' (Evanoff, 2004, p. 447). Shepard (2012b) reports how the increasing diversity of participants in Occupy NY was associated with the development of multi-issue agendas (health, employment, energy, education, etc.) founded on a common cause against expanding inequalities (see also http://www.nycga.net).

The experience of complexity inside and outside the field of activism also provides motivation to those who seek autonomous alternatives to employ a critical reflexive mode of cognition in their analyses and practices. Many media made myths around the ways a capitalist economy works (or fails to work); the existing but constantly denied class conflicts in an advanced society like the US; issues as complex as derivative markets, nature of money, the roots of global crises, climate change, taxation, and socioeconomic inequalities have been challenged in such a thriving virtual vernacular academia since the 2008 GFC (see activist reports like Flank, 2011; Writers for the 99% et al., 2012).

The cosmopolitanism of social democratic and Keynesian think tanks, civil society organizations, and progressive democrats has found a physical and virtual place to encounter unheard personal stories, experiences, and knowledge coming from the Main Street. Perhaps nowhere better than in the Occupy NYC Declaration Flowchart, can we find a visualized conception of *glocal* complexity and the interconnection of grievances (http://occuprint.org). The chart is made of many key words each suggested by participants at their general assembly on 21 September 2011. The draft was published online for broader discussion acknowledging that the grievances are not all inclusive. The declaration chart (Schragis, 2011) has a seemingly paradoxical but sensible sentence, 'Our increasingly interconnected world obscures the underlying truth that all of our grievances are connected.' It adds, 'Let us not be weighed down by the complexity of our situation but united by its singularity as we re-establish a system that protects our rights.' How the singularity of the post-GFC situation has affected the development of transversalism is a question I will try to address briefly in the next section.

The GFC, as a Turning Point?

The 2008 GFC, with its consequent and still persisting economic recession, appeared to challenge more seriously the basic globalist ideas such as the end of the nation-state, the end of ideology, and the end of history. The crisis exposed a few important facts that must be considered when explaining the recent shifts in the GJM. First, it revealed the fragility of the new world economic system and the unsustainable nature of growth even in the core. The moral-managerial bankruptcy of the neoliberal order is not just limited to the post-colonial periphery. With the coming-home crisis, the incompetence of the new world system is now proved to be a historical phenomenon for populations in the North, too. Second, it highlighted the geopolitical imbalances, exposing the significant (though paradoxical and deficient) role the state can play in managing the financial crisis, and thereby dispelled the 'end of nation-state' myth for many observers (Pugh, 2011). Third, it exacerbated growing inequalities within both the North and South; a process that can be summarized as 'Third Worldization' of the majority in the First World and 'First Worldization' of an elite minority in the Third World (Galbraith, 2012). The global Left was able to redefine its goals and strategies as soon as the post-Cold War globalism gained momentum and started to reorder global hierarchies in the 1990s. However, the 2008 GFC not only revealed the crisis of neoliberal globalism but also required the Left to redefine its roles once again by taking the complexity of economic globalization more seriously into account. The demographic configuration of recent job recoveries in the US, for instance, shows signs of a further intersectionally uneven, casualized, gendered-racialized process (Kochhar, 2012). Finally, the crisis underlined the distinction between rising new economies in the South with their pseudo-Keynesian development models, and the demise of the Western share of the global economy in a new multipolar world order.

Accordingly, the links between the state and corporate capitalism now seem to be much more dynamic than what was assumed by many globalists from either the Left or Right. The ascending 'corporate welfare' model of the Post-GFC era has pushed for a more systemic and overt socialization of the loss, as governments accumulated debts, and later imposed austerity while maintaining or even intensifying the process of the privatization of rewards and opportunities through measures like bailouts and corporate tax cuts (see Callinicos, 2012; Kostigen, 2011). However, a number of states (like in Australia) used populist forms of public expenditure including cash distribution and interest rate cuts to maintain demands and public legitimacy. The full impact of the GFC was not felt in the 'real economy' until after the recovery measures had been put in place. Rising unemployment coincided with an increasing turn to austerity as governments sought to claw back from deepening indebtedness. Such populist interventionist reforms and their associated party politics of promising change caused bewilderment and delay in responses to the GFC among civil society and grassroots movements.

This delay can also be partly explained in terms of the persisting globalist legacy of GJM. The enduring residue of globalist perceptions in the Left, despite all the structural decentralizations, made it difficult for many groups to reincorporate national politics into their ideological visions; something that far-right activism could easily do, due to its strong patriotism. The Left's resurrection surfaced with a significant shift towards national politics in both the practical and ideational dimensions. Relatively successful national and regional liberations from neoliberal globalism in Latin America and then finally in the Arab uprisings, with their loud and strong national-regional accents, accelerated this ideological transition in Northern justice activism.

The same logic used to justify decades of rigid structural adjustment, ruthless austerity measures, and demanding debt dependency in the Global South is now being used more bluntly and more aggressively than before to push the welfare state further back in the Global North and its semi-peripheries like Greece and Spain (Johnston et al., 2010). The boomerang effect of neocolonial world order and its neoclassical threat to the sovereignty of even developed nation-states has left no one (except the so-called 1%) secure. The post-GFC movement for justice consists of a rather harmonious multitude of local and national oppositions that have taken part in a globalizing choir of unheard voices.

With economic and financial globalizations in disarray and their asymmetries more clearly exposed thanks to the GFC, many solidarity networks for justice and democracy have now started to move further from their universalistic ambitions and globalist imaginaries by engaging in more contextualized or localized forms of activism (e.g. Occupying Oakland, Occupy Auckland, Occupy Baltimore, Occupy Toronto). As such, the GFC contributed to this shift by incorporating newer and younger voices since the experiences and reactions differed across different communities (Reimer, 2012). The GFC has thereby opened up a new chapter in the history of grassroots struggles for justice.

Using David Harvey's terminology (2006), as soon as the regional 'fixity' of capital finally prevailed over its global 'motion', due to the growing fragmentations in the world economy, the globalist logic started to lose its currency in both mainstream politics and the movements for justice (Schrader and Wachsmuth, 2012). There seems to be a nexus between the disarray of capital and the decentralized GJM—a nexus that has regenerated the movement into new forms of resistance through North–South transversality. Global justice activism after the GFC continued to shift its focus further away from global free trade and global governance towards pushing for radical reforms in the relationship between the state and the market at both the national and regional levels. The spread of the dissident spirit of Arab Spring across the regions in 2011 showed how, this time, an array of national movements for democracy in the South could become inspiring exemplars for Northern activists.

The Occupy movements expanded their scope beyond finance, economy, and even income inequality. Drawing on the legacy of past anti-racist and civil rights resistance, a broad range of ethnic groups participated in the uprising in October 2011 and expressed their personal stories of frustration and ideas for change. As soon as the movement gained momentum, despite its failure in physically occupying Wall Street, it began to branch out geographically, diversify demographically, and transform into further localized protests. It also started to bring out and take action on a vast array of interrelated social issues through the setting up of specialized working groups. Multi-scalar issues such as racism, immigration, migrant workers' rights, foreclosures, police brutality, violence, media, and environment were extensively addressed and debated. Many activists in the movement occupied an intermediating space between high-profile national/global organizations like unions, NGOs, INGOS, and leftist think tanks on the one hand and the subaltern grassroots on the other hand. This unique positioning in fact provided the activists with a better capacity for comprehending complexities. Therefore, the transnationalization processes based on justice globalist agendas have transformed into a *transversalization* process; that is, a process through which justice activism has gained stronger national/local accents on the top of their moderated global imaginary, and cross-regional rhetorical-experiential exchanges have further become the principles of today's resistance (see Greene and Kuswa, 2012).

In other words, we can now perhaps claim with more confidence that the so-called 'global imaginary' (Sassen, 2004; Steger, 2008) is giving way to a multitude of *glocal* imaginaries. The conventional cosmopolitanization of ideologies in the GJM has started to relent at the prospect of growing various vernacular, grassroots, multi-centered, transversal cosmopolitanization processes. The GJM's tendency for international motion is now balanced by the recent local fixities. The tendency for fixity made the Occupy movements evolve further beyond the constitution of transient open spaces for intellectual debate. Liboiron (2012), for instance, shows how ideas about the management of crisis, sustainable alternatives, and recycling waste started to flourish from within the Occupy encampment in New York when activists had to live in the park with no access to energy and sanitation.

Conclusion

By constructing common grounds through dialogical processes, as in the case of the WSF and online public spheres, the Global Justice Movement promoted the possibility of exchanging and accommodating positive elements of cultures, ideologies, and traditions in encountering common sources of problems. This capacity has increasingly been exploited by many local/national activist networks, alongside the shifts in the nexus of disarrayed capital and diversifying global activist networks; this process was later stepped up by the post-crisis activism. Due to the experience of the multi-scalar nature of the recent global financial crisis and the multidimensional nature of inequalities associated with the crisis, these forces cannot detach themselves from the reality of social divisions in favor of an imagined 'globally shared collective future' (Beck, 2002) or world citizenship. Hybridism and the acknowledgment of complexity are among the principles of these new movements.

In this article, I attempted to highlight the realignments and reorientations within the global field of resistance by focusing on Occupy movements. I acknowledge that the contrasts between the recent movements and the earlier ones in the GJM can only be ideal-typically constructed by analysts. In practice, both the pre-GFC and post-GFC phases of mobilizations consist of rival ideological visions. However, the post-GFC uprisings imply a significant reorientation in the ideological landscape of global resistance in favor of more grassroots, pragmatic notions of cosmopolitanism. Would the ascendance of transversalism make the justice movements more vulnerable to risks like the possibility of being captured or diverted by formal politics, or nationalist-populist reactionary perspectives? This ideological reorientation certainly has both advantages and disadvantages. A critical assessment of the consequences of such shifts, especially the realignment of the national vs. global as their core element, is of course needed. However, in this article, I tried to overcome my intellectual temptation to critically appraise, optimistically praise or pessimistically despise the new developments since such an assignment is far beyond the scope of my argument.

There are certainly groups and networks that push for the adoption of nationalistic or populist agendas such as engagement with electoral politics or turning the Occupy movement into a Tea Party of the Left. Occupy movements in fact successfully resisted such temptations for renationalization in 2012. This success however has been achieved at the cost of pushing OWS into 'abeyance'. Nonetheless, as far as the elements of self-reflexivity and transversality persist among groups of activists and occupiers, the prospective movements will be able to address such challenges and more effectively advance modes of opposition depending on the emerging contexts. There is no doubt that developing forms of action and organization that represent the specificity of local struggles and at the same time provide means for global collective actions will remain as a central challenge for the Left. The descendants of Occupy movements will need to draw on the legacies of WSF, the horizontalism of occupiers, the experiences of transversal feminists, and the like when redefining their historical roles.

Acknowledgement

I would like to express my special gratitude to Associate Professor James Goodman and Dr Jonathan Marshall and the anonymous reviewers for their most generous and constructive comments.

References

Ashraf, H. (2011) Claiming space for diversity at Occupy Wall Street, in S. Van Gelder (ed.) *This Changes Everything: Occupy Wall Street and the 99% Movement* (San Francisco: Berrett-Koehler Publishers), pp. 33–35.
Beck, U. (2002) The cosmopolitan society and its enemies, *Theory, Culture and Society*, 19(1–2), pp. 17–44.
Beeman, A. (2012) Post-civil rights racism and OWS: Dealing with color-blind ideology, *Socialism and Democracy*, 26(2), pp. 51–54.
Brassett, J. (2010) *Cosmopolitanism and Global Financial Reform: A Pragmatic Approach to the Tobin Tax* (Abingdon, UK & New York: Routledge).
bruddaone (2011) *A Black Woman Who Occupied Wall Street: Why She Won't Be Going Back*, http://www.dailykos.com/story/2011/10/17/1027186/-A-Black-Woman-Who-Occupied-Wall-Street-Why-She-Won-t-Be-Going-Back.
Buell, J. (2011) Occupy Wall Street's democratic challenge, *Theory & Event*, 14(4), 2011 supplement, http://muse.jhu.edu/journals/theory_and_event/v014/14.4S.buell.html.
Callinicos, A. (2012) Contradictions of austerity, *Cambridge Journal of Economics*, 36(1), pp. 65–77.
Cockburn, C. & Hunter, L. (1999) Transversal politics and translating practices, *Soundings: A Journal of Politics and Culture*, Issue 12(Summer), pp. 88–93.
Cook, N. (2012) Canadian development workers, transnational encounters, and cultures of cosmopolitanism, *International Sociology*, 27(1), pp. 3–20.
Evanoff, R. J. (2004) Universalist, relativist, and constructivist approaches to intercultural ethics, *International Journal of Intercultural Relations*, 28(5), pp. 439–458.
Flank, L. (2011) *Voices from the 99 Percent: An Oral History of the Occupy Wall Street Movement* (St. Petersburg, FL: Red and Black Publishers).
Galbraith, J. K. (2012) *Inequality and Instability: A Study of the World Economy just before the Great Crisis* (New York, NY: Oxford University Press).
Germain, R. D. & Kenny, M. (2005) *The Idea of Global Civil Society: Politics and Ethics in a Globalizing Era* (London & New York: Routledge).
Giri, A. K. (2006) Cosmopolitanism and beyond: Towards a multiverse of transformations, *Development and Change*, 37(6), pp. 1277–1292.
Goodman, J. (2007) Reordering globalism? Feminist and women's movements in the semi-periphery, in M. Griffin-Cohen & J. M. Brodie (eds) *Remapping Gender in the New Global Order* (London & New York: Routledge), pp. 187–204.
Greene, R. W. & Kuswa, K. D. (2012) From the Arab Spring to Athens, From Occupy Wall Street to Moscow: Regional accents and the rhetorical cartography of power, *Rhetoric Society Quarterly*, 42(3), pp. 271–288.
Harvey, D. (2006) *The Limits to Capital* (London & New York: Verso).
Harvey, D. (2012) *Rebel Cities: From the Right to the City to the Urban Revolution* (New York: Verso).
Hayduk, R. (2012) Global justice and OWS: Movement connections, *Socialism and Democracy*, 26(2), pp. 43–50.

Held, D. (2010) *Cosmopolitanism: Ideals and Realities* (Cambridge: Polity Press).
Holton, R. J. (2009) *Cosmopolitanisms: New Thinking and New Directions* (Basingstoke, UK & New York: Palgrave Macmillan).
Hosseini, S. A. H. (2006) Beyond practical dilemmas and conceptual reductionism: The emergence of an accommodative consciousness in the alternative globalization movement, *Portal: Journal of Multidisciplinary International Studies*, 3(1), pp. 1–27, http://epress.lib.uts.edu.au/ojs/index.php/portal/article/view/102/76.
Hosseini, S. A. H. (2009) Global complexities and the rise of global justice movement: A new notion of justice? *The Global Studies Journal*, 2(3), pp. 15–36.
Hosseini, S. A. H. (2010) *Alternative Globalizations: An Integrative Approach to Studying Dissident Knowledge in the Global Justice Movement* (Abingdon, UK & New York: Routledge).
Ibrahim, J. (2013) The struggle for symbolic dominance in the British 'anti-capitalist movement field', *Social Movement Studies*, 12(1), pp. 63–80.
Johnston, J. A., Kouzmin, A., Thorne, K. & Kelly, S. J. (2010) Crisis opportunism: Bailouts and E-SCADs in the GFC, *Risk Management—an International Journal*, 12(3), pp. 208–234.
Jones, R. A. (2012) OWS and the class/race dynamic, *Socialism and Democracy*, 26(2), pp. 30–32.
Juris, J. S. & Pleyers, G. H. (2009) Alter-activism: Emerging cultures of participation among young global justice activists, *Journal of Youth Studies*, 12(1), pp. 57–75.
Juris, J. S., Ronayne, M., Shokooh-Valle, F. & Wengronowitz, R. (2012) Negotiating Power and Difference within the 99%, *Social Movement Studies*, 11(3–4), pp. 434–440.
Kochhar, R. (2012) *The Demographics of the Jobs Recovery*, Pew Research Centre, http://www.pewhispanic.org/2012/03/21/the-demographics-of-the-jobs-recovery/.
Kostigen, T. (2011) *The Big Handout: How Government Subsidies and Corporate Welfare Corrupt the World we Live in and Wreak Havoc on our Food Bills* (Emmaus, PA: Rodale).
Lawson, S. (2011) Cosmopolitan pluralism: Beyond the cultural turn, *Cosmopolitan Civil Societies Journal*, 3(3), pp. 27–46.
Liboiron, M. (2012) Tactics of waste, dirt and discard in the Occupy movement, *Social Movement Studies*, 11(3–4), pp. 393–401.
Maisano, C. & Jacobin Editorial Board (2012) Another Occupy Is Possible—and Necessary, *The North Star*, 15 June, http://www.thenorthstar.info/?p=935.
Marcus, D. (2012) The Horizontalists, *Dissent*, 59(4), pp. 54–59, http://muse.jhu.edu/journals/dissent/v059/59.4.marcus.html.
Massey, D. (1999) Space for co-existence? *Soundings: A Journal of Politics and Culture*, Issue 12(Summer), pp. 7–11.
McDonald, P. M. (2011) Occupy Oakland reflects diversity, unity, and a legacy of activism, *Huffington Post*, 10 November, http://www.huffingtonpost.com/pamela-mays-mcdonald/occupy-oakland-reflects-a_b_1006213.html.
Murray, D. (2010) Democratic insurrection: Constructing the common in global resistance, *Millennium: Journal of International Studies*, 39(2), pp. 461–482.
Patomäki, H. (2013) *The Great Eurozone Disaster: From Crisis to Global New Deal* (London & New York: Zed Books).
Pugh, J. (2011) The stakes of radical politics have changed: Post-crisis, relevance and the state, in B. K. Gills (ed.) *Globalization in Crisis* (London: Routledge), pp. 287–299.
Reimer, M. (2012) 'It's the kids who made this happen': The Occupy movement as youth movement, *Jeunesse: Young People, Texts, Cultures*, 4(1), pp. 1–14.
Robertson, R. T. (2003) *The Three Waves of Globalization: a History of a Developing Global Consciousness* (New York: Fernwood Pub.; Zed Books).
Sassen, S. (2004) Local actors in global politics, *Current Sociology*, 52(4), pp. 649–670.
Schrader, S. & Wachsmuth, D. (2012) Reflections on Occupy Wall Street, the state and space, *City*, 16(1–2), pp. 243–248.
Schragis, R. (2011) *Declaration Flowchart*, Distributed by Occuprint, http://occuprint.org/Posters/DeclarationFlowchart.
Shepard, B. (2012a) Occupy against inequality, *Socialism and Democracy*, 26(2), pp. 26–29.
Shepard, B. H. (2012b) Labor and Occupy Wall Street: Common causes and uneasy alliances, *WorkingUSA: The Journal of Labor and Society*, 15(1), pp. 121–134.
Smith, C., Castañeda, E. & Heyman, J. (2012) The homeless and Occupy El Paso: Creating community among the 99%, *Social Movement Studies*, 11(3–4), pp. 356–366.
Smith, J. & Glidden, B. (2012) Occupy Pittsburgh and the challenges of participatory democracy, *Social Movement Studies*, 11(3–4), pp. 288–294.
Staggenborg, S. (2011) *Social Movements* (New York: Oxford University Press).

Starr, A. & Adams, J. (2003) Anti-globalization: the global fight for local autonomy, *New Political Science*, 25(1), pp. 19–42.

Steger, M. B. (2008) *The Rise of the Global Imaginary: Political Ideologies from the French Revolution to the Global War on Terror* (Oxford & New York: Oxford University Press).

thinking sociology (2011) Is Occupy Wall Street Racially Inclusive?, http://thinkingsociology.wordpress.com/2011/11/27/is-occupy-wall-street-perpetuating-racial-inequality/.

Todd, B. (2011) Racial Fractures and the Occupy Movement, Racialicious.com, http://www.racialicious.com/2011/11/16/racial-fractures-and-the-occupy-movement/.

Uggla, F. (2006) Between globalism and pragmatism: ATTAC in France, Germany, and Sweden, *Mobilization*, 11(1), pp. 51–66.

Uitermark, J. & Nicholls, W. (2012) How local networks shape a global movement: Comparing Occupy in Amsterdam and Los Angeles, *Social Movement Studies*, 11(3–4), pp. 295–301.

West, C. (2011) A love supreme: Deep democratic awakening, *The Occupied Wall Street Journal*, (5), p. 1, http://occupiedmedia.us/2011/11/a-love-supreme/.

Writers for the 99%, et al. (2012) *Occupying Wall Street: The Inside Story of an Action that Changed America* (Chicago, IL: Haymarket Books).

Yuval-Davis, N. & Stoetzler, M. (2002) Imagined boundaries and borders: A gendered gaze, *European Journal of Women's Studies*, 9(3), pp. 329–344.

Dr S. A. Hamed Hosseini is a lecturer and a faculty associated researcher at The University of Newcastle, Australia. He has conducted research on transnational social movements, global social change, globalist ideologies, cosmopolitanism, and transversal identities. His new book, *Alternative Globalizations: An Integrative Approach to Studying Dissident Knowledge in the Global Justice Movement* (Routledge, 2011) establishes a new way of theorizing the (trans)formation of ideas, identities, and solidarities in recent oppositions to capitalist globalization.

Crisis Is Where We Live: Environmental Justice for the Anthropocene

DONNA HOUSTON

Macquarie University, Sydney, Australia

ABSTRACT *This article considers the material imaginations of environmental crisis and justice in the context of the Anthropocene. I argue that political action at the intersections between environmental degradation and environmental change produce 'anticipatory histories' (DeSilvey, 2012) of planetary crisis. 'Anticipatory histories' disorder linear and depoliticised understandings of external crisis and they support different social imaginaries of the relationship between everyday life and geophysical events. Drawing its inspiration from recent environmental justice projects in the United States (New Orleans after Hurricane Katrina and high-level nuclear waste disposal at Yucca Mountain in Nevada), this article explores what environmental justice can teach us about living with environmental crisis and change.*

> In a warmer world . . . socio-economic inequality will have a meteorological mandate. (Mike Davis, 2010)

Environmental Justice in a Changing World

This article considers the material imaginations of environmental crisis and environmental justice in the Anthropocene epoch. A decade ago, the Nobel Prize winning atmospheric chemist Paul Crutzen (2002) argued that we have entered a new geologic era of the Anthropocene (following the Holocene) because human impacts on the planet have become a 'global geophysical force in their own right' (Steffen et al., 2007, p. 614). The Anthropocene is a subject of much commentary and debate across science, the humanities, and popular culture, and its implications push current understandings of human–environment relationships in several urgent directions. First, the Anthropocene represents a time of political and social reckoning—where we are called to collectively witness the consequences of human decisions and the impacts of our 'failing modernisms' on the conditions of planetary life (Rose and Robin, 2004). Second, the Anthropocene emphasises a rapidly diminishing window of opportunity to prevent key ecological tipping points associated with unknowable environmental change (Palsson et al., 2012). Third, it prompts new calls for thought and action that can imagine different relationships between geologic time, the cultural logics of capital and accumulation, and the ontological realities of our species-being (Charkabarty, 2009; Clark, 2010; Roelvink, 2013).

The Anthropocene is an emergent narrative in global environmental politics and it is rapidly gaining momentum (Swyngedow, 2011). One of the key intellectual challenges of the Anthropocene epoch is to reimagine how humans make connections between planetary and everyday life in ethical, sustainable, and ecologically just ways (Gibson-Graham and Roelvink, 2009). While it has not been framed as such, environmental justice is a diverse political project that is firmly embedded in the choices and consequences of the Anthropocene. The political movement for environmental justice emerged in the United States in the late 1970s and early 1980s as a response to a crisis in toxic accumulation in local communities, workplaces, schools, and on American Indian reservations. Over the last 40 years, the movement for environmental justice has proliferated beyond the US context to represent: 'a far-reaching, mobile and evolving frame for understanding and acting on socio-environmental concerns' (Walker, 2009b, p. 356).

The political and imaginative contexts of environmental justice have their roots in a social critique of the Western desire for 'pristine' forms of nature (Agyeman, 2008; Gottleib, 2001). As Julian Agyeman observes: 'the environmental justice project has redefined the term "environment" so that the dominant wilderness, greening and natural resource focus now includes urban disinvestment, racism, homes, jobs, neighbourhoods and communities' (2008, p. 752). For environmental justice activists and scholars, the separation of nature from culture in mainstream environmental movements is a source of environmental inequity and erasure. 'Pristine nature' devoid of human work and action is an exclusionary discourse that ignores the interwoven contexts of eco-social realities in and of an altered and damaged world. Material imaginations of environmental justice emerge out of the 'affective legacies' of Rachel Carson's (1962 [2002]) *Silent Spring* rather than cultural traditions embedded in the wilderness ethic (Lockwood, 2012). Carson's work mobilised private feelings of pain and anger directed towards the destructive practices of industrial modernity (especially the impacts of chemical pollutants) on people and the environment (Ibid.). Public–private imaginations of environmental injustice link personal stories about illness and death to broader and often invisible practices of environmental decision-making that have left places polluted and degraded.

The experiences and imaginaries of environmental injustice are anticipatory and accumulative. They have mobilised politically in countless community struggles to redress the disproportionate siting of pollution and unwanted land-use in working class, communities of colour and they have materialised as public discourse in the form of the 17 Principles of Environmental Justice that were drafted at the First National People of Color Environmental Leadership Summit in Washington DC in 1991. I explore two aspects of the imaginative legacy of environmental justice in this article: (1) that environmental justice projects represent decades of community work that addresses environmental degradation and environmental change; and (2) that the particular contribution of environmental justice for the Anthropocene is that it is a project that materially and imaginatively situates environmental crisis in everyday terms, as something that we live with and strive to transform.

In the narrative that follows, I draw inspiration from two recent environmental justice projects in the United States (post-Katrina New Orleans and the former nuclear waste dump site at Yucca Mountain in Nevada) to explore the imaginative work of environmental justice in the Anthropocene era. I argue that recent scholarly and public commentary on the Anthropocene has a similar preoccupation with reimagining the inhabited contexts of non-pristine and transformed nature, but with a notable difference (Marris, 2011; Robbins, 2013). The Anthropocene epoch registers a different awareness of the scale and temporality of environmental crisis and introduces new terms to the often local and regional contexts of environmental justice scholarship, activism, and debate, such as planetary life, geological time, and species-being. In order to explore the material and imaginative spaces between environmental crisis and justice in a changing world, I use Caitlin DeSilvey's (2012) concept of 'anticipatory history', which she describes as process of understanding change to environments and landscapes 'not as loss or failure but as something altogether more complex' (2012, p. 33). This article uses the idea of 'anticipatory history' to describe the movement between toxic legacies of environmental injustice, public and imaginative work, and the future prospects of inhabiting the world differently. While the Anthropocene cultivates new political–ecological subjectivities that seek to ethically and materially reimagine relationships between people and planetary crisis; environmental justice represents 'thousands of community solutions' to diverse environmental problems that are already underway (Di Chiro, 2011). In the following section, I explore how 'anticipatory histories' of environmental justice can help us to rethink how we tell stories about environmental crisis in the present.

'Anticipatory Histories': Disordering and Inhabiting Crisis

The coming of the Anthropocene and its urgent calls to action has apocalyptic overtones, which are often storied through extreme climatic events (of which in the past year there have been plenty). Yet, the idea that we have arrived at a point in history where humans must alter their present course of development also changes the ways in which we think and talk about environmental crisis. Apocalyptic environmental crisis is a highly problematic discourse and much has been done by human geographers and environmental scholars to disorder its linear trajectories. For example, influential radical geographers such as Cindy Katz (1995) and David Harvey (1998) have both warned that environmental crisis, when presented as an apocalyptic 'end of the world as we know it' narrative, is disempowering and devoid of the particular politics and histories that create crisis in the first place. For Harvey (1998), the danger of evoking metaphors of apocalypse is that it leads to public disenchantment when the imminent collapse does not occur and it also diverts our collective attention away from longer-term, gradual changes that require collective political action and foresight. He argues that imagining an 'end' to nature is a teleological fantasy and that it is far more productive to 'construe ourselves as active agents caught within "the web of life"' . . . than the linear thinking that has us heading off a cliff or crashing into a brick wall' (1998). Katz similarly argues: 'Until the apocalyptic moment human action drives history, but history-become-apocalypse renders human agency moot' (1995, p. 277).

The Anthropocene complicates matters further. While Katz and Harvey's warnings about the ahistorical contexts of apocalyptic thinking are important critical interventions, we do live in times of acute and profound environmental crisis and it is equally important to critically rethink how we live with it (Buell, 2003). New material imaginations of the Anthropocene highlight existing contradictory concepts of nature and change, which are based on linear constructions of time and transformation associated with modernity. Here everything from the evolution of species, to apocalyptic crisis that has us heading into oblivion is tied to stories of progress where time marches forward towards a discernible (but unknown) point where presumably Enlightenment or collapse will be achieved. Within this schema, the progressive story of environmental crisis is particularly difficult to apprehend (for the reasons outlined by Harvey and Katz above) *and* because we are called to act on futures that are yet to materialise (Hulme, 2010). This is also problematic for critical perspectives on justice because terms such as 'species-being' and 'planetary' have yet to be reworked and embedded in enlarged frameworks of environmental justice. It is not surprising, then, that Dipesh Charkabarty writes:

> The task of placing, historically, the crisis of climate change thus requires us to bring together intellectual formations that are somewhat in tension with each other: the planetary and the global; deep and recorded histories; species thinking and critiques of capital. (2009, p. 213)

Or, that in a similar vein Gerda Roelvink observes:

> We are being called . . . to move beyond using species as a (contested) biological term for categorization, such as homo sapiens . . . to consider species as a political-economic collective that has become geological. (2012, p. 2)

The environmental consequences of the Anthropocene require collective action that takes uncertain futures seriously, not as an end point or some utopian ideal, but as a matter of everyday life. Part of this challenge is to develop new understandings of how embodied, everyday, and planetary realities are being reimagined in environmentally just and sustainable ways. This is a provocative undertaking because it means, as Charkabarty suggests, bringing social and geological stories together to produce new understandings and contexts for action.

Caitlin DeSilvey's (2012) notion of 'anticipatory history' is especially useful for framing such a task. Her approach to rethinking environmental change emerges out of a somewhat different context—where anticipatory histories describe how cultural heritage practices can narrate past and future events in climatically dynamic places such as coastlines. For DeSilvey, anticipatory histories are processes that are attentive to the complex relationship between narrative and transience, in other words, to the ways in which we make sense of change in relation to the past and the future of landscapes. Part of the process of engaging with anticipatory histories is to rethink the embeddedness of linear time in understanding major and minor geophysical and social histories. In place of the static creep of linear time, 'anticipatory' concepts of time and space open up different possibilities for understanding human–environment relationships across continuities and discontinuities, foldings, ruptures, memories, and disappearances (DeSilvey, 2012).

The idea of anticipatory history is evocative for rethinking environmental justice in the Anthropocene. Such an approach unsettles the notion of environmental crisis as a series of causes, effects, and responses to an external and finite problem. Outside of exceptional circumstances, environmental injustice is notoriously difficult to attribute to particular causes and effects: did a person get cancer from a lifetime of swimming in a polluted lake or because they ate fast food or smoked cigarettes? One of the most important legacies of Rachel Carson's *Silent Spring* is that it provided a framework for storytelling about the consequences of toxic pollution in terms of body–environment relationships, in other words, what we feel and know to be true despite the absence of conclusive scientific evidence. Thinking about how environmental justice engages with the Anthropocene gives us an opportunity to further explore how disordering the linear consequences of environmental crisis open up different possibilities for engaging with its multiple realities. Anticipatory histories of environmental justice piece together discordant temporalities, scales, and rhythms of inhabiting places (Hinchcliffe, 2003).

Environmental Justice: Between the Accumulation and Anticipation of Crises

The interconnections between the planetary and the everyday tend to become real to us in the event of so-called 'natural' disasters such as hurricanes, cyclones, earthquakes, firestorms, and floods. Disasters of this kind are often narrated as shocks because they are hard to predict and because they partially seem a consequence of Nigel Clark's 'indifferent' nature (2010). Neil Smith (2006) writes that: 'It is generally accepted among environmental geographers that there is no such thing as a natural disaster.' To say that disasters are not particularly natural is to argue that the social and ideological processes assigned to acts of 'nature' are never neutral. To suggest otherwise produces 'depoliticised imaginaries', where Eric Swyngedouw argues that 'nature' becomes an object, an empty signifier devoid of the diverse, historical, and contingent relationships that make up our socio-ecological realities (Swyngedouw, 2011, p. 272).

Understanding the interconnections between environmental crisis and environmental justice in the context of the Anthropocene is equally perilous. Joel Wainwright and Geoff Mann recently observed that 'the negative consequences of climate change sound out in two rhythms that are not synchronized' (2012, p. 3). So-called natural disasters are visible and dramatic, but they can also be attributed to ultimately external forces that tragically but only temporarily interfere with the linear trajectories of human progress. 'There is an almost imperceptible ambient noise of rising seas and plodding upward of food prices,' Wainwright and Mann write, 'but this is hard to hear' (Ibid., p. 3). Imaginaries of environmental crisis that are out of synch with social-ecological realities tend to either attribute too little or too much agency to either humans or an imagined external nature (Clark, 2010).

Environmental justice, by contrast, has tended to avoid this predicament with its 'anthropogenic' framing of people, communities, and justice as lying at the centre of environmental concerns (Walker, 2009b, p. 358). The anthropogenic framing of environmental justice, I think, has more in common with the challenges of rethinking socio-ecological relationships in the Anthropocene. Take one of the movement's popular catchphrases articulated here by Dana Alston:

> For people of color, environmental issues are not just a matter of preserving ancient forests or defending whales. While the importance of saving endangered species is recognized, it is also clear that adults and children living in communities of color are endangered species too. Environmental issues are immediate survival issues. (2010, p. 17)

While a powerful indictment of the class bias of white middle-class mainstream environmentalism that has tended to focus on the conservation of charismatic animals and the preservation of wilderness, this statement is also frequently taken as particular evidence of the anthropogenic character of the environmental justice movement, which has more in common with civil rights and social justice than with ecological thinking. In my view, Alston's phrase emphasises how environmental justice is an ecological movement. The idea that people are environmentally endangered as a consequence of cultural and economic disregard of particular places evokes 'togetherness' with other endangered creatures in the survival of ecological communities. This not only suggests that people, animals, and ecologies are bound up in environmental politics of care and neglect, but also ways in which environmental justice reframes survival as a particular kind of inhabited politics.

Environmental justice activism focuses on struggles for survival and justice in polluted and non-pristine environments. Yet, it is often the non-pristine ecologies that environmental justice movements inhabit that produce its 'anthropogenic' associations, rather than the question of how individuals and collectives frame environmental justice issues. Of course, some community actions for environmental justice are unequivocally focused on human concerns, such as lead paint in schools or the problem of asbestos-lined houses. Yet, when individuals and communities act on these concerns, the stories spread out to encompass broader eco-social relationships that link community and ecological health. Stories about environmental injustice accumulate and constellate to form affective connections between human and nonhuman bodies and places (Houston, 2013; Lockwood, 2012). Thus, the 'justice' component of environmental justice in community activism is often quite imaginative and expansive; it implies a set of politics and responsibilities where not all of us are 'together' in environmental crisis and injury equally and where not 'everyone' imbricated in environmental crisis and injury is human. Indeed, this sentiment is poignantly reflected in the first principle of the 17 Principles of Environmental Justice: 'Environmental Justice affirms the sacredness of Mother Earth, ecological unity and the interdependence of all species, and the right to be free from ecological destruction.'[1]

In the next two sections, I want to illustrate these points by drawing inspiration from two recent examples of places affected by environmental injustice and collective community action in the United States. I argue that community projects that simultaneously address environmental justice and environmental crisis produce 'anticipatory histories' of environmental change—where stories play an important role in reconfiguring past injustices, geo-social relationships, and future eco-social possibilities in and of a damaged world.

Accumulating Crises: Hurricane Katrina

Environmental crisis is often narrated as a shock that unfolds in the present but then recedes in to 'the historical dustbin of inevitable "natural" disasters' (Smith, 2006). We wait for the next storm or earthquake to appear on the horizon. In recent years, however, environmental disasters and extreme events have been harder to dismiss. Unfolding disaster creates global cultural moments of clarity where we see the complexities and injustices of life in the Anthropocene. Indeed, in these moments, when the global media is awash with images and stories of people and animals stranded in flooded, scorched, and scoured landscapes, we see how environmental crisis intersects with everyday life. What often emerges in the mess of aftermath is the 'unnaturalness' of environmental disaster because the crises that are produced are geographically, historically, and socially uneven (Davis, 1999; Smith, 2006). This can be illustrated by the public remembering of ecological disasters such as Hurricane Katrina, which made landfall on the US Gulf Coast on 29 August 2005. During the high point of global public and media attention, the disaster of Hurricane Katrina was depicted as a shock caused by the unpredictability of external and violent 'nature' and an appalling lack of governmental response to crisis, made all the more so because this institutional failure unfolded in one of the world's wealthiest nations.

For a brief time, the media was saturated with horrifying images of dead bodies floating in putrid floodwaters, and of the suffering of the mostly African American residents of the city stranded on rooftops, or on dry patches of road, and in the New Orleans Superdome without adequate food, water, or sanitation (Giroux, 2010, pp. 29–51).[2] Yet, as Henry Giroux (2010) and Cindy Katz (2008) note, while the images of suffering generated much sympathy and anger on behalf of the abandoned residents of New Orleans—the spectacle of Hurricane Katrina also masked an ongoing and ordinary crisis of social reproduction, racism, environmental injustice, and the hostile impacts of neoliberalism and privatisation on the public sector.

CRISIS, MOVEMENT, MANAGEMENT: GLOBALISING DYNAMICS

As Cindy Katz writes: 'Underneath all the physical wreckage and debris, what Katrina and the flood in its wake scoured was the desperately uneven landscape of social reproduction in New Orleans' (2008, p. 16). She goes on to say that:

> The Hurricane hit at the then nadir of a three decades-long deterioration in social wage; a combination of social relations and policies at the national, state, and municipal scales that eroded virtually every aspect of social reproduction, except those associated with militarism and policing. (2008, p. 17)

Hurricane Katrina produced and exacerbated social and environmental inequities that mixed together 'bad elements': extreme weather, toxic pollution (from the petrochemical industry and from wetland destruction), racism, institutional failure, and the systematic abandonment of the economically and socially vulnerable under a neoliberal social contract (Katz, 2008). Hurricane Katrina (before and after) revealed how crisis contains profound injustices that shape past, present, and emergent events. Hurricane Katrina laid bare the failures of the state and the market even as the crisis was being turned into an opportunity for reconstruction.

Nearly eight years on from Hurricane Katrina, there are a number of things to say about how environment and crisis get bound up in cultural and political imaginaries. The first is that, beyond the initial shock of the spectacle of crisis, its everyday and ongoing effects in particular places continue to remain largely invisible. After Hurricane Katrina, Henry Giroux observed that '. . . the images moved all of us, but only it seems for a time. Why is that?' (2010, p. 30). The problem in part is one of distance and proximity. While residents of New Orleans continue to grapple with the ordinary effects of 'post-crisis' reconstruction, broader public attention has gone elsewhere. It seems that when crisis goes from being extraordinary to being ordinary—into the realm of living, gendered, classed and raced bodies struggling with everyday issues such as access to safe housing, jobs, healthcare, healthy ecosystems and education—our collective imaginative capacity to continue to understand ecological crisis as simultaneously everyday, social, and ongoing diminishes. Yet, it is here in the everyday of environmental crisis, where people and other species struggle to survive and live with past trauma and future possibility, where alternative stories and politics of recovery are enacted.

New Orleans after Katrina highlighted a history of accumulated crises through the neoliberal 'abandonment' of people and the environment (Lipsitz, 2006). The collective injury of abandonment is also what currently shapes the politics of the city's reconstruction. In this sense, New Orleans is an 'unfinished story' about the right to define and shape the future city in a context of climate change (Chatterton, 2010). Part of this reshaping requires brining in to proximity social histories of economic injustice with environmental histories. Toxic moulds and sediments, urban flooding, economic justice, and disaster governance intersect at different scales and temporalities, but they all shape the contexts for community planning and redevelopment. It is in this sense that the unfinished story of post-Katrina New Orleans is also, significantly, about the struggle over both public memory and environmental history. The struggle over whose memory is told and whose is forgotten directly relates to the collective task (locally, nationally, globally) of understanding the ways in which political responses to crisis by governments and elites assumes that 'disorder' happens in local communities rather than in the actions of those who are authorised to act on their behalf (Solnit, 2010).

Rebecca Solnit's wonderful book *A Paradise Built in Hell* (2009) focuses on the considerable evidence that demonstrates the ways in which local communities come together to help and support each other in the face of catastrophe. In post-Katrina New Orleans, this cooperation has continued in the flourishing of volunteer organisations and not-for-profit groups in the city. This is also mirrored in a grassroots response to rebuild the city from the bottom up (Smith, 2006). At the same time, the underreported stories of the actions of those assigned to the tasks of rescue and protection of citizens, and the actions of white vigilante groups who targeted and murdered black men in the aftermath have only been recently called to public account (Solnit, 2010). Solnit writes, 'How we remember Hurricane Katrina is also how we'll prepare for future disasters so getting the story right matters for survival as well as for justice and history' (Ibid., p. 1).

Environmental justice stories in post-Katrina New Orleans are about coming to terms with the systematic vulnerabilities and accumulated crises, which were already built in to the urban fabric and that resulted in hundreds of tragic deaths. Flooding in New Orleans is exacerbated by its radically altered and polluted regional hydrology (caused by the development of the oil and gas industry, levee construction, wetland destruction, and urban sprawl). Environmental justice stories in New Orleans are also world-making in the sense that they can anchor urban projects that reconfigure socio-ecological-justice possibilities. The recent project to revitalise the city's Lafitte Corridor into a sustainable urban greenway is an excellent example.[3] The Lafitte Corridor project brings together embodied cultural and environmental connectivities in a post-disaster frame: a desire to create walkable, convivial spaces, a reinvestment in community place making, and the sustainable management of ground and stormwater in urban contexts.

While relatively small in scope, projects like the Lafitte Corridor redevelopment demonstrate important exercises in imagination that recreate urban life as a series of metabolic exchanges (Davis, 2010). Such projects also demonstrate that healthy and environmentally just communities and economies are embedded in a much larger problem of revitalising and restoring the regional hydrological system to functional health. Environmental justice projects are firmly embedded in people–environment hybrids that do not entirely view environmental crisis and degradation in terms of total loss or failure—but in terms of a broader confluence of goals that evoke injury, pain, and trauma but also the hopeful work that comes with inhabiting the politics of crisis and seeking to transform it (Gibson-Graham and Roelvink, 2009). Mike Davis (2010) observes that cities in the Anthropocene will remain the 'ground zero of convergence' between processes of disordering and inhabiting crisis. But he goes on to say that: 'the ecological genius of the city remains a vast, largely hidden power' (p. 43). Urban environmental justice projects that abound in post-disaster landscapes such as New Orleans offer glimpses into the future problems and prospects of this.

Anticipating Crises: Yucca Mountain, Nevada

The three-decade-long struggle against the disposal of high-level radioactive waste at Yucca Mountain in Nevada is also an example of environmental justice work at the boundaries between toxic legacy and environmental change. Between 1987 and 2010, the US Department of Energy focused on Yucca Mountain (located in the transition zone between the Mojave and Great Basin deserts, approximately 100 miles north-west of Las Vegas) as the only site selected for the geologic disposal of commercial radioactive wastes.[4] Despite vigorous protests from local residents, American Indian, environmental, and anti-nuclear proliferation groups, the state of Nevada, and many scientists, the US federal government pressed ahead with the study and licensing of the Yucca Mountain Project, which cost the American public over US$10.5 billion in taxpayer money. In 2010 the Obama administration officially put an end to the Yucca Mountain Project, citing inconclusive science and public opposition as the reasons for the project's demise (Stover, 2011).

CRISIS, MOVEMENT, MANAGEMENT: GLOBALISING DYNAMICS

The public struggle over the burial of radioactive waste at Yucca Mountain pitted tens of thousands of years of geological formation in the interdesert American west against the 'technical fixes' of modern era. Located on the former Nevada Test Site, Yucca Mountain became a site of contested social and environmental history after the US Department of Energy began its plans to bury 70,000 metric tons of high-level nuclear waste in a layer of volcanic tuff 1,000 feet below the ground. The dynamism of the landscape (shaped by water, plate tectonics, and fire) became a key factor in narrating the site's unsuitability for the excavation of radioactive wastes. This in turn produced various cultural projects that explored different regional, cultural, and historical scales of environmental injustice and the argument that the science of nuclear waste disposal at Yucca Mountain was driven by politics (Shrader-Frechette, 2003). Environmental justice groups mobilised these arguments in their public memory-work, which performed multiple stories of opposition to nuclear waste dumping: including deep environmental histories of the geology of the Great Basin and Mojave deserts, 500 years of internal colonisation of American Indians, with the social and industrial legacies of the Cold War.

Environmental justice activists at Yucca Mountain worked at these various intersections because they were tasked with gathering alternate evidence about how nuclear development impacts on everyday life and regional environments. The enactment of opposition to nuclear waste disposal built upon diverse public and scientific collaborations such including the scientific monitoring of local water; educating communities about health and American Indian land and food justice; publicly articulating the embodied experience of living and working with radioactive materials through art and community memory-work; addressing environmental racism and American Indian land rights; and engaging in imaginative and storytelling praxis as a means of reshaping the future possibility of the region (Houston, 2013).

The imagined possibility of not having a large nuclear waste facility in Nevada was materialised in the project's demise. But some of the future eco-social possibilities drawn into the anti-nuclear waste struggle remain uncertain. For example, the Western Shoshone, on whose land Yucca Mountain is located, continue to fight for their land rights in the region. Environmental justice organisations such as the Western Shoshone Defense Project and the Shundahai Health Network focus on the political tasks of making connections between nuclear colonisation, environmental injustice, and American Indian land rights. While the nuclear waste dump at Yucca Mountain has been averted, these organisations continue to enact and sustain environmental justice work around human rights and ecological justice in relation to gold mining, water extraction, and environmental degradation in the Great Basin. Anticipatory histories of crisis rethink ways of articulating justice in particular places, by drawing on different configurations of past practices and future possibilities. At the same time, the unfinished businesses of Western Shoshone land justice at Yucca Mountain remains a counterpoint for future socio-ecological action.

Work-in-a-Changing-World

Environmental justice projects offer glimpses into life in the Anthropocene where toxic legacies and geophysical environmental change converge. The stories of post-Katrina New Orleans and Yucca Mountain, Nevada denote both successes and failures in grappling with the enormity of environmental problems and acting upon them. Environmental justice, I have argued, is in practice an expansive community framework that is particularly suited to working in altered and damaged ecologies—and connecting the realities of environmental degradation to the lived contexts of everyday life. In post-Katrina New Orleans and in rural Nevada, environmental justice activists have forged alternative visions of place that highlight the importance of sustaining everyday life and creating alternative futures. At Yucca Mountain, this vision manifested as the absence of a nuclear waste dump and the risks posed to localities through the transportation of highly radioactive materials (Solnit, 2004). In New Orleans, this vision materialised in the visible histories of environmental injustice and the community work underway to enact sustainable change. These two examples show us how environmental crisis is both inescapable and ordinary. But this does not mean that it is necessarily apocalyptic and apolitical. Environmental crisis is ordinary because it impacts on the most fundamental elements of everyday life—how we sustain our bodies, families, communities, livelihoods and places in relation to the living/dying earth.

In the Anthropocene epoch, we need to tell stories about environmental justice and the kinds of work-in-the-world that is performed in the articulation and framing of its concerns and relationships. This is important, because when new ideas and concepts (such as the Anthropocene) manifest and gain political traction, it is easy to get caught up in calls for new forms of sociality around eco-social problems and gloss over actions and dialogues that are already underway. Perhaps more importantly, it is necessary to capture the 'anticipatory histories' of environmental justice in our collective imaginings of the Anthropocene, the stories that remind us of the consequences of toxic contamination on people, animals, ecologies, and places and what is at stake when we think about the kinds of ecologies that exist in the places where we live. Environmental justice work in New Orleans and at Yucca Mountain offer glimpses into the possibilities for engaging with these broader issues, but they also highlight current limitations in our thinking about the social ecologies of environmental degradation. The Anthropocene, whether it is a new geologic age or a twenty-first century moment in popular culture, prompts us to ask and act on difficult questions: what kind of species pollutes its own living space and how can we continue to ignore the accumulative impacts? This, I believe, is where the toxic and affective legacies of the *Silent Spring* meet a new set of ethical and planetary responsibilities. Environmental justice for the Anthropocene is fraught with possibility and peril. The project sets out complex tasks to rethink the consequences of toxic pollution at embodied, local, bioregional, and planetary scales. And it is here that the evolving, storied platforms of environmental justice have the potential to develop 'more-than-human' capacities in ways that continue to support the movement's underlying principles and practices. Crisis is, after all, where we live.

Notes

1. The 17 Principles of Environmental Justice were drafted at the First National People of Color Environmental Leadership Summit convened in Washington DC (Oct 24–27) in 1991. They can be found at http://www.ejnet.org/ej/principles.html.
2. Rebecca Solnit (2010) and Henry Giroux (2010) both discuss how the media spectacle after Hurricane Katrina reproduced racist stereotypes that associated black people with disorder and looting and ignored the actions of vigilante groups and the police in managing the crisis of the aftermath.
3. See Friends of Lafitte Corridor (LOFC), http://www.folc-nola.org
4. In 1987 the US federal government amended the Nuclear Waste Policy Act (1982) to consider only Yucca Mountain (which was originally one of seven selected sites) for the excavation of radioactive waste. Popularly known as the 'Screw Nevada Bill', the amended act was argued to privilege politics over science and ignored the fact that 80% of Nevadans opposed Yucca Mountain (Shrader-Frechette, 2003).

References

Agyeman, J. (2008) Toward a 'just' sustainability? *Continuum: A Journal of Media and Cultural Studies*, 22(6), pp. 751–756.

CRISIS, MOVEMENT, MANAGEMENT: GLOBALISING DYNAMICS

Alston, D. (2010) The Summit: Transforming a movement, *Race, Poverty and the Environment*, 2(3/4), pp. 14–17.
Buell, F. (2003) *From Apocalypse to Way of Life: Environmental Crisis in the American Century* (London and New York: Routledge).
Carson, R. (1962 [2002]) *Silent Sprint*, 40th Anniversary ed. (Bsoton and New York: Mariner Books)
Chatterton, P. (2010) The urban impossible: A eulogy for the unfinished city, *City*, 14(3), pp. 234–244.
Charkabarty, D. (2009) The climate of history: Four theses, *Critical Inquiry*, 35, pp. 197–222.
Clark, N. (2010) *Inhuman Nature: Sociable Life on a Dynamic Planet* (New York: Sage Publications).
Crutzen, P. (2002) Geology of mankind, *Nature*, 415 (3 January), p. 23.
Davis, M. (1999) *Ecology of Fear: Los Angeles and the Imagination of Disaster* (New York: Vintage Books).
Davis, M. (2010) Who will build the ark? *New Left Review*, 61 (January–February), pp. 29–45.
DeSilvey, C. (2012) Making sense of transience: An anticipatory history, *Cultural Geographies*, 19(1), pp. 31–54.
Di Chiro, G. (2011) Acting globally: Cultivating a thousand community solutions for climate justice, *Development*, 54(2), pp. 232–236.
Gibson-Graham, J. K. & Roelvink, G. (2010) An economic ethics for the Anthropocene, *Antipode: A Journal of Radical Geography*, 41(Supplement 1), pp. 320–346.
Giroux, H. (2010) The media and Hurricane Katrina: Floating bodies and disposable populations, in G. Martin, D. Houston, P. McLaren & J. Suoranta (eds) *The Havoc of Capitalism: Publics, Pedagogies and Environmental Crisis* (Rotterdam: Sense Publishers), pp. 29–52.
Gottlieb, R. (2001) *Environmentalism Unbound: Exploring New Pathways for Change* (Cambridge, MA/London: The MIT Press).
Harvey, D. (1998) Marxism, metaphors, and ecological politics, *Monthly Review*, http://monthlyreview.org/1998/03/01/marxism-metaphors-and-ecological-politics.
Hinchcliffe, S. (2003) 'Inhabiting'—Landscapes and natures, in K. Anderson, M. Domosh, S. Pile & N. Thrift (eds) *Handbook of Cultural Geography* (London: Sage), pp. 207–225.
Houston, D. (2013) Environmental justice storytelling: Angels and isotopes at Yucca Mountain, Nevada, *Antipode: A Journal of Radical Geography*, 42(2), pp. 417–435.
Hulme, M. (2010) Cosmopolitan climates: Hybridity, foresight, meaning, *Theory, Culture & Society*, 27(2–3), pp. 267–276.
Katz, C. (1995) Under a falling sky: Apocalyptic environmentalism and the production of nature, in A. Callari, S. Cullenberg & C. Biewener (eds) *Marxism in the Postmodern Age: Confronting the New World Order* (New York and London: The Guildford Press), pp. 276–282.
Katz, C. (2008) Bad elements: Katrina and the scoured landscape of social reproduction, *Gender, Place & Culture*, 15(1), pp. 15–29.
Lipsitz, G. (2006) Learning from New Orleans: The social warrant of hostile privatism and competitive consumer citizenship, *Cultural Anthropology*, 21(3), pp. 451–468.
Lockwood, A. (2012) The affective legacy of Silent Spring, *Environmental Humanities*, 1, pp. 123–140.
Marris, E. (2011) *Rambunctious Garden: Saving Nature in a Post-Wild World* (New York: Bloomsbury).
Palsson, G., Szerszynski, B., Sörlin, S., Marks, J., Avril, B., Crumley, C., Hackmann, H., Ingram, J., Kirman, A. et al. (2013) Reconceptualizing the 'Anthropos' in the Anthropocene: Integrating the social sciences and the humanites in global environmental change research, *Environmental Science & Policy*, 28(April), pp. 3–13.
Robbins, P. (2013) Ecological anxiety disorder: Diagnosing the politics of the Anthropocene, *Cultural Geographies*, 20(1), pp. 3–19.
Roelvink, G. (2013) Rethinking species-being in the Anthropocene, *Rethinking Marxism: A Journal of Economics, Culture & Society*, 25(1), pp. 52–69.
Rose, D. & Robin, L. (2004) Ecological humanities: An invitation, *Australian Humanities Review*, 31–32 April, http://www.australianhumanitiesreview.org/archive/Issue-April-2004/rose.html.
Shrader-Frechette, K. (1993) *Burying Uncertainty: Risk and the Case Against Geologic Disposal of Nuclear Waste* (Berkeley: University of California Press).
Smith, N. (2006) There is No Such Thing as a Natural Disaster. Understanding Katrina: Perspectives from the Social Sciences, http://understandingkatrina.ssrc.org/Smith/.
Solnit, R. (2004) *Hope in the Dark: Untold Histories, Wild Possibilities* (New York: Nation Books).
Solnit, R. (2009) *A Paradise Built in Hell: The Extraordinary Communities that Arise in Disaster* (New York: Viking).
Solnit, R. (2010) Reconstructing the story of the storm: Hurricane Katrina at five, *The Nation*, http://www.thenation.com/article/154168/reconstructing-story-storm-hurricane-katrina-five.
Steffen, W., Crutzen, P. & McNeill, J. (2007) Are humans now overwhelming the great forces of nature?, *AMBIO: A Journal of the Human Environment*, 36(8), pp. 614–621.

Stover, D. (2011) The 'scientization' of Yucca Mountain, *Bulletin of Atomic Scientists*, http://www.thebulletin.org/web-edition/columists/dawn-stover/the-scientization-of-yucca-mountain.

Swyngedouw, E. (2011) Depoliticized environments: The end of nature, climate change and the post-political condition, *Royal Institute of Philosophy*, 69(Suppl.), pp. 253–274.

Wainwright, J. & Mann, G. (2012) Climate Leviathan, *Antipode: A Journal of Radical Geography*, 45(1), pp. 1–22.

Walker, G. (2009a) Beyond distribution and proximity: Exploring the multiple spatialities of environmental justice, *Antipode: A Journal of Radical Geography*, 41(4), pp. 614–636.

Walker, G. (2009b) Globalizing environmental justice: The geography and politics of frame contextualization and evolution, *Global Social Policy*, 9(3), pp. 355–382.

Donna Houston is a lecturer in the Department of Environment and Geography at Macquarie University in Sydney.

Global Justice Organising in Australia: Crisis and Realignment after 9/11

ELIZABETH HUMPHRYS
University of Sydney, Australia

ABSTRACT *The 's11' protest in Melbourne in 2000 saw 20,000 demonstrators successfully blockade the Asia-Pacific Summit of the World Economic Forum and led to the cohering of the Global Justice Movement (GJM) in Australia. The 9/11 attacks, a year later to the day, halted that momentum and seemingly caused movement crisis and retreat. While some accounts, such as the* Wall Street Journal's *editorial 'Adieu Seattle?', argued the 'global security crisis' trumped movement claims and strategy, the experience of activists in Australia is better conceptualised as rearticulation and realignment in response to elite hegemonic practices. This article argues that 9/11 was not the cause of movement collapse in Australia, but that its consequences exacerbated internal movement weaknesses. Further, it argues that despite the return of anti-systemic movements — in the form of the* Indignados *and Occupy movements in particular — the global justice frame has remained weak in Australia.*

Introduction

The success of the Seattle protests against the Ministerial Meeting of the World Trade Organization (WTO) in November 1999 brought a new movement to global attention (Cockburn et al., 2000; Starr, 2000). Building from a number of campaigns throughout the previous decade—such as for cancelling third world debt, corporate responsibility, environmental justice, and fair work—Seattle saw a new political movement critical of global processes and structures come to public attention. This was not the beginning of the GJM in either the Global North or South; however, it was a key turning point given that it occurred in the heart of the world's biggest economy. Seattle and the new movement's concerns went beyond single issues to encompass critiques of the world system, with a focus on the systemic rather than simply the sectional or symptomatic (Callinicos, 2003a; Wallerstein, 2002). It took place in a context of growing dissatisfaction with contemporary global political economy and converging criticisms of global priorities and structures in the neoliberal era (Ayres, 2004). The successful demonstrations and blockade of the summit venue became a model for other events in North America, Europe, and elsewhere—including Australia.

From 11 to 13 September 2000 in Melbourne, Australia, the Asia-Pacific Summit of the World Economic Forum (WEF) was successfully blockaded and disrupted as part of a series of events organised by the s11 Alliance, nongovernment organisations (NGOs), unionists, and radical activists. At the peak of the demonstration, approximately 20,000 activists took part on the second day of 12 September (Boyle, 2001; Bramble and Minns, 2005, pp. 106–7). Yet despite the vibrancy and size of the demonstration, dubbed 's11' after the date on which the three days of protest began, the GJM in Australia was surprisingly short lived. This article looks at the 'seemingly paradoxical sequel' (Hadden and Tarrow, 2007) to the success of s11 in the rapid decline of the GJM after 9/11 and the commencement of the 'War On Terror'. This experience of crisis and collapse was not common to every country, and the movement grew in parts of Europe in the same period (especially in Italy and Spain). But in Australia, in the shadow of the twin towers attack, there was a disintegration of anti-systemic campaigning. Even with the return of the Occupy movement almost a decade later, anti-systemic mobilisation remains weak locally compared to other Western countries.

This article and research deploys a Gramscian-Marxist framework that considers social movements as part of an internally differentiated social totality, and prioritises the question of movement-relevant research. It is essential to view social movements as an arena of contestation and dialogical relations, with an emphasis on their dynamic internal space where broader contradictions and tensions are articulated. The alternative, to view social movements in a primarily instrumental sense, is to see them removed from societal totality and to analyse them as separate entities from the political and economic structures that envelop them. There is also a potential trap in reifying social movements, seeing them as merely things and not for their more inherent nature or essence as comprising social relations. The line of antagonism that a movement addresses may be between the movement and dominant social groups, but the line of antagonism in terms of class and social conflict is also inside the movement driving its internal dynamics.

Movement-relevant research proposes a movement-engaged methodological approach. Such a methodological framework operates from the 'ground up' and involves 'direct engagement with movements in the formulation, production, refinement, and application of the research' (Bevington and Dixon, 2005, pp. 197–201). Activists were asking the questions explored by this research in the period after 9/11, as they individually and collectively assessed the collapse of the movement. It was for this reason that this research was undertaken. In developing and executing the project, opportunities were sought to advance key ideas and concepts with GJM activists, and ongoing research findings were presented to a number of activist and academic forums.

The research included semi-structured interviews with 15 activists involved in the GJM from 1999 to 2002, the contents of which were analysed and coded using the NVIVO software. Formal interviews were supplemented by discussion via email, phone or in person as necessary. Semi-structured interviews were identified as the most appropriate method, as the research concerned a loosely organised movement that was largely no longer active in a coherent sense, and this made methods of field observation difficult (Blee and Taylor, 2002, p. 93). Further, the issues canvassed were not suitable for exploration through structured interviews or surveys as they involved detailed subjective examination of a complex phenomenon in an effort to develop a theoretical framework (Ibid., pp. xv–xvi).

The GJM in Australia did not have membership lists (Burgmann, 2003, p. 283). Therefore, to ensure that an appropriate range of activists were interviewed a process of 'mapping' the movement was undertaken. This map was initially constructed from the researcher's knowledge as an activist within the movement, and from relevant literature and movement ephemera. Meetings were held with seven activists (six of whom were additional to those interviewed) to enhance and 'test' the map. The map 'illustrates' the movement along a number of trajectories: movement antecedents; post-Seattle movement events; GJM campaigns and initiatives; and independent media associated with the movement.[1]

Activists considered to be 'reflexive activists' (Maddison and Scalmer, 2006, p. 7) were associated with each 'branch'. In general, official leaders of organisations were excluded because of a concern that their responses would be limited by their role as spokespeople of their respective organisations (that is, giving the organisation's 'line') (Blee and Taylor, 2002, pp. 93–4). Interviewees were chosen to reflect a diversity of backgrounds and situations within the movement more generally, and activists who were involved in single-issue campaigns as well as those who sought to work between organisations and sections of the movement were identified. The selection of interviewees was ultimately a 'purposeful sample' and not a 'probability sample' (Hackett and Carroll, 2006, p. 165). It is acknowledged that several of the interviewees had an existing activist relationship with the author. While being an insider has benefits, including access to activists and the ability to build rapport and trust (Blee and Taylor, 2002, p. 97), there are also a number of difficulties and risks. These issues had to be accounted for in choosing interviewees, conducting the interviews, and analysing the data. While constant attention was paid to the issue of bias, it would be erroneous to say the research results were entirely immune from it.

Background: Movement Formation

Movement identity has always been a strategic area of interest for social movement scholars, as it is fundamental to movement formation and sustainability over time (Melucci, 1995). Prior to s11 in Australia, in what would later be called the GJM, there was no well-developed internal collective identity *as* a movement. The s11 activities initiated a qualitative shift in three ways. Firstly, s11 led to clear self-awareness by the movement of a collective identity and a common project (Flesher Fominaya, 2010, p.380). As one activist, Amanda, said: 's11 was the point in history that allowed the movement to coalesce. Events [can be a] catalyst for movements to form as opposed to being the activities that movements do.' Secondly, there was an immediate impact in opening up public debate as a result of the blockades, in turn giving the movement confidence. Environmental activist Paul noted, 'suddenly we were having a fantastic debate about ... what we want. ... I think that was a real peak in terms of informed, broad-based mainstream debate about preferred futures.' And finally, the movement came to view itself as being on the offensive (for a better world) as opposed to only defensive struggle against regressive policies and actions taken by elites and the state. Numerous activists described their involvement in terms of creating something, rather than just fighting cutbacks and conservative political decisions.

The GJM after s11 was buoyant, with activists initiating a range of actions and events. For several months in the first half of 2001 this included weekly pickets of a Nike superstore over unfair labour practices, each time costing the corporation between $10,000 and $15,000

(Whyte, 2001). Anti-systemic and anti-capitalist groups formed around the theme of sexual equality/liberation/freedom groups formed in a number of cities and played a central role in the movement (Humphrys, 2007; Pendleton, 2007). Other activities included growing radical independent media projects (Garcelon, 2006; Meikle, 2003), fair trade and debt campaigns (Hunt, 2002; Ranald, 2006), and attempts to forge movement unity through joint broad-based actions on May Day 2001 involving both institutional and extra- or anti-institutional elements (in particular trade unions) (Hubbard, 2001; Kingston, 2001).

Movement Decline

While the events of 9/11 presented the movement with particular challenges, it is not the case that the GJM in Australia collapsed only because of the terrorist attacks. It is important to recognise the 'numerous ways in which September 11 [2001] has become a metaphor and symbolic turning point' (Kalantzis, 2004, p. 582) for geopolitical and societal changes, and in the process has obscured more complex circumstances. Clearly 'the political events following the September 11 attacks in 2001 gave rise to a dramatic shift in the consent/coercion balance of the neoliberal world order' (Stephen, 2009, p. 487), but there were a range of responses and outcomes across the Global North. In Europe the GJM more effectively took up the questions of the US invasion of Afghanistan and Iraq, but in the US and Australia the movement was unable to do this despite a significant and vibrant anti-war movement (Hadden and Tarrow, 2007). Activists argued that although the movement's trajectory of decline could not be separated from 9/11 and its aftermath, it was primarily internal and pre-existing limitations that most contributed to the movement's crisis. As Haddon and Tarrow note of the United States, it is insufficient to explain the decline on the basis of American (or Australian) 'exceptionalism', as such 'an explanation is not dynamic: it cannot explain why participation in the GJM either rose or fell' (Ibid., p. 360). Nor can the decline be attributed to a more general decrease or collapse in social movement activity in Australia, as there were a number of other large and vibrant movements active in the same period.

Activists noted the following when they argued the movement had declined: decreased attention in the public sphere and media to movement issues; a decline in protest numbers; a narrowed spectrum of participants and organisations in movement protests; and, internal disagreements resulting in a splintering of organising alliances. In relation to the first of these, a review of key terms in articles in 100 local, regional, and national Australian newspapers[2] supports the view that public space for the issues of the GJM was decreased (see Table 1). In the period after Seattle and s11, increased coverage was given to the question of globalisation and dissent to it, but a dramatic falling away in the wake of 9/11.

In addition, the period after 9/11 saw a rapid decline in the size of public demonstrations. The number of protesters at s11, estimated at between 15,000 and 20,000, was a clear highpoint. As Table 2 details, after the demonstration in October 2001 in Brisbane (organised as a GJM protest against the Commonwealth Heads of Government Meeting (CHOGM) summit but cancelled in the wake of 9/11), it was not until the protests against the G20 in Melbourne in November 2006 that the GJM could once again mobilise more than 1,000 demonstrators at an explicitly GJM demonstration. Interviewees involved in both GJM and anti-war organising argued that anti-war mobilisations were *consciously* not organised under the rubric of the GJM but rather the singular demand of 'no war', and that the ideological framing on demonstrations reflected this. Consequently, those demonstrations have been set aside from the key protest events.

Table 1. Penetration of key topics in the Australian Media

Key Terms:	Anti-globalisation	Globalisation	Globalisation & protest	TOTAL	Key GJM mobilisations
1998	10	752	32	794	
1999	7	1,045	79	1,131	Seattle (Nov)
2000	216	2,310	523	3,049	s11 (Sep)
2001	612	2,960	647	4,219	CHOGM Brisbane (Oct)
2002	347	1,566	272	2,185	Sydney WTO (Nov)
2003	159	1,201	142	1,502	
2004	109	1,129	77	1,315	
2005	190	1,316	141	1,647	Sydney Forbes (Aug)
2006	113	1,353	127	1,593	Melbourne G20 (Nov)
2007	123	1,358	117	1,598	Sydney APEC (Sept)
2008	61	1,124	47	1,232	
2009	54	785	48	887	

Note: 'Anti-globalisation' was the more commonly used term in the mainstream media to describe the GJM, but is one usually rejected by activists as inaccurate (Buttel and Gould, 2004, pp. 40–1; Burgmann, 2003, p. 247).

Table 2. Key GJM protests events in Australia

Event	Date	Place	Size
j18 (pre Seattle)	18 June 1999	Sydney	500
s11	11–13 September 2000	Melbourne	15,000–20,000
m1 2001	1 May 2001	Most capital cities	18,000
CHOGM	6 October 2001	Brisbane	2,500
m1 2002	1 May 2002	Most capital cities (Largest: Sydney)	3,000 (1,000)
WTO	November 2002	Sydney Homebush	1,000 500
Forbes	30 August 2005	Sydney	1,000
G20	November 2006	Melbourne	2,000

*Figures for m1 2001 and m1 2002 (GJM May Day mobilizations) are from the independent Left newspaper *Green Left Weekly*, Issue 447 (2001 figures) and Issue 491 (2002). The figures for j18, WTO and Forbes from Goodman 2010. Figure for CHOGM from Conachy 2001. Figure for G20 protest from Anon 2006.

The constituency of protests also narrowed in this same period, causing a qualitative change to the form of the movement. Interviewees emphasised that the diversity of the movement at s11 and at m1 in 2001—which saw unions and NGOs jointly involved in demonstrations with extra- or anti-institutional movement forms—had dwindled. There were attempts, in particular by trade activists, to bring the institutional and extra- or anti-institutional elements together for the anti-WTO protests in Sydney in November 2002, but activists reported that internal demarcation was growing. The protest against the Forbes Global CEO Conference in August 2005 in Sydney saw little cooperation between the institutional and extra- or anti-institutional sections, and by the time of the G20 protests in November 2006 in Melbourne the dynamic of cooperation between those elements had been all but lost.

The splits in organising collectives over various protests, a number of which occurred before 9/11, were another symptom of a dynamic of internal rupture and exposed the internal brittleness of the movement (such as the significant split directly prior to the anti-CHOGM demonstration over whether or not activists should blockade the venue). While extra- or anti-institutional elements might have been the stronger force at the anti-WEF demonstrations in 2000, over time these networks proved more difficult to maintain. Moreover, in the challenging times for the GJM after 9/11 many activists looked to the stability of institutional sections in order to channel their efforts; this was particularly the case with activists becoming involved in electoral politics through the Australian Greens. A majority of activists interviewed remarked that the Australian Greens were the key beneficiary of the success of the s11 demonstration and GJM in Australia, especially in relation to the Greens' opposition to the Iraq war and campaigning to end the mandatory detention of asylum seekers.

Evidence from Activists

There was a complex set of factors affecting the movement and generating or contributing to movement crisis. In an effort to illuminate the overall dynamic of movement crisis and collapse, Table 3 summarises the data from the interviews on drivers of movement decline. The table lists all 17 drivers of movement decline that were raised by *more than one activist* during the interviews, each one listed on a separate row, and discussed in detail below. The table then breaks down the characteristics of each of the drivers of decline into sub-categories. In the table, 'X's indicate which categories describe each of the drivers of movement decline. In terms of the sub-categories, the table first delineates whether each element was due to dynamics that were imposed mainly from outside the movement ('externally driven') or developed within its internal constitution ('internally manifested'). A further delineation is made within these two categories, regarding whether the origin of these external and internal dynamics was to be found mainly in objective ('structural') or subjective ('ideological') processes. While in some cases an identified driver of decline neatly fits into just one of these sub-categories, in many there is overlap. Furthermore, a Marxist methodology starts with the recognition that the 'inside' and 'outside' of a movement form a differentiated social totality, just as there is a dialectical unity between the subjective and objective. Nevertheless, greater analytical clarity can be gained by categorising the nature of drivers of movement decline in this way. Precisely because totality is internally differentiated, drawing a distinction between inside and outside, or subjective and objective, allows us to gain a richer concrete understanding of the processes at work and their origins. Importantly, such an approach also militates against simplistic and one-sided notions of why the GJM declined, such as the idea (mentioned above) that it was simply the events of 9/11 that were causative.

Factors Arising from Outside the Movement

While the post-9/11 drive to war in Afghanistan and Iraq was principally an external factor, initiated and pursued outside the GJM's immediate sphere of influence, it had ideological consequences affecting GJM cohesion. As mentioned above, a key issue identified by activists was that space for debate in the media and wider public sphere about GJM issues was closed or reduced by the events. One activist stated that the debate about globalisation of the preceding

Table 3. Analytical framework for the external and internal factors related to decline of the GJM in Australia

	Externally driven		Internally manifested	
	Structural	Ideological	Structural	Ideological
Narrowing of space for debate in public sphere	X	X		
Violence from state at movement protests	X		X	X
Legislative restrictions on protest & movement introduced after 9/11	X		X	
Decline in size of movement in North America, change to shape of movement in Europe	X			
Post-9/11 drive to war in Afghanistan and Iraq	X			X
Elites emboldened		X		
Use of fear by elites		X		
Dichotomous frame re-established: horizontal frame of 'clash of civilisations' between the civility of the west / incivility of terrorists		X		
Racialisation of the other / re-emphasis of nationalism		X		
Differentiation within GJM / lack of cohesiveness			X	X
Weak nature of movement collective identity				X
Lack of flexibility of movement in changed circumstances			X	
Challenge to frame of 'who is the enemy'				X
Incoherent alternative vision to capitalism & imperialism				X
Inability to meld anti-systemic analysis & critique of war				X
Lack of democratic infrastructure to dialogue problems / challenges			X	
Disagreement on nature of the political subject (i.e. who can / will change the world)			X	X

years no longer appeared in the media, while another emphasised that while some conversation continued it was within a new frame that did not allow for a deeper questioning of the structures of society:

> [What we are left with is] Huntington's Clash of Civilizations thesis.... There's nothing there about global capital and its role in constructing this whole war. What we're seeing is institutionalized globalized Islamaphobia and ... it's a blanket kind of ideological directive about who the enemy is and what nation states need to do to crush the enemy inside and without.

September 11 was seen as a trigger to allow a new dichotomous framework of civilisation/terrorism to be asserted, obscuring the more complex debates about globalisation and global justice. As Mary Kalantzis identifies, '[p]roductive big-picture doubt [had] quickly been displaced by race certitude' and in this environment 9/11 became 'less a turning point than an alibi to return to an old story' (2004, p. 583).

Perhaps the first structural impact on the movement in Australia was the cancellation of CHOGM in Brisbane in October 2001 because of fears of a terrorist attack. The movement had been organising for a protest at CHOGM focusing on justice for asylum seekers, third world debt, and the role of corporate globalisation (Ensor, 2001). Significant effort had also been made by the prominent GLBTIQ activists to mobilise against the attendance of Zimbabwean President Robert Mugabe, who had described gays and lesbians as worse than pigs and dogs (Laurence and Humphrys, 2001). When CHOGM was cancelled, the planned rally and blockade morphed into a protest against the impending US invasion of Afghanistan. However, given that the focus of the original protest was no longer there, the event was relatively small (see Table 2).

Some activists spoke of how, in the immediate aftermath of the attacks, they or others felt that GJM protests should not occur. Some argued it would be disrespectful to those who had died in the 9/11 attacks, while others were afraid of what might happen in light of previous police violence and increasingly aggressive language from governments involved in the Coalition of the Willing. One interviewee noted the feeling among US activists he was in contact with at the time:

> I remember all these mainstream NGOs in the US called off participating in demonstrations [in New York and Washington against the World Bank and IMF] and you weren't allowed to demonstrate, it was disrespectful to demonstrate and everyone really quickly came into line in terms of being under attack.

Activists argued that this external driver exacerbated already established tensions regarding police violence at demonstrations, in play prior to 9/11, and in particular that this was a contentious issue between institutional and extra- or anti-institutional groups or organisations.

Many commentators have argued that 9/11 served as an excuse to use repression to silence dissent, primarily through increased surveillance and legislative restrictions on political protests (Burgmann, 2003, p. 325; Campbell, 2002; Marcuse, 2003; Starr, 2006). There were two elements to this dynamic, the first being that protest policing now included 'criminalization and pre-emptive attacks on protesters' and the second 'that the property crimes which some sectors of the alterglobalization movement occasionally enact was not only being characterized as violence but was also being investigated as "terrorism"' (Starr, 2006, p. 61). While there were attempts before 9/11 to increase surveillance and policing of protesters (McCulloch, 2000, 2001), this became more audacious and included restricting activists' physical movement on the basis of what they might do rather than what they had done (Goodman, 2010, p. 353). New laws were used to both intimidate protesters with the threat of arrest without charge and to conflate them with 'terrorists' (Devine, 2001).

Global elites also increasingly welcomed inside their summits 'respectable' movement participants (such as leading spokespeople from NGOs) and activists argued this was a way of disrupting unity and appearing to take on board protesters' concerns. Activists saw this external pressure as consequential, as it divided more radical elements from the institutional elements that were given 'a seat at the table'. It was also clear that the elites were learning how to manage demonstrations more effectively (Della Porta et al., 2006; Gillham and Noakes, 2008). The confusion and failures of the police at s11 and Seattle (De Armond, 2001) were replaced with renewed and reshaped interventions in Genoa in 2001 and elsewhere. On occasion elites changed venues to avoid protests, such as relocating the 2002 Sydney WTO meeting from the central business district to a remote suburban location at Homebush (Stainsby, 2003). Though it is worth noting that such management of protests by elites is not unidirectional, and the nature of protest management itself engenders response. The repressive handling of the protest at Genoa resulted in the killing of a protester, and this is turn provoked further mass protests across Italy.

CRISIS, MOVEMENT, MANAGEMENT: GLOBALISING DYNAMICS

Internal Factors and Pre-Existing Weaknesses

Weaknesses that limited movement coherence and effectiveness prior to the 9/11 attacks were set aside temporarily in the general upswing of activity. These weaknesses were articulated as a struggle for direction:

> I think that to a degree [the summit strategy] had run its course... and 9/11 happened at roughly that point, it kind of knocked it over probably faster than would have happened for a whole range of reasons. I mean, we had the invasion of Iraq, we had the criminalization of dissent in a way that hadn't happened before, and a lot of US foundations stopped funding anti-corporate globalization work. So I think it hastened that decline... rather than caused it.

In the post-9/11 environment some factors that were previously seen by activists as strengths became growing problems. Chief among these was the differentiation within the movement (its 'unity in diversity'), which became a perceived barrier to organising given there was little democratic space in which to resolve political differences. While there were spaces in which to organise specific events or protests (such as 'spokescouncils'), there was a lack of general spaces in which to debate out movement strategy and politics. While activists had hoped that regional and local social forums might provide this opportunity, efforts to establish an Asia-Pacific Social Forum did not progress and the Australian capital city social forums struggled to establish themselves as broad and inclusive settings. As such, the GJM in Australia was unable to deal coherently with the implications of the War on Terror and to articulate a united response across the movement. This resulted in both ideological and organisational fragmentation and was increasingly seen by activists as a barrier to effective organising.

There were growing ruptures between more radical and more conservative elements, in particular over violence at demonstrations and the heavy-handed tactics of police. Many interviewees remarked that while the violence may have come as little surprise to more radical organisers, more conservative activists became wary of organising blockades in particular. This was also linked to two intertwined internal issues. Firstly, many interviewees spoke of a lack of internal space to debate and discuss issues confronting and potentially dividing the movement, including how to deal with police violence. Paul noted:

> I think it was actually a really complex debate that was going on [about why the terrorist attacks occurred] and complex debates are hard to capture in the mainstream... also remember that we have this really broad movement, so it's not even like there was place where that debate could happen in a single place.

Activists indicated that those spaces did not emerge, and not that their efforts to create such spaces were hindered by internal or external forces. This situation was seen as an important organisational failing, arising from the expectation the movement should 'naturally' generate such forums. Secondly, some argued that not enough had been done prior to 9/11 to establish trust between movement elements, to better develop collective identity (which in turn may have assisted to establish permanent spaces for debate).

While many activists saw themselves as involved in and building the wider GJM, some noted they had identified with the movement because of involvement with specific campaigns. This was important in light of the fact that a weaker sense of collective identity emerged in the absence of large-scale mobilisations. Giulietta stated:

> [I was] involved in campaigns and projects around anti-racism, housing, and squatting and other kinds of social centre movement projects that I think intercepted with issues around globalization. ... It didn't consciously label itself as part of the globalization movement. But of course there

were issues that we were dealing with, and the intellectual and political origins, it kind of tipped its cap to [and] was necessarily part of those [GJM] struggles and ideas.

Without summit protests and their organising structures, there were few places to discuss through practical and political matters. The pre 9/11 debates around 'summit hopping', 'global versus local', and whether the GJM was 'a movement of movements' took on new meaning as the impact of several ideological factors played out inside the movement, including an inability to combine the movement's anti-systemic analysis with a critique of war and imperialism:

> ... the Left had to learn again how to construct the peace movement or anti-war movement at the same time as trying to integrate that with an anti-systemic or anti-capitalist, anti-corporate power perspective. We haven't done that very successfully. ... I think they've been able to do that more successfully in Europe, integrate those two perspectives and maintain them.

In some countries there was a more direct path from the pre- to post-9/11 periods for GJM activists, which involved a better integration of global justice and anti-war demands. But this was not the case in the United States or, as argued by interviewees, in Australia. In Western Europe 'the global justice movement continued to expand, both internationally and internally' (Hadden and Tarrow, 2007, p. 370). For example, mobilisations across Italy were not only large but managed to link the issues of globalisation and war (Callinicos, 2003b, p. 137). In Barcelona, activists were able to mobilise 300,000 people (Paczynska, 2008, p. 7) around the demand of 'No to a Europe of Capital and War'. The Barcelona Social Forum, itself a GJM body, initiated and called the local anti-war protest that were part of the internationally coordinated anti-war demonstrations of February 2003. Furthermore, Donatella della Porta has emphasised in research on the European GJM that it was reasonably well grounded in the community (Della Porta, 2005b) and that the European movement managed the question of 'deliberative democracy' with some degree of success (Della Porta, 2005a).[3]

By contrast, although the anti-war protests in Australia were large and vibrant,[4] interviewees remarked that there was not much of an anti-capitalist flavour even if many of the same activists were involved in organising them. This failure to integrate the demands of global justice, anti-war, and imperialism was not accidental, as the adoption of the more singular 'no war' demand was deliberate and seen as necessary to build a broad-based anti-war movement:

> we basically adopted the line that we should say 'no war' ... and we quite deliberately [did that]. ... [As t]he main focus of the protest movement against the war, we deliberately excluded any questions of global economic power ... and that was probably a mistake.

Activists argued that although significant numbers of campaigners entered the anti-war movement in 2002 and after, it was less a case of movements joining together but of seepage of activists from the GJM into the larger anti-war movement. Henry argued that in the process, the anti-systemic perspective was lost:

> it not only changed global politics, but it changed the shape of the movements as it were, so it went from being an anti-globalisation movement to being this defensive stop the war kind of movement.

As Jennifer Hadden and Sidney Tarrow detail in their analysis of the movement in the United States after 9/11, there was an erosion ('spillout') of the GJM as the anti-war movement grew—as opposed to both movements enhancing each other in a process of 'spillover' (2007, p. 360). They also note that there was no decrease in political action or shrinking of movements more generally in the wake of 9/11, but that the decline of the GJM can be found in the spillout into anti-war and electoral work (Ibid., pp. 360, 372). A similar dynamic was observable in Australia where there were large mobilisations around the Iraq war, for refugee rights, and against anti-union or anti-worker legislation brought in by the conservative government (the 'WorkChoices' legislation). These movements were successfully built at the same time that the GJM was collapsing. Yet the GJM was unable to promote itself effectively within these political fields.

Conclusion

In the decade between the close of the Cold War and the launch of the War on Terror alter-globalisation critiques developed, revealing power relations intrinsic to global economic organisation in the epoch of neoliberalism. The alternative perspectives that emerged illuminated the more fundamental geopolitical relations inherent to capitalism. However, as the impact of s11 and 9/11 demonstrate, counter-hegemonic movements do not develop along an orderly path. They are permeated by the ideas and agendas of ruling elites and, as in the case of the GJM in Australia, are vulnerable to the politics of fear and the constraints of wartime dissent. The GJM was subject to the impact of world events, and in the Australian case its internal fragility meant that it struggled to cope with a new environment. Under the weight of 9/11, a multiplicity of factors came together to provide a moment of transition from an offensive to a defensive stance. While this path was not pre-ordained, contingent internal and external dynamics worked together to offer not a stepping-stone, taking the movement forward through discussion and debate, but a paralysing and debilitating process in the absence of internal democratic spaces which may have enabled the clarification of ideas. In this period the movement shrank and qualitatively narrowed in terms of its diversity.

The experience of the GJM post-9/11 is instructive for political movements today. 'In the last decade', suggests Ruth Reitan, there has been a rearticulation and realignment emerging where:

> US-NATO imperial overstretch has combined with casino capitalism's catastrophic effects at last coming home to roost in the economic core. What is emerging is something that was always latent, as an aspiration, in the movement strands. But with time it has grown more pronounced, as the movements have moved from resisting to experimenting, from protesting to proposing and, in some places, imposing: coalescing into a demand and the practice of democracy, now! Thus, what began nearly two decades ago as anti-globalization morphed for a time into alter-globalization and global peace and justice or simply the movement of movements, and now seems to be congealing into a counter-hegemonic project of and for global democratization. (Reitan, 2012, pp. 323–4)

The protests of the Arab Spring, the Occupy movement, and the Spanish *Indignados* have inspired activists to once again mobilise opposition against the current geopolitical order. While in Australia these have been short-lived expressions, the immediate size and vibrancy of events such as Occupy Sydney and Occupy Melbourne demonstrate that wider concerns around inequality and 'globalisation' have not disappeared. The Occupy protests are not a simple rearticulation of the GJM and its concerns; a decade of war imposed on Iraq and Afghanistan by the 'Coalition of the Willing' has altered things dramatically (Humphrys, 2012).

In addition, the economic crisis unfolding since 2007–2008 has only continued to highlight the failure of elites to address economic disadvantage—an issue that was at the centre of the GJM. The economic system has also been shown incapable of achieving its other key aim of perpetual economic growth. Australia may have avoided the worst of the financial and economic crisis due to an ongoing resources boom, but the resultant 'two-speed' economy, with growing inequalities and deepening casualisation of work, has reduced living standards and left people feeling increasingly insecure (Scalmer, 2012). It is in this context that events such as Occupy have reawakened anti-systemic politics. As research completed at a key Occupy Sydney rally demonstrates, unequal wealth and corporate control and influence were the key concerns of those who attended (Jackson and Chen, 2012, p. 2). Given that the ongoing Occupy camps were small (mass rallies peaked at around 2,000 participants), and there has been little success in attracting institutional players (such as unions and NGOs) into the movement, the question of how to build a sustainable movement on this newly (re)emerging sentiment remains.

In this way, while 9/11 was a key event in the crisis experienced by the GJM in Australia, the management of 9/11 and the global economic downturn by elites has itself engendered responses opening new opportunities for mobilisation. Rather than seeing movement disintegration as simply failure, the reflexive processes of the activists interviewed for this study underline that movements and activists equally learn in retreat:

> Movement success or failure is often treated in the literature as an all or nothing proposition: either movements meet their objectives or they fail. . . . [but] if our focus shifts from movement outcome to development, the relation between failure and success becomes more complex and raises the possibility that scholars should consider what seems to be an oxymoron: the possible benefits of 'failure' for social movements. (Flesher Fominaya, 2010, p. 400)

Just as the GJM arose from its campaign and movement antecedents in fair trade, anti-corporate, and anti-neoliberal activity, so it has played a role in the movements since—and in particular since the re-emergence of global anti-systemic struggle in the last few years. It is in this context that the legacy of the GJM continues to play an important role.

Acknowledgements

The author is grateful for the feedback provided by the anonymous reviewers of the article as well as by James Goodman, Jon Marshall, Tad Tietze, and Kate Davison.

Notes

1. A brief discussion on how the program was used in this research is available on the Tinderbox website (http://www.eastgate.com/Tinderbox/Using/SocialInquiry.html). The full movement 'map' can be viewed at Enclosure A, Humphrys (2011).
2. These figures are based on searches of the Newsbank database, a complete full-text database of more than 100 local, regional, and national newspapers in Australia (paid advertisements are excluded).
3. While activists raised these two aspects as important to movement decline in Australia, further research might usefully assess to what extent the 'internal' factors that appear as limitations in Australia were present in the European case.
4. The key anti-war rally in Sydney was estimated to have between 250,000 and 400,000 participants, making it the largest demonstration in Australian history.

References

Anon (2006) G20 protest turns violent, *ABC News Online*, 18 November, http://www.abc.net.au/news/newsitems/200611/s1791848.htm.
De Armond, P. (2001) Netwar in the Emerald City: WTO protest strategy and tactics, in J. Arquilla & D. Ronfeldt (eds) *Networks and Netwars: The Future of Terror, Crime and Militancy* (Santa Monica, CA: Rand Corporation), pp. 201–235.
Ayres, J. M. (2004) Framing collective action against neoliberalism: The case of the 'anti-globalisation' movement, *Journal of World-Systems Research*, 10(1), pp. 11–34.

CRISIS, MOVEMENT, MANAGEMENT: GLOBALISING DYNAMICS

Bevington, D. & Dixon, C. (2005) Movement-relevant theory: Rethinking social movement scholarship and activism, *Social Movement Studies*, 4(2), pp. 185–208.

Blee, K. M. & Taylor, V. (2002) Semi-structured interviewing in social movement research, in B. Klandermans & S. Staggenborg (eds) *Methods of Social Movement Research* (Minneapolis: University of Minnesota Press), pp. 92–117.

Boyle, P. (2001) The politics of the new movement for global solidarity, *Links: International Journal of Socialist Renewal*, 17, http://links.org.au/taxonomy/term/14.

Bramble, T. & Minns, J. (2005) Whose streets? Our streets! Activist perspectives on the Australian anti-capitalist movement, *Social Movement Studies*, 4(2), pp. 106–121.

Burgmann, V. (2003) *Power, Profit and Protest: Australian Social Movements and Globalisation* (Crows Nest: Allen & Unwin).

Buttel, F. H. & Gould, K. A. (2004) Global justice movement(s) at the crossroads: Some observations on the trajectory of the anti-corporate globalisation movement, *Journal of World-Systems Research*, 10(1), pp. 37–66.

Callinicos, A. (2003a) *An Anti-Capitalist Manifesto* (Cambridge: Polity).

Callinicos, A. (2003b) The anti-capitalist movement after Genoa and New York, in S. Aronowitz & H. Gautney (eds) *Implicating Empire: Globalisation & Resistance in the 21st Century World Disorder* (New York: Basic Books), pp. 133–150.

Campbell, B. (2002) NYC after 9.11, *CounterAction*, 1, pp. 10–11.

Cockburn, A., St. Clair, J. & Sekula, A. (2000) *5 Days that Shook the World* (London: Verso).

Conachy, J. (2001) Anti-war protests in Australian cities, *World Socialist*, http://www.wsws.org/articles/2001/oct2001/aust-o20.shtml.

Della Porta, D. (2005a) Making the polis: Social forums and democracy in the global justice movement, *Mobilization: An International Quarterly*, 10(1), pp. 73–94.

Della Porta, D. (2005b) The social bases of the global justice movement: Some theoretical reflections and empirical evidence from the First European Social Forum, Civil Society and Social Movements Programme Paper Number 21 (Geneva: United Nations Research Institute for Social Development).

Della Porta, D., Andretta, M., Mosca, L. & Reitan, H. (2006) *Globalisation from Below: Transnational Activists and Protest Networks* (Minneapolis: University of Minnesota Press).

Devine, M. (2001) Protesters find any army will do as they embrace terror, *Sydney Morning Herald*, 15 November, p. 16.

Ensor, T. (2001) Common—wealth?: CHOGM and third world debt, Stop CHOGM resources, http://pandora.nla.gov.au/pan/21728/20011003-0000/www.stopchogm.org/resources.html.

Flesher Fominaya, C. (2010) Creating cohesion from diversity: The challenge of collective identity formation in the global justice movement, *Sociological Inquiry*, 80(3), pp. 377–404.

Garcelon, M. (2006) The 'Indymedia' experiment: The Internet as movement facilitator against institutional control, *Convergence*, 12(1), pp. 55–82.

Gillham, P. F. & Noakes, J. (2008) Police and protester innovation since Seattle, *Mobilization: An International Quarterly*, 12, pp. 335–240.

Goodman, J. (2010) Provoking 'Globalist Sydney': Neoliberal summits and spatial reappropriation, *Globalizations*, 7(8), pp. 347–357.

Hackett, R. A. & Carroll, W. K. (2006) *Remaking the Media: The Struggle to Democratise Public Communication* (New York: Routledge).

Hadden, J. & Tarrow, S. (2007) Spillover or spillout? The global justice movement in the United States after 9/11, *Mobilization: An International Quarterly*, 12, pp. 359–376.

Hubbard, L. (2001) Trades hall to take May Day action against anti-worker corporations, *Media Release*, www.vthc.org.au/index.cfm?section=52&category=52&viewmode=content&contentid=1848.

Humphrys, E. (2007) 'With their bodies on the line': Activist space and sexuality in the Australian alter-globalisation movement, Paper presented at the Queer Space Conference (University of Technology Sydney), www.dab.uts.edu.au/conferences/queer_space/proceedings/globalisation_humphrys.pdf.

Humphrys, E. (2011) From Offence to Defence: The Australian Global Justice Movement and the Impact of 9/1, master's thesis, University of Technology Sydney, http://epress.lib.uts.edu.au/research/bitstream/handle/10453/20390/02Whole.pdf?sequence=2.

Humphrys, E. (2012) From global justice to Occupy everywhere: The antecedents to a new movement, *Overland Journal*, Special Issue: 'Occupy Overland', http://overland.org.au/previous-issues/issue-occupy/feature-elizabeth-humphrys/.

Hunt, J. (2002) *The Jubilee 2000 Campaign in Australia: An Evaluation* (Melbourne: Jubilee Australia).

Jackson, S. & Chen, P. (2012) Understanding Occupy in Australia, *Journal of Australian Political Economy*, 69, pp. 5–28.

Kalantzis, M. (2004) September 11: Mixed metaphor, *Signs*, 29(2), pp. 582–584.
Kingston, M. (2001) M1, *Sydney Morning Herald*, 1 May.
Laurence, K. & Humphrys, E. (2001) Fuck your profiteering: People die while you play business, *Stop CHOGM Resources*, http://pandora.nla.gov.au/pan/21728/20011003-0000/www.stopchogm.org/resources.html.
Maddison, S. & Scalmer, S. (2006) *Activist Wisdom* (Sydney: University of New South Wales Press).
Marcuse, P. (2003) On the global uses of September 11 and its urban impact, in S. Aronowitz & H. Gautney (eds) *Implicating Empire: Globalisation & Resistance in the 21st century world disorder* (New York: Basic Books), pp. 271–285.
McCulloch, J. (2000) Globalising violence: Civil protest is being used as a pretext for paramilitary policing, *Arena Magazine*, 50, pp. 10–11.
McCulloch, J. (2001) Paramilitary surveillance: S11, globalisation terrorists and counter-terrorists, *Current Issues in Criminal Justice*, 13(1), pp. 23–35.
Meikle, G. (2003) Indymedia and the new net news, *M/C Media and Culture Journal*, 6, http://journal.media-culture.org.au/0304/02-feature.php.
Melucci, A. (1995) The process of collective identity, in H. Johnston & B. Klandermans (eds) *Social Movements and Culture* (Minneapolis: University of Minnesota), pp. 41–63.
Paczynska, A. (2008) Turtles, puppets and pink ladies: The global justice movement in a post-9/11 world, Center for Global Studies, Working Papers in Global Studies, No. 1 (Washington, DC: George Mason University).
Pendleton, M. (2007) Looking back to look forward: The past in Australia queer anti-capitalism, 1999–2002, *Melbourne Historical Journal*, 35, pp. 51–71.
Ranald, P. (2006) The Australia-US Free Trade Agreement: A contest of interests, *Journal of Australian Political Economy*, 57, pp. 1–27.
Reitan, R. (2012) Theorizing and engaging the global movement: From anti-globalization to global democratization, *Globalizations*, 9(3), pp. 323–335.
Scalmer, S. (2012) The world of all of us, *Overland Journal*, Special Issue: Occupy Overland, http://overland.org.au/previous-issues/issue-occupy/feature-sean-scalmer/.
Stainsby, M. (2003) Beyond summit-hopping? G8's retreat to Kananaskis and the way ahead, *Socialism and Democracy*, 17(2), pp. 191–215.
Starr, A. (2000) *Naming the Enemy: Anti-Corporate Movements Confront Globalization* (Sydney: Pluto Press).
Starr, A. (2006) '. . . (Excepting barricades to prevent us from peacefully assembling)': So-called 'violence' in the Global North alterglobalization movement, *Social Movement Studies*, 5(1), pp. 61–81.
Stephen, M. D. (2009) Alter-globalization as counter-hegemony: Evaluating the 'postmodern prince', *Globalizations*, 6(4), pp. 483–498.
Wallerstein, I. (2002) New revolts against the system, *New Left Review*, 18, pp. 29–39.
Whyte, N. (2001) Nike protests defy police intimidation, *Socialist Worker*, p. 11.

Elizabeth Humphrys is a Ph.D. candidate in the Department of Political Economy, University of Sydney, Australia. She is a co-editor of *Interface: A Journal for and About Social Movements*.

Reinscribing the City: Art, Occupation and Citizen Journalism in Hong Kong

FRANCESCA DA RIMINI
University of Technology Sydney, Australia

ABSTRACT *As neoliberal restructuring destroys historic precincts in Hong Kong, these spaces' social and living histories take on new meanings for the city's disenfranchised citizenry. In 2006 the impending demolition of Hong Kong's iconic Star Ferry Pier and Queen's Pier inspired a new form of spatial and cultural politics, which spawned unanticipated civic participation in the struggle to own the city. A lengthy cycle of oppositional actions interwove imaginative interventions, occupations, and investigative reportage, creating 'temporary affective spaces' around the piers. Contributors to the online citizen journalism site Hong Kong In-Media reframed sentimental mainstream media narratives by connecting urban development to political agency. The grassroots piers movement is significant because it seeded a new social movement in Hong Kong, one which shares resonances with Chinese protest culture and the global Occupy movement. Moreover, the organically constituted social formation of protesters perhaps materialises the philosophical concept of the 'multitude'.*

Introduction

Issues of spatial justice have propelled a new turn in social movement practice in Hong Kong in recent years. Battles over controversial urban development projects are intertwined with ongoing struggles around citizenship and enfranchisement. Significantly, the right to own the city, to protect local community cultures and daily ways of life, is inspiring collective experimentation with participatory democracy. This article looks at an urban renewal project which demolished two historic piers during 2006–2007. The political significance of this struggle is fourfold. Firstly, the campaign strengthened the city's existing preservation movement. Secondly, it challenged Hong Kong's non-representative mode of governance. Thirdly, its locally differentiated form of resistance shared similarities, and displayed notable differences, with comparable battles worldwide over the neoliberalised metropolis. Finally, and most importantly for this article, the campaign seeded what some have described as a new social movement in Hong Kong, one which combined spatial, symbolic, and discursive politics. Participants harnessed the cooperative cognitive aptitudes informational capitalism demands, creating social experimentation, enduring networks, and an enduring mode of resistance which would nourish future campaigns.

Neoliberalism, the political project to restore the ruling class's power by processes of state deregulation making room for private accumulation, forms part of the backdrop to the narrative about the piers (Chung and Ngai, 2007; Harvey, 2005). Neoliberalism has different 'spatial contours' in different places, arriving relatively late in East Asia to confront an environment 'dominated by developmentalism and its legacies' (Park et al., 2011, pp. 20, 8). Hong Kong's neoliberalisation processes began in the 1980s and deepened and accelerated after the 1997 financial crisis, when a new government discourse of 'small government and big market' became code for the construction of an 'entrepreneurial state' built on the privatisation of 'lucrative public assets' (Chung and Ngai, 2007, pp. 66, 74). The neoliberal economic regime was 'institutionalised and made official ideology' via Hong Kong's Basic Law, which stipulates among other things low tax rates, free flow of capital, and free trade (Ngok, 2011, pp. 687–9). Consequently, neoliberal restructuring has affected health services, public housing, transportation, and the labour regime (Chung and Ngai, 2007; Mathews et al., 2012; Park et al., 2011). This global capital hub now possesses 'one of the highest rates of inequality worldwide' according to the United Nations; contributing factors include low pay, long working hours, high rents, and privatisation of public housing (Ku, 2009, p. 512).

The piers preservation campaign is a case study in the evolution of social movement practice during Hong Kong's intensification of neoliberalisation. The emergent movement drew inspiration from key events in Hong Kong and China's protest cultures, and from Western activism, including the creation of Temporary Autonomous Zones. Significantly, it birthed a new form of political agency untethered to traditional 'polite' civil politics, and independent of organisations with defined hierarchies and programmes. Instead this nimble form manifested qualities of new social movements (NSM) worldwide like the anti-globalisation and Occupy movements: individualistic, experiential, experimental, self-organised, building social relations uniting class and cultural divides. Perhaps also the movement's subjects resemble what Autonomist theorists conceive as the 'multitude', a plural, networked social body experimenting with alternatives to capitalism and other oppressive forms of power.

The Politics of Space

Gentrification, Land Reclamation, and Urban Renewal in Hong Kong

Gentrification, the frontier in the 'urban wilderness' produced by capital's cyclical movement, is intertwined with globalisation processes aimed at revitalising the profit rate (Lees et al., 2008; Smith, 1986). Gentrification's geographical 'reorderings and restructurings' are vital both to capital accumulation and the 'dynamics of class struggle' (Harvey, 2000, p. 31).

Hong Kong is a metropolis of almost 7 million people. Its distinctive spatial restructuring is rooted in the government's developmentalist ideology and its desire to actualise a 'modern global city,' with the metropolis becoming a land regime producing revenue from land sales and development taxes (Ku, 2012, pp. 5–6). Land reclamation extends income-generating spaces for the government (Lung, 2012). By the mid-1990s landfill projects had shrunk Victoria Harbour's original 6500 hectares by over 50% (Ku, 2012, p. 6). Chinese developers have contributed to the regime since the real estate market's financialisation in the late 1960s, connecting boom and bust cycles of real estate and stock equities markets (Tang et al., 2012). Government-appointed urban specialists who advocated redeveloping 'pockets of decay' built popular acceptance of the land (re)development regime 'hegemony' while heritage-related administrative structures, policies, laws, and consultation increased public perception of rationality (Ibid., p. 95; Lung, 2012, pp. 123–6). However, consultative processes are opaque with the government withholding substantive information and crushing 'irrational' views (Tang et al., 2012, p. 97).

The intensification of spatial reordering has propelled struggles that link architectural preservation to self-identity and daily life. Major contested developments include the Star Ferry Pier, Queen's Pier, King Yin Lei Mansion, various Urban Renewal Authority projects in Wanchai, and Central's Graham Street open market (Lung, 2012). Consequently, grassroots groups have proliferated with newcomers SEE Network, Heritage Watch, and Heritage Hong Kong advocating alongside the Conservancy Association and the Institute of Architects. Such self-organisation suggests that heritage is no longer regarded as an elite issue. However, campaigns have had mixed results, with whole precincts demolished and local residents dispossessed.

A Case Study in New Social Movements: The Piers Preservation Movement

The social impact of increasing participation in Hong Kong's urban development struggles is exemplified by the campaign to save two piers. According to academic and media activist Chong Iam Ip, the Star Ferry Pier (SFP) and nearby Queen's Pier (QP) in Hong Kong's Central District reflected Hong Kong's 'postwar development of colonial modernity' (2007, p. 3). Queen's Pier was part of the new waterfront built on reclaimed land in 1954. Like its 1920s' predecessor, this stylistically 'modern utilitarian' space served as the dis/embarkation place for British royalty and colonial governors, and would become an important recreational site for residents (including many of the 260,000 female migrant domestic workers), and a locus for political demonstrations (Lai, 2010; Law, 2002). The Star Ferry had been well patronised, servicing millions of passengers annually (Ng et al., 2010). Over time the SFP had been relocated, its third iteration in 1957 featuring a distinctive clock. Perhaps citizens' 'indifferent' attitude to both piers' 1950s' reconstruction arose because for the first time in this city of 'aristocrats and commercial elites' the government had provided public spaces for 'ordinary people' (Ibid., pp. 416–17).

Symbolically, this section of harbour frontage signified both the 'localisation process of colonial administrative power' and also the locus of anti-colonial movements (Lam, 2007b). The 1966 Star Ferry riots, the Chinese Language Movement, Protect Daiyu Island movement, and rallies against inflation, rent hikes, and tax increases had all occurred there (Lam, 2004, pp. 115–24; Ku, 2012). However, the socio-cultural significance of the piers and their surrounds was 'largely untapped' before the 2006–2007 preservation campaigns which rediscovered powerful instances of situated social activism (Ku, 2012, p. 8). Previously opposition had typically focused on government policy rather than lived histories.

In 1999 the Hong Kong Special Administrative Region (HKSAR) government announced their phased land reclamation plan entailing the construction of a highway, shopping mall, and seaside park. However, they hid the demolition of the two piers. Negotiations (often clandestine) that exclude specific groups of stakeholders are one hallmark of neoliberalisation.

Members of a transnational elite class promote public–private partnerships (PPP) to finance 'infrastructure projects with limited public budgets' (Bankwatch Network, 2012). Yet despite mounting evidence of this model's failures few governments have repudiated it. In this instance, the Hong Kong Harbourfront Commission (2010, p. 3) would eventually acknowledge that 'the community may have different views or concerns about PPP, particularly on the issue of public accountability'.

Consistent with its 'bureaucratic-economic mode of governance,' the government ignored commissioned research and alternative preservation plans (Ku, 2012, p. 7; Lam, 2007a). The media tended to avoid preservation issues as heritage remained associated with elite interests. An intransigent planning authority was unswayed by non-confrontational protests, and although the Society for Protection of the Harbour's 10,000-strong rally in 2004 had secured the Harbour Protection Ordinance, this would apply only to future projects (Ip, 2007, p. 4; Ku, 2012, p. 7). Ultimately artistic provocations reawakened public interest in the piers, and the ensuing collective reflection seeded a new set of social actors who would use non-institutional means to mobilise escalating cycles of action.

In June 2006 Leung Po, an artist and one of the editors of the citizen journalism website Hong Kong In-Media (HKIM), critiqued the 'malady of the city' whose symptoms included an independent book store's closure and the impending piers' demolition (Lam, 2007a, p. 61). Other HKIM readers/writers ran with the theme, establishing what would become a discursive and organisational space for the piers preservation movement. I expand on HKIM's critical role later.

In August artists/educators Choi Tsz-kwan, Ger, and Tsang Tak-ping encouraged their Youth Centre students to create a series of Sunday afternoon performances and art installations in the square adjacent to the SFP. Some works expressed loss, mourning, and anger, while others highlighted social history (Lam, 2007a, p. 58). Although the mainstream media (MSM) focused solely on the interventions' nostalgic mood, passers-by 'made their own reading[s] of the artwork/performance' (Ibid., p. 59). Over the ensuing weeks months a visible 'folk spirit' animated the pier, transforming the site into a 'spectacle to be read' Ku (2012, p. 10). Formal groups like the Conservancy Association and the Action Group on Protection of the Harbour organised walks, cruises, and a carnival to further the cause (Ibid.). The SFP clock tower became a campaign icon when independent magazine *SEE Network* uncovered its heritage value as the city's only existing antique mechanical clock (Ibid., p. 9). Editor Patsy Cheng started an online campaign augmented by workshops. Local artist Karden Chan created two woodblock prints, one of the distinctive SFP clock tower and the other of chess players at QP, with both images used in campaign materials (DeWolf, 2009). Chan's choice of medium referenced the May Fourth Movement of 1919 when Beijing students used woodblock prints to communicate emancipatory ideas about Western styles of sociopolitical reform.

Crucially, emotional responses elicited by the various art interventions were 'politicised' into a grassroots citizen campaign initiated by cultural and media activists. Chu Hoi-dick's HKIM article questioned the effectiveness of '"photo-shooting" gestures of protest', kick-starting an online discussion about imposed developments (Lam, 2007a, p. 62). Ger critiqued the artistic provocations, reframing the fight as being about 'participation in the city in the cultural and historical context, not simply as common memory, not as mere personal emotions' (Ibid.). Movement participant Yeung Yang reflected on the relationship between 'organised social action' and 'personal transformation', suggesting that activism required people to understand how their bodies 'relate to social space' (Ibid., pp. 62–3). When the Secretary for Housing, Planning, and Lands argued that because the clock tower's most valuable aspect was its 'collective memory', which could be incorporated into the waterfront's future design, activists transformed the nostalgic discourse by critiquing the ideas of 'living space' and 'living history' (Ku, 2012, p. 10). Movement participants gathered local historical knowledge to mobilise actions. Their critical approach to 'memory work' is exemplified by the recuperation of the 1966 Star Ferry Riots narrative (Ibid., pp. 11–12).

When the young worker So Sau-chong protested a fare increase in 1966 by staging a lone hunger strike at the SFP, his subsequent arrest motivated thousands to join an escalating series of mass riots that culminated in one casualty and 1,465 arrests. Significantly, So's symbolic gesture had provoked the 'first mass protests involving many young people confronting a local issue', leading the colonial government to implement many social reforms, even if mainly to bolster their own legitimacy (Ku, 2012, p. 12). The riots are noteworthy also for the 'narrowly focused and depoliticised' official discourse on citizenship and community they propelled, reflecting a concept of dutiful citizenship that emphasised 'civic obedience and responsibility instead of rights and critical judgement' (Lam, 2005, pp. 310–11, 320). Social and economic conditions produced by the regime's political and class structure had caused the riots, yet class divisions were maintained by 'stigmatising' the post-riots welfare changes not as a civic right but as 'charity' (Chung and Ngai, 2007, p. 71; Scott, 1989, p. 92). Participants in the contemporary movement used this 'almost forgotten event' to illuminate the SFP's spatial connection to a 'tradition of activism in local history' (Ku, 2012, pp. 12, 15–16). Some would later stage a hunger strike at SFP, noting in a communiqué the 'irony' of the changing times (Ibid.). Whereas So had protested against a foreign colonial government, they were protesting HKSAR's postcolonial government which still ignored the people's will.

HKIM became the central platform for news, reflection, and mobilisation. The campaign's horizontal networked form encouraged spontaneous responses to unfolding events. When demolition commenced in late November 2006, people rallied at government offices and a human chain flanked the construction site. Momentum increased when citizen journalists uncovered that the Secretary for Home Affairs had lied about a consultative committee's support of the demolition. Subsequent actions included a second human chain, a 36-hour occupation of the construction site, and a sit-in outside an official's home. The confrontation's escalation triggered the campaign's 'radical turn' and caused a 'small political crisis', generating MSM coverage and the first substantive government intervention (Ip, 2007, p. 3; Lam, 2007a, p. 63). The 'brutal' crushing of the clock tower and dumping of its remains outraged the public, as did the excessive police force against occupying activists (Lam, 2007b). A 'loose alliance' of participants grew out of the movement's radicalisation, and this social formation (subsequently naming itself Local Action) would later lead the QP struggle (Ku, 2012, p. 13).

Media academic and activist Clemencia Rodriguez (2001, p. 22) likens citizens' media to a 'multitude of small forces' surfacing and bursting 'like bubbles in a swamp'. In this instance citizen reporters unearthed controversial news that the government would construct a People's Liberation Army berth. What would it mean for residents if Central's waterfront were to be dominated by 'four symbolic landmarks' representing money, consumerism, state power, and military power? These would erase the architectural signifiers of civil struggles and diminish possibilities for uncommodified social life.

One distinguishing feature of the piers' movement was participants' use of diverse modes of protest to build an enduring, broad-based resistance movement combining long-term strategy with short-term tactics (Ip, 2007). While other rallies and campaigns had often employed entertaining skits that imbued an 'air of carnivalesque' (Lai, 2010; Law, 2002, p. 1641), the piers movement embraced more improvised and risky expressive forms. Activists integrated Internet and mobile phone communications, building an 'organic, flexible network' through which new actors were mobilised (Ku, 2012, p. 13). For example, when police detained some participants in a candlelight vigil to celebrate the SFP's 49th birthday, people texted friends and circulated calls on HKIM requesting support for the arrestees (Ip, 2007). This built movement momentum by drawing in new participants. Similarly, a 49-hour hunger strike launched after the clock tower demolition on 16 December inspired numerous citizens to visit in solidarity. On 17 December, 200 people broke the police cordon outside Government House. The hunger strike ended with a collective chant modifying Mao Tse-tung's use of a classical proverb: *A single spark can start a prairie fire!*

After the SFP's demolition people used HKIM to continue movement-building dialogic processes, including discussion forums on urban planning and localised cultures. Local Action network's demographic base comprised people in their 20s and 30s affiliated with minor NGOs, the pro-democracy movement, and urban campaigns. The QP campaign would provide the next experimental field for agenda-setting spatial and cultural forms of protest, niches that 'conventional organisations and institutional politics' had left open (Ku, 2012, p. 13).

Reappropriating Queen's Pier: Temporary Affective Spaces

In 1985 activist philosopher and poet Hakim Bey (1985) published his concept of the Temporary Autonomous Zone (TAZ). Since then, this 'poetic fancy' inspired by historical pirates' 'intentional communities' has been imaginatively realised by activists worldwide. A TAZ is likened to 'an uprising which does not engage directly with the State, a guerrilla operation which liberates an area (of land, of time, of imagination) and then dissolves itself to re-form elsewhere/elsewhen, *before* the State can crush it' (Ibid., no page numbers). Moments of insurrection contain possibilities of freedom beyond those of rapidly co-opted or corrupted revolutions. Self-managed events like underground free raves, workshops, or occupations can be TAZs, leaving behind material traces of the collective doing and spirit (graffiti, built structures, gardens, media, etc). The short-term occupation of public spaces by the global Occupy movement is another example (Samman et al., 2012). During the piers campaign movement participants re-created QP as a space of social flows, creativity, protest, and celebration. Local Action aimed to 'strengthen people's attachment to QP by making it a "temporary autonomous zone" ... independent of the interference by the police', according to Ip (2007, p. 6).

As noted earlier, the QP had been a symbol of colonialism. When the last governor left, it became also a symbol of decolonisation, recolonisation, and continuing disenfranchisement. The pier and its surrounds reflected the life of the city, used for socialising, fishing, sailing, and demonstrations (Henderson, 2008). The large community of Filipina women working as live-in domestics in Hong Kong also congregated in Central's public parks and walkways, as they were 'unwelcome' in privately controlled spaces like shopping malls (DeWolf, 2007). By reappropriating the pier as a TAZ, Local Action expanded its symbolic meanings, staging events 'to be read and lived/performed simultaneously' (Ku, 2012, p. 14). People sleeping, cooking, and eating together on site became small infectious acts of civil disobedience. Network members combined symbolic, discursive, and spatial practices to investigate people's space in the 'dual sense of common folk and autonomous citizens', building a 'new form of political subjectivity rooted in civil society' (Ibid.).

Local Action networked with other groups such as Civic Frontier and Pan-Democrats, organisers of the 318 (18 March 2007) rally demanding universal suffrage. A manifesto-style press release referenced local examples of interrelated concerns: neoliberal privatisation of the common, environmental dangers, the destruction of small businesses and homes, unequal distribution of resources and community infrastructures, and right of abode for immigrant workers (Let's work together, 2007).

> Universal suffrage is a practice of democracy; we also need to practice direct participation in all kinds of planning issues that affect our life and living space directly. We want and we are practicing democracy now. (Ibid.)

This text evidences the piers movement's maturing political critique, which localised ideas from various sources including, it seems, anarchism, Autonomism, and critical geography. The movement supported the formation of a more pluralistic social subject whose members had complementary claims to ownership of the city. For example, piers activists worked with Filipino community organisations (DeWolf, 2007). The often 'invisible' Filipina and Indonesian migrant domestic workers had increasingly engaged in activist struggles, distinguishing events (including the 2005 anti-WTO protests) with cultural and artistic performances (Lai, 2010). Such pluralism and inclusiveness are critical elements of NSMs in general, suturing traditional divides.

After the pier officially closed on 26 April 2007 several Local Action members maintained a 24-hour guard on site, and three started a hunger strike on 28 July. The group convinced the Secretary for Development to attend discussion forums on 29 July, marking the first time a high-ranking official had met activists publicly (Poon, 2007). However, some tension existed among activists, with one complaining that patient court challenges to 'idiotic planning decisions' did not attract as much media attention as 'chaining yourself to a pole' (Ibid.). The 'emerging radicalism' challenged those civil society 'collaborators' who preferred cordial relations with officials (Ip, 2007, p. 12).

An online photographic essay by P. H. Yang (2007) dedicated to Local Action's 'brave and courageous' members begins with a portrait of SFP arrestee Ho Loy whom the press had dubbed 'Woman Warrior of Star Ferry'. MyRadio host Dr Lo Wing Lok interviews two hunger strikers, as a group sings 'We Shall Overcome'. A night shot captures a neon SOS sign on the eve of QP's closure. A protester dressed as the SFP clock tower looms behind a government representative. Three hunger strikers lie on mattresses surrounded by banners and flowers. A banner proclaims 'Protect our culture and history', drawing attention to the now-demolished clock tower. And finally, images of joyous defiant celebrations.

Analysing elements of some specific movements and projects, and taking a line of flight from Bey's TAZ, the concept of a 'temporary affective space' or TAS takes form (da Rimini, 2010). A TAS is constituted by the self-produced, self-managed socialised technologies and creative experiences experienced by a 'company of strangers' who gather as bodies and telepresences around an aim/campaign/issue. These spaces and the affective interactions they inspire interweave rage and hope, nurturing social experimentation in hacking the future, transmitting possibilities across local/translocal/global networks. Building alternative worlds is demanding work, so shared (tel)embodied experiences offer replenishment. Future research could determine how the digital builds upon or complements these processes, and how TAS (spatial, performative, creative) and telepresence (discursive, performative, critical) combine to produce subjectivity. In our loose affinity networks perhaps we become multitude through the transit from being strangers to familiars.

Many events during the piers campaigns, from the art students' performance works, to the occupations and hunger strikes, to celebrations, created temporary affective spaces. Certainly people engaged intellectually with urban planning issues, as evidenced by online discussions and articles. But more than this, movement participants' experiences at the piers created emotional and sensorial connections to the issues, to the threatened physical spaces, to the metropolis itself, and to one another. Arguably a new kind of sociality and subjectivity arose from this affective ground.

Antecedents, Enablers, and Agency

Evolving Modes of Dissent and Movement Building

Mass demonstrations have become a prominent feature of Hong Kong's political landscape, reinvigorating the pro-democracy movement and challenging citizens' purported political apathy and conservatism (Lee and Chan, 2008). Each year on the anniversary of the 1997 handover to China the 'seven-one' rallies argue for specific rights. In 2003 an unprecedented 500,000 people protested the HKSAR regime and national security legislation threatening press freedom (Ibid.). Protesters reported feeling that they made history, with the term 'July 1 effect' signifying the protest's potential effects on participants and society (Cheng, 2009; Lee and Chan, 2008). The government withdrew the legislation to prevent the most serious post-handover political crisis from triggering mainland struggles (Lai, 2007, p. 146). Subsequent rally attendances have fluctuated, with the 2012 event drawing an estimated 400,000 (England, 2012).

A second important annual event is the candlelight vigil in Victoria Park held on 4 June to commemorate the Tiananmen Square protests and associated massacre. In 1989 the PRC government had brutally repressed the popular, peaceful student-led movement which had spread to hundreds of Chinese cities. Just before the massacre in Beijing a million Hong Kong citizens had rallied in solidarity with mainland demonstrators, a 'vast majority . . . marching for the first time' ever (Cheng, 2007, p. 92). A panicked authoritarian mainland hierarchy inserted Article 23 into the Basic Law 'to prevent the SAR from becoming a base for subversion against the motherland', and instituted 'tougher measures' to counter pro-democracy forces (Wo-Lap Lam, 2007, p. 36). Today's Tiananmen-themed protests reflect an unwavering desire for democracy throughout greater China, with the 2012 vigil attracting an estimated 180,000 people (Chui and Boehler, 2012).

Both the seven-one and 4 June protests take conventional forms tolerable for HKSAR, if not for Beijing. They have a fixed route/location and duration, and the organising bodies (Civil Human Rights Front and Hong Kong Alliance in Support of Patriotic Democratic Movements in China, respectively) do not encourage civil disobedience. Furthermore, individualised expressions of opposition tend to be subsumed into the unified whole of the mass march and vigil. Despite these limitations the protests have energised the pro-democracy movement. Social scientist Chan Kin-man described the 2003 seven-one as a 'post-modern style of mobilisation' in its deployment of IT and Internet-supported media and social networks (quoted in So, 2011, p. 371). Nevertheless, these modes still differ from the more individualistic and socially generative oppositional forms which arose during the piers campaign, which has implications for the kind of democracy each movement strives for.

Hong Kong's Changing Mediascape

In the late 1990s the Hong Kong mediascape included 50 daily newspapers, over 600 periodicals, four television services, a public broadcaster, and two commercial radio stations. However, local radio was highly regulated, television remained tied to government, and print media had become increasingly monopolised (Ip, 2009). As the political spectrum further factionalised (pro-Hong Kong versus pro-China), MSM scope and courage further diminished (Lai, 2007, p. 11).

In contrast, the less controllable 'instrumental mobilisation forces' of BBSs, Internet radio, and web-based forums had helped galvanise attendance at protests in 2003 (Ip, 2009, p. 56). Paradoxically these oppositional channels had arisen from a localised crisis of informational capitalism, when many ICT companies closed during the 2002 dotcom collapse. Subsequently a newly constituted body of unemployed geeks established online forums and webcast platforms. Over half a million people participated in the 2004 'seven-one' protest, spurred by the proposed National Security Bill that would criminalise 'activities suspected of "sedition" and "subversion"' (Ibid., p. 57). Consequently, more independent media and approaches emerged, with online sites such as HKIM and People's Radio Hong Kong connecting activists and 'ordinary' Internet users (So, 2011, p. 376).

The Genesis of Hong Kong In-Media

Hong Kong In-Media was born in this period of mass mobilisations, flourishing online initiatives, and the intensification of neoliberalisation (Da Rimini, 2010, pp. 48–59). Existing alternative media, pro-democracy parties, and grassroots organisations existed in a segmented, factionalised field riven by ideological and historical tensions (Cheng, 2007, 2011). However, a 'new generation' of more radical political activists who dismissed pro-democracy political parties 'as part of the political establishment' was emerging (Cheng, 2007, pp. 24–5). Such activists sometimes operated 'outside existing channels' to advocate causes ranging from 'environmental protection, community-building, gay rights, labour grievances, [and] services for under-privileged groups' (So, 2011, p. 376). These mainly youth-led movements reflected increasing support for 'post-materialist values' (Ngok, 2011, p. 707).

Democratic media activism is 'less likely to constitute a movement in itself than a nexus between movements' (Hackett and Carroll, 2008, p. 4). It is something 'sticky' whose substantive content, collective means of production, and social relationships draws people towards it, forming new networks. Desiring a new space of politics, in 2004 some local intellectuals, students, and activists brainstormed how they could advance a citizens' movement. They drew inspiration from Asian practices including South Korean citizen journalism, Taiwanese blog culture, and Malaysian social service practices (Ip and Lam, 2009). Because this nascent media activism project identified itself as a 'very localised process' engaging with the democratisation movement, Hong Kong–China relations, and press freedom, it reflected some of the annual protests' concerns (Lam, 2006a). However, it also explicitly sought to transform locals' 'habits and interests' into 'something more radical' (Lam quoted in Hadl, 2007).

The HKIM semi-open citizen journalism was launched in October 2004. It aimed to 'facilitate the development of a participatory democratic society' in Hong Kong by engaging with grassroots organisations, intellectuals, activists, public, and 'border-crossing perspectives', to build a 'critical atmosphere for individual and collective social praxis' (Lam, undated). The project refused to adopt a clear ideological stance, which resulted in a 'friendly split' with some NGOs. By 2005 around 4,000 people were visiting HKIM, comparable to Hong Kong's small and medium-sized newspaper readership (Ip, 2006). A dozen people shared the editorial and administrative workload, with 100 regular contributors, hundreds of periodic columnists, and 3,000 registered users producing content and a sense of community.

The Anti-WTO Protests of 2005 and HKIM's Evolution of 'Action Media'

In mid-December 2005 Hong Kong hosted the Sixth Ministerial Conference of the World Trade Organization (WTO). The associated anti-WTO protests attracted numerous Asian social movement groups and regional journalists (Sohi, 2006). Immediately prior to the protests HKIM organised the New Media and Social Transformation conference for local and regional media groups.

Neo-Marxist sociologist John Holloway describes activism as a 'community of doing, a collective of doers, a flow of doing through time and space' (2005, p. 26). The HKIM conference spatialised alternative networks and created 'social flows', experimenting with participatory democracy through cooperative communicative labour. HKIM members challenged the assertions, hierarchies, and enclosures perpetuated by the WTO with knowledge, porous networks, and the power of the common. They researched regional trade treaties, organised a petition against police brutality, networked with regional affiliates, translated articles for an international portal, and published articles.

The accumulated anti-WTO events built upon the changing local resistance culture. By consolidating solidarity among Asian social movements they advanced a 'sense of "joint struggle"', as a 'shift in geopolitical-economy of neoliberalism' was already under way (Sohi, 2006, pp. 357–8). Hong Kong activists reported being deeply affected by their experiences, and by protesters' (especially the 1,500+ Korean contingent's) determination (James, 2006). An anti-WTO evaluation session highlighted the need to connect 'inter-locals and the international-local movement' via forms of cultural production whereby people could develop mutual 'emotional ties, sympathy and appreciation' (Lam, 2006b).

The praxis of 'action media' grew out of this ground. Action media is a 'representation and materialisation circle, reconfiguring and redefining the Real', explains a HKIM founding member, Oiwan Lam (undated). The concept is loosely defined as 'movement action' combined with 'media practice' (Lam, 2006a). Crucially, this subjective, experiential form of activism requires the media activist to 'jump into the story of his/her own construction', becoming part of the unfolding narrative and its framing (Lam, 2007a, p. 64). When media activists enter the fray, they move beyond the discursive realm into the spatial domain, creating possibilities for new social subjects. The praxis recalls the still influential 'Tactical Media' praxis:

> when the cheap >do it yourself< media, made possible by the revolution in consumer electronics and expanded forms of distribution (from public access cable to the internet) are exploited by groups and individuals who feel aggrieved by or excluded from the wider culture. Tactical media do not just report events, as they are never impartial they always participate and it is this that more than anything separates them from mainstream media. (Lovink and Garcia quoted in Apprich, 2013)

Informational Capitalism, Metropolis, and Multitude

We can examine the form of political agency the piers movement generated through the lens of Autonomist theory. It argues that as industrial and agricultural processes become increasingly informationalised, informational capitalism becomes the dominant productive paradigm. The 'historical tendency' of informationalism—expressed through new modes of ordering framed variously as 'cognitive capitalism' or 'biocapitalism' (see Marazzi, 2011, pp. 57,. 49)—extends beyond industrialism's spatialised production sites (factory, office, school) into the whole of life. In this 'social factory' individuals' linguistic, creative, cognitive, and affective capacities are continuously exploited, with the aim to '*fuse* work and worker, to *put to work the entire lives* of workers' (Marazzi, 2008, p. 50, emphasis in original).

Today's 'precarious' workers must enact the knowledge, social connections, and professional networks they create outside of official working hours. These expectations now extend outwards from infocapitalism's heartlands to workers of the Global South and Periphery (see So, 2011, pp. 366–7 on Hong Kong's 'new poor'; Cheng, 2011, p. 53 on Hong Kong's under-remunerated graduates; and Ngok, 2011, pp. 699–700 on Hong Kong's 'transformation into a post-industrial economy'). However, such pervasive exploitation holds emancipatory keys, as people can draw upon the same cognitive capacities, and tools of information production and distribution, to build experimental alternatives to capitalism (Virno, 2004).

The metropolis is the exemplary site of social struggle in the post-industrial era, just as the factory was in the industrial era (Hardt and Negri, 2009, pp. 249–60). This locus of serendipitous encounters and cooperative labour gives rise to a new political subject, a differentiated multiplicity of individuals Autonomists name the 'multitude' (Hardt and Negri, 2004). Although the multitude is inherently ephemeral it (re)coalesces in crisis, as the post Global Financial Crisis anti-austerity riots and occupations worldwide demonstrated. This 'field of the common' is simultaneously a 'field of conflict' whose ability to tolerate internal differences and contradictions is part of its 'beauty' (Hardt quoted in Hawthorne, 2011).

Hong Kong's piers movement produced a new social subject. Movement participants believed that everyone had the right to shape the metropolis and protect localised culture (Ngok, 2011; So, 2011). This pluralistic subject could withstand different political positions (liberalism, anarchism, etc.), class/ethnic divides (e.g. Hong Kong citizens, migrant domestic workers), and a programme open to all. Participants' cooperative labour and affinity networks suggest that in some sense they were becoming multitude, experimentally redeploying the skills and aptitudes informational capitalism demands. Many became involved because they had been moved by others' courage and imagination in the face of localised neoliberal restructuring and cultural/spatial dispossession, exacerbated by continuing disenfranchisement. Autonomist theory links the multitude to anti-capitalism and anti-globalisation drivers, but the Hong Kong experience suggests more complexity, specificity, and differentiation.

Like NSMs elsewhere, the piers movement was constituted by 'new kinds of networks and flows of communication, action, and experience', rather than by fixed ideologies and programmes, and 'embodied intersubjectivity' was as important as 'functional imperatives' (McDonald, 2006, pp. 63–4). Some locals regarded it as a 'postmodernist' movement, 'spontaneous, loosely organised, with diversified participants and non-materialist objectives, mobilised via information technology or mass media' (Ngok, 2011, p. 707). But like the Occupy movement or the Anonymous network, a horizontal, non-ideologically driven project open to spontaneity can disturb both antagonists and allies (Knappenberger, 2012). Hence, some moderate groups would criticise the piers activists as being 'unorganised mobs without strategies' (Ip, 2007, p. 8).

Urban development creates its own internal crises. Despite the QP's demolition in February 2008 the preservation campaign achieved 'miracle' status because of the protesters' tenacity. The reconstructed tourist-oriented Disneyesque pier simulated 'past traditions and childhood fantasies' (Ku, 2012, p. 10). The complex boasted an exclusive restaurant, but ferry fares increased and some routes were permanently closed. Consequently, ferry patronage dropped by 18% with commuters preferring buses and rail, worsening air pollution (DeWolf, 2011). The Star Ferry Company Limited pinned its hopes on shop rentals, advertising revenue, more tourism infrastructure, and government subsidies (Ibid.). In 2012 the company again sought state assistance and permission for more fare increases in 2013, predicting a major increase in its operating deficit otherwise (Mok, 2012).

Although the enduring agency of the new social actors emerging from the movement is beyond this article's scope, evidence exists that the movement has significantly influenced subsequent struggles. To give just one example, the campaign against the express rail link (XRL) in

2009–2010 used symbolic and spatial actions to reject the 'gospel of developmentalism' and challenge the regime's legitimacy, again arousing much public sympathy (Ngok, 2011, pp. 708–10).

Conclusion

Although obvious comparisons with the global Occupy movement exist, especially in the highly visible occupation of iconic public spaces and the recoding of these sites by a suite of expressive cultural practices, some important differences remain. Firstly, notwithstanding differentiated localised concerns, the Occupy phenomenon is characterised by its very generalised aims and ideological positions (anti-capitalism, anti-globalisation, anti-neoliberalism, ending of student debt, etc.). In contrast, the piers movement had a specific short-term goal: to stop the demolition of the SFP and QP. Its longer-term aim was to foster participatory democracy, and continued popular involvement in urban development struggles citywide would offer a path towards this. Secondly, Occupy in many cities has failed to gain popular traction, and consequently it has been easier for government and MSM to marginalise and dismiss. The piers movement, however, gained immense support from the general public, who identified with the loss of familiar ways of social and cultural life that renewal projects were creating throughout the city. MSM eventually used the activists' reframing of the narrative in their own accounts, and the government made cursory (or cosmetic) efforts to broaden input into planning processes. Thirdly, whereas Occupy events and actions often required formal processes of reaching consensus (affinity groups, general assemblies, etc.), the piers movement encouraged spontaneous individualised responses to many arising situations, with self-reflexivity happening later, usually online. Finally, in most instances Occupy's ongoing legacy in the various places that hosted occupations is hard to quantify. In comparison, the piers movement was the impetus for a new social movement in Hong Kong, recuperating direct action practices from the 1950s and 1960s, and combining them with contemporary nomadic forms of spatial and symbolic politics, where occupation is only one tactic among many.

Questions of democracy were at the heart of the piers movement, but what distinguished this movement from the annual protests, the reinvigorated pro-democracy movement, and organised forms of civic activism was its commitment to a more radical form of participatory democracy. This commitment was realised in the movement's organisational form (horizontal, networked) and its exploration of how people could use this form to create common visions and build consensus for action. The metropolis is as much an imaginary construct as it is a material one. Struggles over the city are about everyday life and living history. Hence participants could reappropriate physical spaces by occupying them, and remake them as microcosms of a new metropolis which refused to subsume social, cultural, and affective dimensions to neoliberal economics, projecting a city that required shared egalitarian forms of stewardship. These occupations created not only 'temporary autonomous zones' but, significantly, 'temporary affective spaces' whose resonance would last long after destruction of the piers and their surrounds.

Acknowledgements

The author thanks the three anonymous peer reviewers whose insightful critique helped me to produce a more comprehensive analysis of the subject; the author also thanks Glenn Mason for editorial assistance.

References

Apprich, C. (2013) Remaking media practices—from tactical media to post-media, *Mute*, 14 February, http://www.metamute.org/editorial/lab/remaking-media-practices-%E2%80%93-tactical-media-to-post-media.

Bankwatch Network (2012) *Overpriced and Underwritten: The Hidden Costs of Public-Private Partnerships*, http://bankwatch.org/public-private-partnerships/resources.

Bey, H. (1985) *T. A. Z.: The Temporary Autonomous Zone, Ontological Anarchy, Poetic Terrorism*, Autonomedia, http://www.hermetic.com/bey/taz_cont.html.

Cheng, J. Y. (2007) The pro-democracy movement: A lost decade? *China Perspectives*, (70), pp. 14–26.

Cheng, J. Y. (2009) The Tiananmen incident and the pro-democracy movement in Hong Kong, *China Perspectives*, (78), pp. 91–100.

Cheng, J. Y. (2011) Challenge to the pro-democracy movement in Hong Kong, *China Perspectives*, (2), pp. 44–60.

Chui, C. & Boehler, P. (2012) Tiananmen protesters gather in Hong Kong in remembrance, *Bloomberg News*, 5 June, http://www.bloomberg.com/news/2012-06-04/tiananmen-security-normal-as-anniversary-held-amid-party-turmoil.html.

Chung, C. Y. & Ngai, P. (2007) Neoliberalization and privatization in Hong Kong after the 1997 financial crisis, *China Review*, 7(2), pp. 65–92.

da Rimini, F. (2010) Socialised technologies, cultural activism and the production of agency, Ph.D. thesis, University of Technology, Sydney.

DeWolf, C. (2007) *Losing More Than Just a Clock Tower*, http://www.urbanphoto.net/blog/2007/10/30/losing-more-than-just-a-clock-tower.

DeWolf, C. (2009) *An Alternative Vision*, http://jmsc.asia/hkindesign/?p=35.

DeWolf, C. (2011) The Star Ferry's Long Farewell, http://www.urbanphoto.net/blog/2011/03/31/the-star-ferrys-long-farewell.

England, V. (2012) Hundreds of thousands protest as Hu Jintao visits Hong Kong, *The Guardian*, 1 July, http://www.guardian.co.uk/world/2012/jul/01/protest-hu-jintao-hong-kong.

Hackett, R. A. & Carroll, W. K. (2008) Building our media: Community broadcasting, social movements and media democratization, *Global Media Journal—Australian Edition*, 1(1), pp. 1–6.

Hadl, G. (2007) In-Media, Indymedia and Interlocals-A Dialogue, *Interlocals*, 2 March, http://interlocals.net/?q=node/272.

Hardt, M. & Negri, A. (2004) *Multitude: War and Democracy in the Age of Empire* (New York: Penguin Books).

Hardt, M. & Negri, A. (2009) *Commonwealth* (Cambridge, MA: Belknap).

Harvey, D. (2005) *A Brief History of Neoliberalism* (Oxford: Oxford University Press).

Hawthorne, N. (2011) Another Hardt interview, *What in the hell . . . ?* [blog], 26 November, http://crashcourse666.wordpress.com/2011/11/26/another-hardt-interview.

Henderson, J. C. (2008) Conserving Hong Kong's heritage: The case of Queen's Pier, *International Journal of Heritage Studies*, 14(6), pp. 540–554.

Hill, R. C., Park, B.-G. & Saito, A. (2011) Introduction: Locating neoliberalism in East Asia, in B.-G. Park, R. C. Hill & A. Saito (eds) *Locating Neoliberalism in East Asia: Neoliberalizing Spaces in Developmental States* (London: Wiley-Blackwell), pp. 1–26.

Holloway, J. (2005) *Change the World Without Taking Power*, 2nd ed. (London and Ann Arbor, MI: Pluto Press).

Hong Kong Harbourfront Commission (2010) *Public-private Partnership and Design Concept and Development Approach for Site 4 in the New Central Harbourfront*, (Hong Kong).

Ip, I.-C. (2006) *What Is The Net?*, http://www.zonaeuropa.com/20061211_1.htm.

Ip, I.-C. (2007) Beyond civil society: A case study of media activism and historical preservation movement in Hong Kong, paper presented to the OURMedia—NUESTROSMedios VI International Conference, Sydney, Australia, 9–13 April 2007.

Ip, I.-C. (2009) Hong Kong: The rise of a new political force, in O.-W. Lam & I.-C. Ip (eds) *Info-Rhizome: Report on Independent Media in the Chinese-Speaking World (2008/09)* (Hong Kong: Hong Kong In-Media), pp. 48–68.

Ip, I.-C. & Lam, O. (2009) Editorial note: Grassroots power/Info-rhizome, in O.-W. Lam & I.-C. Ip (eds) *Report on Independent Media in the Chinese-Speaking World (2008/09)* (Hong Kong: Hong Kong In-Media), pp. 1–4.

James, D. (2006) The meaning of Hong Kong WTO, *Common Dreams*, 14 January, http://www.commondreams.org/views06/0114-29.htm.

Knappenberger, B. (2012) *We Are Legion: The Story of the Hacktivists* (Venice, CA: Luminant Media).

Ku, A. S.-m. (2009) Contradictions in the development of citizenship in Hong Kong: Governance without democracy, *Asian Survey*, 49(3), pp. 505–527.

Ku, A. S.-m. (2012) Remaking places and fashioning an opposition discourse: Struggle over the Star Ferry pier and the Queen's pier in Hong Kong, *Environment and Planning D-Society & Space*, 30(1), pp. 5–22.
Lai, C. P. (2007) *Media in Hong Kong: Press Freedom and Political Change, 1967–2005* (New York: Routledge).
Lai, M.-y. (2010) Dancing to different tunes: Performance and activism among migrant domestic workers in Hong Kong, *Women's Studies International Forum*, 33(5), pp. 501–511.
Lam, O. (2006a) Struggles against neoliberal globalization and independent media. Hong Kong, http://ahoi.pbwiki.com/mediastruggle.
Lam, O. (2006b) Connected without connection: beyond the cliches of technology breakthrough and networking. Hong Kong, http://ahoi.pbworks.com/internetmedia.
Lam, O. (2007a) What is that star? Media cultural action in the claiming of space, in F. da Rimini (ed.) *A Handbook for Coding Cultures* (Sydney: d/Lux Media Arts & Campbelltown City Council), pp. 58–66.
Lam, O. (2007b) The Queen's Pier preservation campaign—D-day, *Interlocals*, http://interlocals.net/?q=node/109.
Lam, O. (undated), Introduction to Hong Kong In-Media. Hong Kong, http://ahoi.pbworks.com/IntroInMediaHK.
Lam, W.-M. (2004) *Understanding the Political Culture of Hong Kong: The Paradox of Activism and Depoliticization* (Armonk, NY: M. E. Sharpe).
Lam, W.-M. (2005) Depoliticization, citizenship, and the politics of community in Hong Kong, *Citizenship Studies*, 9(3), pp. 309–322.
Law, L. (2002) Defying disappearance: Cosmopolitan public spaces in Hong Kong, *Urban Studies*, 39(9), pp. 1625–45.
Lee Chi Leung (translator) (2007) FAQ on Queen's Pier campaign, *Interlocals*, 2 July, http://interlocals.net/?q=node/117.
Lee, F. L. F. & Chan, J. M. (2008) Making sense of participation: The political culture of pro-democracy demonstrators in Hong Kong, *The China Quarterly*, 193, pp. 84–101.
Lees, L., Slater, T. & Wyly, E. (2008) *Gentrification* (New York: Routledge).
Let's work together (2007) Let's work together: People's planning for our Home and our Land—318 Rally (Destination at Queen Pier) 2007, http://beyondthestars.wordpress.com/2007/03/15.
Lung, D. (2012) Built heritage in transition: A critique of Hong Kong's conservation movement and the Antiquities and Monuments Ordinance, *Hong Kong Law Journal*, 42(121), pp. 121–142.
Marazzi, C. (2008) *Capital and Language: From the New Economy to the War Economy* (Los Angeles: Semiotext(e)).
Marazzi, C. (2011) *The Violence of Financial Capitalism* (Los Angeles: Semiotext(e)).
Mathews, G., Ribeiro, G. L. & Vega, C. A. (eds) (2012) *Globalization from Below: The World's Other Economy* (London: Routledge).
McDonald, K. (2006) *Global Movements: Action and Culture* (Malden, MA: Blackwell).
Mok, D. (2012) Star Ferry seeks fare rises or subsidy, *South China Morning Post*, 14 August, http://www.scmp.com/article/974035/star-ferry-seeks-fare-rises-or-subsidy.
Ng, M. K., Tang, W. S., Lee, J. & Leung, D. (2010) Spatial practice, conceived space and lived space: Hong Kong's 'Piers saga' through the Lefebvrian lens, *Planning Perspectives*, 25(4), pp. 411–431.
Ngok, M. (2011) Value changes and legitimacy crisis in post-industrial Hong Kong, *Asian Survey*, 51(4), pp. 683–712.
Park, B.-G., Hill, R. C. & Saito, A. (eds) (2011) Introduction: Locating neoliberalism in East Asia, in *Locating Neoliberalism in East Asia: Neoliberalizing Spaces in Developmental States* (London: Wiley-Blackwell).
Poon, A. (2007) Hong Kong turns activist, *Asia Sentinel*, 2 August, http://www.asiasentinel.com/index.php?option=com_content&task=view&id=608&Itemid=173.
Rodriguez, C. (2001) *Fissures in the Mediascape: An International Study of Citizens' Media* (Cresskill, NJ: Hampton Press).
Samman, A., Coombs, N. & van Houwelingen, P. (eds) (2012) *Journal of Critical Globalisation Studies*, Issue 5 'Imperialism, Finance, #Occupy', http://www.criticalglobalisation.com/issue5/JCGS-ISSUE-5.pdf
Scott, I. (1989) *Political Change and the Crisis of Legitimacy in Hong Kong* (Honolulu: University of Hawaii Press).
Smith, N. (1986) Gentrification, the frontier, and the restructuring of urban space, in N. Smith & P. Williams (eds) *Gentrification of the City* (Boston: Allen & Unwin), pp. 15–34.
So, A. Y. (2011) The development of post-modernist social movements in the Hong Kong Special Administrative Region, in J. Broadbent & V. Brockman (eds) *East Asian Social Movements: Power, Protest, and Change in a Dynamic Region* (New York: Springer), pp. 365–78.
Sohi, J. (2006) Anti-WTO movement in Hong Kong: The 'battle of Hong Kong' and implications for Asian social movements, *Inter-Asia Cultural Studies*, 7(2), pp. 353–358.
Tang, W.-S., Lee, J. W. Y. & Ng, M. K. (2012) Public engagement as a tool of hegemony: The case of designing the new central harbourfront in Hong Kong, *Critical Sociology*, 38(1), pp. 89–106.

Virno, P. (2004) *A Grammar of the Multitude: For an Analysis of Contemporary Forms of Life* (Los Angeles and New York: Semiotext(e)).
Wo-Lap Lam, W. (2007) Beijing's policy towards Hong Kong and the prospects for democratisation in the SAR, *China Perspectives*, (70), pp. 34–39.

Francesca da Rimini is an established and prolific Internet artist, engaged in numerous collaborations. She is a post-doctoral researcher at the Cosmopolitan Civil Societies Research Centre, University of Technology Sydney and co-author of *Disorder and the Disinformation Society: The Social Dynamics of Networks and Software* (Routledge, 2013).

Religious Globalisms in the Post-Secular Age

ERIN K. WILSON* & MANFRED B. STEGER**

*University of Groningen, The Netherlands
**University of Hawai'i Manoa, USA and RMIT University, Melbourne, Australia

ABSTRACT *This article explores the interconnections between mounting global crises and the emergence of the post-secular. Specifically, the article argues that the post-secular is both a description of and a response to shifting global realities in the twenty-first century. It describes the crisis of secular rationalism, brought about in many ways by an overemphasis on economic rationalism and neoliberalism (Steger et al., 2013). Yet, as noted by Jürgen Habermas (2006, 2008), Mariano Barbato (2010), and Justin Beaumont and Paul Cloke (2012), the post-secular offers a way of resisting, reforming, and potentially revolutionizing these dominant secular, rationalist, neoliberal frameworks that presently shape global politics and society. We suggest, however, that the influence of globalization has been undertheorized in these previous studies. In particular we argue that the intersection between the post-secular and emerging global political ideologies of market and justice globalisms is having a profound impact on religious movements, generating 'religious globalisms' that offer alternative responses to global crises around finance, poverty, and climate.*

During the same 30-year period that marked the ascendancy of neoliberal economics and information and communication technology, religion has experienced a dramatic resurgence in the global public sphere. The 'return of religion' and the concurrent 'crisis of secularism' (Calhoun et al., 2011; Petito and Hatzopoulos, 2003) have defied the expectations of many scholars and policymakers. Still steeped in the modernist 'secularization of politics' thesis, these commentators cast religion as a largely spent force, seemingly spiraling toward its inevitable demise as secular rationalism was gaining supremacy around the world (Berger, 1967; Fox, 2001, pp. 54–5; Marx and Engels, 1992 [1848], p. 24; Weber, 1918, pp. 139, 142–3). Both traditional and new forms of religion, however, have refused to heed such sweeping pronouncements of their impending death. Instead, they have thrived in the global political landscape of the twenty-first century while, paradoxically, secularism has encountered a serious problem of political legitimization (Berger, 1999; Casanova, 1994; Hurd, 2008; Mavelli, 2012a; Philpott, 2002; Wilson, 2012).

How can we explain that religion's growing political influence across the globe has been *helped* by globalization, democratization, international law, and technology—forces that were supposed to secure the ultimate victory of rationalism and secularism? While several theories have been put forward in response to this question, two incisive theses have appeared in a recent study on the subject. Its authors suggest, firstly, that the dramatic and worldwide increase in the political influence of religion occurring in the last few decades has been driven by religious people's desire for freedom for their communities to assemble and publicly profess their faiths and programs. In other words, the resurgent religions have benefited from, rather than been hindered by, globalization and other forces of the modern, secular world. The authors' second thesis suggests that various forms of 'political theology'—sets of ideas that religious communities hold about political authority and justice—have been *strengthened* as a result of the shifting relationship between the spheres of politics and religion fueled by the globalization of secularism (Toft et al., pp. 9–10).

While sharing these scholars' sensitivity to the impact of globalization on religion's political comeback, we suggest that understanding the significance of this phenomenon requires that we move beyond generalizations and explore, precisely, what sort of globalization dynamics facilitate what kind of religious resurgences. While helpful in general terms, Toft, Philpott, and Shah's identification of 'globalization' as driving our current transition into a post-secular era remains far too broad to help us understand which manifestations of globalization may contribute to the perceived resurgence of 'political theology' and the emerging troubles of secularism (Bretherton, 2010; Habermas, 2006; Mendieta and Vanantwerpen, 2011; Steger, 2008; Wilson, 2012).

In this article, we argue that 'globalization'—understood as neoliberal economic globalization—is contributing in many ways to an increasing questioning of secular rationalism as the main arbiter of acceptable knowledge in contemporary global politics. We further suggest that the post-secular is producing multiple religious globalisms—religiously infused political ideologies that inspire the faithful to pursue a particular vision for society—that operate as both supporters of and loci of resistance to dominant forms of neoliberal globalization. We identify three such religious globalisms—neoliberal religious globalisms, religious justice globalisms and neotraditional religious globalisms—though this list is by no means exhaustive.

The concept of the post-secular is still fluid, with multiple debates about its meaning and application (Mavelli and Petito, 2012). Yet notions of 'resistance' and 'alternatives' feature prominently in efforts to define and describe this emerging phenomenon. The post-secular challenges the dominance of secularism, particularly militant forms of secularism that police the borders of the public sphere and limit expressions of religious argumentation and belief from entering therein. Contrary to the assumptions of such militant secularism, which argues that religion is irrational and causes only violence and chaos when permitted in the public sphere, the post-secular argues that religion can also be an important source of meaning and identity, one that can open up alternative ways of being in and responding to the world, that can positively contribute to the pursuit of justice and emancipation for humanity (Barbato, 2010; Beaumont and Cloke, 2012; Habermas, 2006; Mavelli and Petito, 2012).

CRISIS, MOVEMENT, MANAGEMENT: GLOBALISING DYNAMICS

Resisting such dogmatic rejections of religion as irrational and prone to wreak chaos and violence on the public sphere (Dombrowski, 2001, p. 4; Rorty, 2003), we are nonetheless conscious that religion manifests at the global level in a variety of ways, positive and negative, constructive and destructive. We share with other observers the 'post-secular' conviction that the religious beliefs of billions of people constitute an important source of meaning and identity that routinely traverse the conventional secular–sacred divide (Cavanaugh, 2009; Eberle, 2002, p. 304; Strenski, 2010). Let us be clear we are not suggesting a return to arrangements where religion dominated the public sphere or the state-sponsored privileging of specific religious practices in the public sphere. Nonetheless, we point to the possibility that religion can open up alternative ways of being in and responding to the world that can positively contribute to emancipatory forms of resistance to oppressive and discriminatory practices (Barbato, 2010; Beaumont and Cloke, 2012), while remaining critical of religion's own tendencies to domination and exclusion.

The majority of academic literature dedicated to identifying post-secular forms of resistance has focused on the local, the individual and abstract-theoretical frameworks. Beaumont and Cloke (2012), for example, have examined the ways in which local faith-based organizations in urban contexts challenge the processes and values associated with neoliberal policies of deregulation, privatization, and liberalization that contribute to poverty and marginalization. Mariano Barbato (2010) has highlighted the language of the pilgrim as an important source of resistance for individuals in addressing the materialistic urges of late capitalism, while Luca Mavelli (2012b) has emphasized the individual body as an important site of post-secular resistance in revolutionary social contexts such as the Arab Spring. Habermas's work on the subject (2006, 2008) epitomizes the abstract-theoretical conceptualization of the post-secular as a form of resistance to dominant forms of secular rationalism that can work to exclude other useful contributions to public debate, in particular religion. Within international relations, post-secular analysis has been limited by the discipline's traditional focus on the nation-state, so far failing to adequately take into account the multi-tiered structures of authority and governance in contemporary global politics (Camilleri, 2012, pp. 1030–1, 1033).

Given the centrality of processes of globalization in the emergence of the post-secular as a form of resistance (Barbato, 2010; Beaumont and Cloke, 2012), it seems imperative to also consider how post-secular resistance and engagement is manifesting at the global level. This is the task we undertake in this article, thereby also addressing Camilleri's (2012) recent call for post-secular theorizing that goes beyond the nation-state. We examine how the post-secular both informs and takes shape as global projects of political practice and resistance—especially at the ideological level in the form of what we call 'religious globalisms' (Steger, 2009).

We begin by outlining the key features of the neoliberal and secular rationalist crises relevant for our analysis. We then explore the interconnections between globalization, resistance, and the emergence of the post-secular. In the main section of this article, we examine how the post-secular at the global level is constituted and enacted in terms of three distinct types of religious globalisms. We characterize two of these variants as forms of post-secular global resistance that contest the dominance of neoliberal market globalism (and its religious variant) by explicitly resorting to religious argumentation. Finding conceptual variations both within and between each of these belief systems, we nonetheless argue that 'religious globalisms' fall into a category that differs from the two previously identified sub-families of 'globalisms,' namely 'market globalism' and 'justice globalism'.

Neoliberalism, Secularism, and Global Crisis

In the last few years, 'crisis' has become a ubiquitous signifier, often appearing in tandem with the familiar buzzword 'globalization'. Across political, social, economic, and cultural dimensions, globalizing forces, such as economic and political integration, population flows and technological advances both generate and respond to new 'global problems' including financial volatility, climate change, increasing food scarcity, pandemics such as AIDS and SARS, widening disparities in wealth and wellbeing, increasing migratory pressures, manifold cultural and religious conflicts, and transnational terrorism (Gills, 2010; Houtart, 2010).

Despite a lack of consensus about the best solutions to contemporary global problems, there is emerging agreement about their causes. Political leaders and activists across a wide center-to-left spectrum have specifically identified neoliberal economic policies that promote rampant growth at the expense of the environment, human dignity, and social cohesion as a key factor contributing to global crises. Economists point to the inherent instability in neoliberalism (Crotty, 2009; Patomäki, 2009), even those who were once faithful disciples of market globalism (Soros, 2008; Wolf, 2009). Advocates for action on climate change stress that the earth's finite resources cannot support a global economic system and ideology that is geared around infinite consumption and growth.[1] Recent global food crises have been clearly linked to rising speculative trade in food staples, such as rice, wheat, and maize (Chand, 2008; Schutter, 2010). Thus, pundits are increasingly questioning neoliberalism's utility as a policy framework.

The perceived failure of neoliberalism has contributed to a reconsideration of secular rationalism's dominance as the main arbiter of acceptable public reasoning. After all, as critics from the global justice movement (GJM) have emphasized, neoliberalism operates according to strict rationalist logic, with little consideration of moral or ethical issues (George, 2001; Grassroots Global Justice, 2009; Steger, 2009; World Council of Churches, 2009). The neoliberal emphasis on market forces—the economistic core of the larger ideological constellation we call 'market globalism'—ignores a wealth of alternative sources of meaning and values that constitute important components of the human experience.

As recent critiques have pointed out, much the same applies to secular rationalism (Bleiker, 2009; Habermas, 2006; Wilson, 2012). For too long, public and academic discourses, particularly within Western contexts, have been governed by strict secular rationalist logic. This prevailing dynamic has excluded not only religious arguments and ideas from consideration in public debate (Eberle, 2002; Rorty, 2003), but also emotions and aesthetics by deeming these too 'subjective' (Bleiker, 2009). The legitimate framework for public debate consisted of secular-rational arguments judged acceptable to a majority of citizens (Dombrowski, 2001; Rawls, 1999).

However, as Christopher Eberle (2002, pp. 313–14) has observed, the assumptions surrounding the acceptability of secular grounds over religious grounds made especially by liberal scholars are misleading (see e.g. Rawls, 1999; Rorty, 2003). Eberle argues that the term '"secular" connotes "natural" and "universal", whereas "religious" connotes "supernatural" and "particular"' (2002, p. 313). However, he goes on to note that 'secular' justifications for particular beliefs, values, and principles are not universal and natural, but are in many cases culturally specific. While most liberal scholars argue that secular grounds are the only acceptable justifications because they are rational and universal, Eberle (Ibid., p. 314) points out that they are seen to be rational and universal precisely because they are made within a particular cultural setting that establishes secular thought as rational, universal, and acceptable. As he puts it, 'Secular grounds, then, are cultural grounds, grounds we find plausible, in large part, because we have been socialized into one culture and not another' (Ibid.).

Globalization—the proliferation of connectivity across world-time and world space—constitutes a central dimension of this crisis of secular rationalism, for it undermines such specific cultural criteria. Increased migration flows often generate heterogeneous and hybrid populations with different (and sometimes contradictory) value and knowledge systems. Growing global interconnections mean that people who lead vastly different lives according to vastly different worldviews must work together to generate acceptable approaches to dealing with common problems and pursuing the common good. Notions of the common good are also increasingly conceived and articulated at the global level in cosmopolitan terms, not just at the level of the national (Erskine, 2002). As Eberle (2002, p. 316) suggests, in such diverse contexts, there arise serious problems with valuing the secular over the religious that may lead to biases, tension, and conflict in political decision-making. Additional critiques of the dominance of secular rationalism have emerged in recent years from scholars interested in the aesthetic (Bleiker, 2009), alternative sources of knowledge (Hulme, 2009, 2010), not to mention scholars of religion in public life (Arkoun, 2003; Bretherton, 2010; Habermas, 2006, 2008; Wilson, 2012). These authors note how 'the primacy of logos over mythos' has led to a marginalization of 'religion's existential, symbolic and prophetic dimensions' within the academic study of religion (Arkoun, 2003 cited in Kassab, 2009, p. 175). Moreover, they object to the privileging of 'reason as the faculty of true knowledge, differentiated from knowledge based on the representations of the imagination' (Arkoun, 2003, p. 31).

The Post-Secular as Description and Response to Global Crises

In this context, we suggest that the post-secular may best be understood as both a description of and a response to these global epistemological and ontological problems. It defines an emerging social condition where neither religious belief nor secular rationalism rules as the dominant *mentalité* of our time. Consider, for example, Charles Taylor's claims regarding the conditions of a secular age. He argues that engaging with religion or having a belief system become one option amongst many. Further, he suggests '[T]he presumption of unbelief has become dominant in more and more . . . milieux; and has achieved hegemony in certain crucial ones, in the academic and intellectual life, for instance; whence it can more easily extend itself to others' (Taylor, 2007, p. 13). For Taylor, then, the chief characteristic of the secular age is where non-belief becomes the default option.

We suggest that in a post-secular age, non-belief is no longer the default position and is itself considered one option amongst many others. Religion is rehabilitated into the public sphere, becoming a legitimate option for challenging dominant political ideological paradigms. This can be seen particularly in the role of faith-based organizations, who are increasingly filling the gaps left by the neoliberalization of the state and campaigning for broader change on issues such as immigration policy and climate change (Beaumont and Cloke, 2012; WCC, 2005; Wilson, 2011). Let us be clear we are not suggesting that belief becomes the default option once again. Rather, in a post-secular age, the default option is either one of pluralism, where both belief and non-belief coexist, sometimes peacefully, sometimes violently, or where, in fact, there is no default option on this matter at all. To put it differently, the post-secular does not represent the end of modernity, nor of the Enlightenment project, but rather 'a continuation of the enlightenment by another means, the production of a New Enlightenment, one that is enlightened about the limits of the old one' (Caputo, 2001, pp. 60–1, cited in Camilleri, 2012, p. 1026).

As a response to the contemporary global situation, we suggest the paradigm of post-secularism represents an attempt to make sense of the continuing and in some cases revived presence of religion in secular societies. The rise of the religious right in the United States as well as the increasing importance of migrant religions in European countries such as the Netherlands (Mepschen et al., 2010; Uitermark and Gielen, 2010) are but two examples of the importance of public religions in the twenty-first century. In this context of ongoing public religious influence, Mavelli and Petito argue that the post-secular has emerged as 'a form of radical theorising and critique prompted by the idea that values such as democracy, freedom, equality, inclusion, and justice may not necessarily be best pursued within an exclusively immanent secular framework' (2012, p. 931).

This form of post-secular critique has profound implications for political debate and reasoning in the public sphere. Habermas (2006) has pointed out that, to a large extent, the rules around contemporary political debate and the types of reasoning permitted within the public sphere are premised on certain key assumptions of secularization theory—namely that religion is predominantly a historical relic, a phenomenon that will die out with the spread of modernization and rationalization (Berger, 1967; Deneulin and Rakodi, 2011). With the end of the Cold War and the events of 9/11, it has become abundantly clear that religion is not dying out, but is taking on new significance and alternative forms (Casanova, 1994; Hurd, 2008; Juergensmeyer, 2008; Leustean and Madeley, 2009; Philpott, 2009).

Habermas (2006, pp. 8–9) insists that we must rethink the parameters of acceptable public reasoning and in particular reassess the requirements that have been placed on religious citizens. He considers it inequitable to expect religious citizens to translate the reasoning for their arguments into secular language, when we do not place the same translation requirement on secular citizens (Ibid., pp. 10–11). Further, he argues that secular society loses an important source of meaning and identity when it refuses to allow religious reasoning and language into the public sphere (Ibid., p. 10). Habermas is not the first commentator to question the exclusion of religious language and reasoning from the public sphere (see e.g. Stout, 2004), nor even the first to employ the term 'post-secular' (see e.g. Connolly, 2000; Thomas, 2005). Arguably, however, his recent writings have acted as a catalyst for the present debates about the meanings and uses of the term (Mavelli and Petito, 2012, p. 936). By arguing that the inclusion of religious language in public debate is not only necessary but also desirable, Habermas calls into question particular assumptions about what is acceptable and what is not in political debate. Our post-secular age, he seems to suggest, can no longer afford to cling to rationalism as an indispensable foundation or even make confident judgments as to what should be considered 'rational' or 'irrational'.

While endeavoring to push us beyond secularist boundaries of public reasoning, several recent critiques have pointed out that Habermas's arguments remain embedded within secular Enlightenment structures that maintain the divisions between secular and religious reasoning and privilege scientific rationalism (Mavelli and Petito, 2012, p. 936; Pabst, 2012, pp. 1003–4). His proposition holds that religious argumentation has an important contribution to make within civil society, but he draws the line at religious arguments being employed within the parliamentary sphere and in public law- and political decision-making (Habermas, 2006, p. 10). Considered in this light, his proposals are not so revolutionary and in fact do not depart that much from the parameters laid out by John Rawls (1999). Indeed, Dallmayr (2012, p. 968) points out that the notion of secular public reasoning to which all people have access is a myth of the Enlightenment. Key secular thinkers, like Rawls and Habermas themselves, have constantly required interpretation and translation, as have the judgments of the courts, to make them more accessible by a majority of people (Ibid.). Consequently, secular public reasoning is not the neutral, self-contained, and wholly intelligible discourse that Habermas makes out and thus not so different from religious reasoning (Ibid.).

Yet what both Habermas and his critics have in common is a recognition that the liberal secular political project, at least within the West, is in trouble. We suggest that Habermas's argument, along with those of other post-secular theorists (e.g. Beaumont and Cloke, 2012; Barbato, 2010; Camilleri, 2012; Mavelli and Petito, 2012) are indicative of a broader malaise affecting many societies. None of the major voices mentioned earlier, from political and economic elites, to global civil society and right-wing reactionary extremists, appear capable of producing a convincing narrative that explains the core dynamics of contemporary global crises. Growing cynicism in Western contexts about dominant forms of politics provides evidence of our thesis. Elections in Australia, the UK, and the Netherlands around the end of the 2000s and more recently in Italy all resulted in hung parliaments, resolving eventually into minority governments. At the same time, levels of voter participation have been steadily declining in Canada, France (Elections Canada, 2003), and the USA (CNN Wire, 2012), with record low voter turnout in the UK (*The Guardian*, 2012) and the highest number of informal votes cast in the 2010 Australian Federal elections since 1984 (Australian Electoral Commission, 2011).

While such events have occurred before, the fact that such tight election results and such poor voter participation are occurring in multiple countries around the world, combined with growing citizens' movements such as Occupy, the Indignants, the 99%, and the Arab Spring, suggests that there is growing dissatisfaction with politics as usual and particularly with neoliberal economics, occurring on a global scale (Agathangelou and Soguk, 2011; Balardini, 2012; Hickel, 2012; Mavelli, 2012b; Sadiki, 2009, p. 211). People around the globe are willing to resist dominant forces in their quest for 'another world'—even if those alternatives have proven to be quite elusive.

Religious Globalisms as Response to Neoliberal Crisis

While many faith-based organizations are proposing alternative visions for society to that being pushed by market-driven processes of globalization, ironically, it is the influence of neoliberalism, in particular globalization driven by neoliberal economic policies, that has contributed to opening up space in contemporary politics for faith-based organizations and religious actors to exercise political influence.

Religious actors have taken this opportunity in a variety of different ways. Some have embraced neoliberal market ideology and adopted it into their theological doctrine and practical activities. Others have vigorously opposed market globalism, through the promotion of more social justice centered policies and doctrines, as well as highly conservative and at times violent and reactionary measures. We briefly outline some key features of these different religious globalisms below.

Neoliberal Religious Globalisms

One way of responding to neoliberal crisis is to argue that markets have not yet been sufficiently 'liberated'. This line of argument—the way out of the Great Recession is more neoliberalism—became particularly obvious during the 2012 US Presidential campaign when Governor Mitt Romney attacked President Barack Obama for seeking to reregulate the US economy in the wake of the Great Financial Crisis (Caldwell, 2012). As the name suggests, neoliberal religious globalists have embraced large portions of market globalism, endorsing its imperatives of market-driven economic growth, material prosperity, and conspicuous consumption. They promote a view of the common good centered on raising material standards of living through massive participation in market activities (Lynch, 2011). Hence, like market globalists, neoliberal religious globalists place great faith in the market and finance to solve their own and the world's most pressing problems.

Several examples of the alignment of neoliberalism with religious movements exist within national contexts, such as Hindu nationalism in India (Rao, 1998; Saxena and Sharma, 1998, p. 249) and Confucianism in Japan and China (though this link is contested; Hussein, 1998, pp. 304–5). Yet arguably the most significant marriage between neoliberalism and religion at the global level has occurred in certain forms of Christianity (primarily, but not exclusively Pentecostalism) (Vasquez, 2008, pp. 164, 174). Examples include the Hillsong Church, which originates in Sydney but maintains a vibrant web of churches across five continents (Hillsong Church, 2012), Joyce Meyer Ministries, Joel Osteen's Lakewood Church, T.D. Jakes's Potter's House (Olsen, 2006), the Catholic El Shaddai Ministries in the Philippines (Wiegele, 2005), and the Redeemed Christian Church of God, a Nigerian church with global networks (Knibbe, 2011). All of these churches promote a view of the Christian life and faith that is globally applicable and consistent with neoliberal assumptions such as a strong emphasis on the individual (Maxwell, 1998); the belief that wealth is essential for a good life; that the market and global finance are essentially benign and governed by the Invisible Hand of God and therefore are beyond rational criticism (Rosin, 2009). The following excerpt from a pamphlet written by Mike Verlade, pastor of El Shaddai ministries in the Philippines and strongly influenced by Pat Robertson's The 700 Club, provides a clear example of how prosperity gospel operates:

> And believe me, God's glorious source of miracle supply in Christ Jesus is not affected by recession, political unrest, inflation, strikes, fire, bankruptcies, earthquakes, and other calamities. Hence anyone who believes and puts into practice continuously this miracle of seed-faith principle, by faith expressing itself through love of God and neighbor, wins God's favor and protection. And as naturally as a seed of palay [rice] sown on fertile soil grows and multiplies, so does your seed faith offering, given to the right mission or ministry, open God's source of miracle supply! (Verlade, 1994, pp. 4–6 cited in Wiegele, 2005, p. 20)

These assumptions are also reflected in the commodification of various dimensions of Christian rituals, including sermons and worship music. Hillsong Church, for example, has a multimillion dollar business based on the sale of its worship music albums (Price, 2011).

The doctrine behind these global Christian networks that fits so tightly with the claims of market globalism is known primarily as the prosperity gospel (Hladky, 2012, p. 82; Vasquez, 2008, p. 164). Prosperity gospel makes use of verses in Christian scriptures, such as the prayer of Jabez, in 1 Chronicles 4:10, that proclaim God's desire to bless all people (Houston, 2002; Wilkinson, 2000). Prosperity doctrine explicitly preaches that such blessings take the form of material wealth and that people must 'bless' others—give their money away (primarily to the church)—in order to make way for God to bless them. Christians who give generously will also reap generously, receiving immediate and manifold blessings from God (in monetary form) in their earthly life, not just as their 'heavenly reward' (Hladky, 2012; Houston, 2002; Wiegele, 2005; Wilkinson, 2000).

Critiques of prosperity gospel are numerous. Some theologians argue that by placing such a strong emphasis on the individual and market forces, prosperity gospel becomes centered on human beings rather than on God, and hence contradictory to much Christian doctrine (Lioy, 2007). Sociologist Paul Gifford notes that prosperity gospel's strong emphasis on the individual privatizes responsibility for social problems and discourages people from challenging the established economic order (Gifford, 1991, pp. 65–6 cited in Maxwell, 1998, p. 351). In this way, prosperity gospel works to reinforce the core claims of market globalism: that no one is in charge of global markets, that neoliberal globalization benefits everyone, and that it is divine providence at work in markets and finance that will resolve the world's problems (Steger, 2009). Neoliberalism becomes a means not only by which people can help themselves, but by which God provides assistance and reward. It promotes very specific understandings of what human flourishing and the common good are that are in many ways at odds with other aspects of Christian doctrine and practice.

Religious Justice Globalisms

In almost complete opposition to the ideological claims of neoliberal religious globalism, other religious organizations have responded to the current crisis of neoliberalism by seeking to transform the dominant paradigm. They challenge the views that financial wellbeing should primarily be considered an individual responsibility and that the market and finance provide the primary means through which social ills can be overcome. These religious justice globalists project the post-secular as the kind of popular resistance envisioned by thinkers like Habermas (2006), Barbato (2010), and Beaumont and Cloke (2012). Articulating a sense of urgency as the global financial crisis or large-scale food crises are ravaging the Global South, many religious justice globalists employ sacred imagery and stories to generate alternative visions for how politics and society can operate in ethical ways that are rooted in religious values. Let us briefly examine two concrete examples: the World Council of Churches (WCC) and some forms of Islamist activism in the Middle East.

The WCC has been actively opposing neoliberalism and defending the rights of the poor since the 1970s.[2] It provides the framework for a global network of churches, NGOs, and indigenous communities that engage in campaigns and research relating to the multiple crises of neoliberalism. The religious justice globalism of the WCC is strongly influenced by liberation theology, particularly the 'preferential option for the poor' (WCC, 2005).[3] In this way, the WCC echoes global Catholic networks that have championed liberation theology and placed emphasis on social welfare against the rising influence of privatization and neoliberalism, particularly within the Latin American context (Gutierrez, 1998).

Employing explicitly religious language, the WCC has put forward a proposal titled 'Alternative Globalization Addressing Peoples and the Earth' (AGAPE). This alternative to market globalism deliberately employs biblical imagery in its acronym, *agape*, the Greek word for the sacrificial love described by St Paul in 1 Corinthians 13:

> The churches and the ecumenical family will be called to move beyond critique of neoliberal globalization to stating how God's grace can *transform* this paradigm. The call will be for an ecumenical vision of life in just and loving relationships, through a search for alternatives to the present economic structures. (WCC, 2005, Foreword)

In line with other critics of neoliberal globalization, the WCC argues that neoliberalism's focus on wealth creation means that everyone and everything is perceived as a commodity that can be bought, sold, and traded. Money and wealth become privileged over all other dimensions of human life; competition between the individual and the community increases. Such commodification on the global scale has detrimental effects on the wellbeing of both people and the environment (WCC, 2005, pp. 3–4). Hence, the WCC promotes a globally coordinated response to neoliberal crises rooted in the alternative values of diversity, cooperation, and global solidarity. It insists that resources are managed democratically and sustainably so that coming generations may enjoy an equal share in the abundance of God's grace and provision (Ibid., pp. 4–5). This overarching vision of 'justice globalism' is then translated into concrete policy proposals addressing global poverty, climate change, health, peacebuilding, and a host of other concerns.

Similar expressions of such justice-globalist values and concerns can also be found in the Arab world where both Christian and Islamic communities have articulated an equally strong concern for human rights, justice for the oppressed, and opposition to market globalism with particular emphasis on the Middle East (Kassab, 2009, p. 174). In Islamic articulations of religious justice globalism, the critique of secular rationalism is more explicit than in Christianity, primarily because in the Middle East secularism has become associated with what many people perceive as the failed project of nationalism. As Sadiki (2009, p. 208) notes, 'Islamists from al-Turabi to al-Farhan consider the state's providential role towards its poor citizens both a civil and religious duty.' The failure of several Middle Eastern states—such as Jordan, Sudan, and Egypt—to protect their citizens' rights to food, education, basic health care, and housing has been a primary catalyst for numerous forms of open resistance throughout the region. Indeed, the so-called 'Arab Spring' represents but the latest and most powerful of such events (Hickel, 2012; Kassab, 2009; Sadiki, 2009, pp. 207–8).

The core concept of 'redistributive justice' links Islamic justice globalisms to more secular political versions of justice globalism. As Sadiki points out,

> Formulations of social justice in Islam may vary in practice and scope according to context, but what makes its conception paradigmatically distinct and common to all Muslim societies is its community-based redistributive system. Through this system, the offsetting of material inequalities and injustices is equally binding on all members and groups constitutive of the Islamic community. (2009, p. 203)

Such an emphasis on redistributive justice also reveals important ideological affinities to other justice-globalist core concepts such as equality and solidarity. Resonating with the WCC argument that humans ought to be good stewards of the resources that God has given to them,[4] Islamic justice globalists hold that 'Godly bounties or favours (ni'am) must be managed in accordance with God's sanctions, by balancing the earthly with the heavenly as well as the individual with the communal' (Sadiki, 2009, p. 202).

The widespread current phenomenon of so-called 'bread riots' in the Middle East, including but not limited to the Arab Spring, encapsulates Islamic opposition to neoliberal economic practices and the pursuit of socially just alternatives. Some scholars have speculated that the increasing frequency of bread riots reflects growing popular dissatisfaction with the dominant social, economic, and political realities in the Middle East. As Sadiki (2009, p. 201) puts it, '"Bread" is used here in a generic sense to refer to free education, health care, and other services.' Bread riots have frequently occurred in countries in the region that have had to implement World Bank and IMF austerity reforms as a condition of loans. Islamist opposition parties, such as the Islamic Action Front (IAF) in Jordan, have been instrumental in opposing these measures, utilizing social justice arguments from Islamic theology. For example, IAF-connected theologian Abu Faris argues that anything that impinges on the believers' dignity (karamah) and upsets the moral and social fabric of society, as do price increases on food items, must be opposed (Ibid., p. 208). This Islamist critique of market globalism clearly converges with a central claim of secular justice globalism: neoliberalism causes widespread social crises.

CRISIS, MOVEMENT, MANAGEMENT: GLOBALISING DYNAMICS

Neotraditional Religious Globalisms

A third category of religious globalisms also reacts to neoliberal crisis by opposing the ideological imperatives of market globalism, albeit for entirely different reasons and from an entirely different standpoint than that of religious justice globalists. These neotraditional religious globalisms frequently engage in acts of violent resistance against the encroaching influences of secular neoliberalism. Substantial research already exists on the relationship between religion and violence (e.g. Appleby, 2000; Girard, 1977; Juergensmeyer, 2000, 2008; Laustsen and Waever, 2000; Seul, 1999). Our focus here is particularly those violent neotraditionalist religious movements that oppose neoliberal globalization. The most prominent actors in this category (and consequently, the most researched) are global expressions of 'reactionary' or 'radical' Islamism as embodied in organizations such as al-Qaeda and Jemaah Islamiya (Karam, 2004; Kepel, 2004; Mandaville, 2007; Steger, 2009). These neotraditional versions of Islamism oppose neoliberal market globalism to ensure the global ideological dominance of their own political agenda. Within this worldview, the aggressive reinvigoration of religion becomes a way of dealing with the stresses, uncertainties, and inequalities wrought by the rapid changes in contemporary society, many of which are induced by neoliberalism (Haynes, 2007, p. 85; Spickard, 2013). This militant agenda embraces 'justice' not as a universal value but as a religiously and culturally specific idea rooted in neotraditionalist interpretations of sacred scripture that are frequently used to justify reactionary and exclusionary ideological claims. The primary targets of their 'resistance' to what they perceive as acts of aggression committed by the 'immoral forces of global unbelief [*kufr*]' are the mass consumption and indulgent lifestyles nurtured in the West and encouraged by secular market globalists (Steger, 2009).

Yet other equally violent reactionary global religious movements have also made their mark in recent times. The most recent example is that of Anders Breivik in Norway. Although an individual acting alone, Breivik claimed to be a member of an anti-Islamist organization, the Knights Templar (Pidd, 2012). Breivik's thought was heavily influenced by conservative, reactionary Christian globalist ideology, seeing 'European Christendom' as under threat from Islam (Cohen, 2011). As Cohen (Ibid.) points out, Breivik is far from being alone in expressing such views. Organizations expressing similar views exist around the globe, including Christian Identity in the United States, the English Defence League, and neo-Nazi organizations (Ibid.). The hallmarks of such conservative religious globalisms are violent racism towards non-whites and condemnation of 'liberal whites' (Barkun, 1997). This brand of religious globalism is opposed more to increased migration, the growing porousness of state borders, and the decline in state sovereignty in some areas, rather than to specific dynamics of neoliberalism per se. As such, it is possible to argue that these militant neotraditional religious movements are an attempt to promote strong religious identities in the face of mounting secularist challenges (Juergensmeyer, 2008; Seul, 1999, p. 562). Spickard (2013) points to Hindu nationalists, alongside Islamist movements as examples of this type of aggressive religious identity politics. Yet the phenomena to which such movements are directly opposed are also arguably outcomes of neoliberal globalization. Consequently, these movements represent an alternative form of resistance to the secularist as well as the neoliberal project.

Conclusion

Neoliberal globalization has undoubtedly contributed to the reinvigoration of global public religion, as suggested by Toft et al. (2011), but to date little has been revealed about the specific dynamics of this relationship. Concurrently, the notion of the post-secular offers a powerful form of alternative theorizing as well as challenge to dominant secular approaches. Yet its possibilities have so far been underemployed at the level of the global (Camilleri, 2012). In utilizing the post-secular to explore religious resurgence in relation to emerging global political ideologies, this article has made a first step towards addressing these gaps. Highlighting the crucial role of neoliberal crisis as a specific dynamic of globalization that facilitates new forms of religious engagement and resistance in our post-secular age, this essay presents the basic outline for a new typology of religious globalisms: neoliberal religious globalisms, religious justice globalisms, and neotraditional religious globalisms.

Yet other types of religious globalisms exist and require exploration such as emerging eclectic forms like Falun Gong, Soga Gakkei, and so-called 'New-Ageisms' (Neumann, 2011). Moreover, careful conceptual mapping exercises of the different strands within the three major types of religious globalisms introduced in this article will also aid scholars and policymakers in their efforts to better understand the ideological dynamics that fuel the global resurgence of religion.

Acknowledgements

The authors wish to thank James Goodman, Jon Marshall, and three anonymous reviewers for their helpful comments on earlier drafts of this article.

Notes

1. Interview with T. Gilbertson, Research Fellow, Transnational Institute, delegate to COP15, Copenhagen, Denmark, 18 December 2009; Interview with J. Kennedy, delegate to COP15, World Council of Churches, Copenhagen, 17 December 2009.
2. Interview with F. Dove, Executive Director, Transnational Institute, The Netherlands, 3 December 2010; Interview with Kennedy, 17 December 2009.
3. Interview with Rogate Mshana, Director, Justice, Peace and Creation programme, World Council of Churches, December 2010.
4. Interview with Kennedy, 2009.

References

Agathangelou, A. M. & Soguk, N. (2011) Rocking the kasbah: Insurrectional politics, the 'Arab Streets' and global revolution in the 21st century, *Globalizations*, 8(5), pp. 551–558.
Appleby, R. S. (2000) *The Ambivalence of the Sacred: Religion, Violence and Reconciliation* (Lanham, MD: Rowman and Littlefield).
Arkoun, M. (2003) Rethinking Islam today, *Annals of the American Academy of Political Science*, 588(1), pp. 18–39.
Australian Electoral Commission (2011) Analysis of informal voting, House of Representatives 2010 Federal Election' Research Report Number 12, 29 March, http://www.aec.gov.au/about_aec/Publications/Strategy_Research_Analysis/paper12/files/informality-e2010.pdf.
Balardini, F. (2012) The self destructive logic of capitalism and the Occupy movement, *Socialism and Democracy*, 26(2), pp. 35–38.
Barbato, M. (2010) Conceptions of the self for post-secular emancipation: Towards a pilgrim's guide to global justice, *Millennium Journal of International Studies*, 39(2), pp. 547–564.
Barkun, M. (1997) *Religion and the Racist Right: The Origins of the Christian Identity Movement* (North Carolina: University of North Carolina Press).
Beaumont, J. & Cloke, P. (2012) Introduction, in J. Beaumont, P. Cloke & J. Vranken (eds) *Faith-Based Organisations and Exclusion in European Cities* (Bristol: The Policy Press), pp. 1–36.
Berger, P. L. (1967) *The Sacred Canopy: Elements of a Sociological Theory of Religion* (New York: Random House).

Berger, P. L. (1999) The desecularization of the world: A global overview, in P. L. Berger (ed.) *The Desecularization of the World: Resurgent religion and World Politics* (Grand Rapids, MI: W.B. Eerdmans), pp. 1–18.
Bleiker, R. (2009) *Aesthetics and World Politics* (Basingstoke: Palgrave Macmillan).
Bretherton, L. (2010) *Christianity and Contemporary Politics* (Chichester: Wiley-Blackwell).
Caldwell, L. A. (2012) Economy in focus during Obama, Romney showdown, *CBS News*, 3 October, http://www.cbsnews.com/8301-250_162-57525673/economy-in-focus-during-obama-romney-showdown/.
Camilleri, J. A. (2012) Postsecularist discourse in an age of transition, *Review of International Studies*, 38(5), pp. 1019–1039.
Casanova, J. (1994) *Public Religions in the Modern World* (Chicago: University of Chicago Press).
Cavanaugh, W. T. (2009) *The Myth of Religious Violence* (Oxford: Oxford University Press).
Chand, R. (2008) The global food crisis: causes, severity and outlook, *Economic and Political Weekly*, 28 June, pp. 115–123.
CNN Wire (2012) Election results 2012: Voter turnout lower than 2008, 2004, report says, http://www.abc15.com/dpp/news/national/election-results-2012-voter-turnout-lower-than-2008-and-2004-report-says.
Cohen, R. (2011) Breivik and his enablers, *The New York Times*, 25 July, http://www.nytimes.com/2011/07/26/opinion/26iht-edcohen26.html?ref=andersbehringbreivik&_r=0.
Connolly, W. E. (2000) *Why I Am Not a Secularist* (Minneapolis: University of Minnesota Press).
Crotty, J. (2009) Structural causes of the global financial crisis: A critical assessment of the 'new financial architecture', *Cambridge Journal of Economics*, 33(6), pp. 563–580.
Dallmayr, F. (2012) Postsecularity and (global) politics: A need for radical redefinition, *Review of International Studies*, 38(5), pp. 963–973.
Deneulin, S. & Rakodi, C. (2011) Revisiting religion: Development studies thirty years on, *World Development*, 39(1), pp. 45–54.
Dombrowski, D. (2001) *Rawls and Religion: The Case for Political Liberalism* (Albany, NY: State University of New York Press).
Eberle, C. J. (2002) *Religious Conviction in Liberal Politics* (Cambridge: Cambridge University Press).
Elections Canada (2003) Explaining the turn-out decline in Canadian Federal Elections, http://www.elections.ca/content.aspx?section=res&dir=rec/part/tud&document=trends&lang=e.
Erskine, T. (2002) 'Citizen of nowhere' or 'the point where circles intersect'? Impartialist and embedded cosmopolitanisms, *Review of International Studies*, 28(3), pp. 457–478.
Fox, J. (2001) Religion as an overlooked element of international relations, *International Studies Review*, 3(3), pp. 53–73.
George, S. (2001) A short history of neoliberalism: Twenty years of elite economics and emerging opportunities for structural change, in F. Houtart & F. Polet (eds) *The Other Davos: The Globalization of Resistance to the World Economic System* (London and New York: Zed Books), pp. 7–16.
Gills, B. K. (2010) The return of crisis in the era of globalization: One crisis or many?, *Globalizations*, 7(1), pp. 3–8.
Girard, R. (1977) *Violence and the Sacred* (Baltimore: Johns Hopkins University Press).
Grassroots Global Justice (2009) Stimulating environmental justice. Statement on sustainable economic development, 16 March, http://www.ggjalliance.org/system/files/EJ%20Stimulus%20Final%203-16-09.pdf.
Guardian, The (2012) UK elections historic turnout since 1918, http://www.guardian.co.uk/news/datablog/2012/nov/16/uk-election-turnouts-historic.
Gutierrez, M. A. (1998) The Argentine Catholic Church in front of the programs of structural adjustment, *International Review of Sociology*, 8(2), pp. 253–266.
Habermas, J. (2006) Religion in the public sphere, *European Journal of Philosophy*, 14(1), pp. 1–25.
Habermas, J. (2008) Notes on post-secular society, *New Perspectives Quarterly*, 25(4), pp. 17–29.
Haynes, J. (2007) *Religion and Development: Conflict or Cooperation?* (Basingstoke: Palgrave Macmillan).
Hickel, J. (2012) Neoliberal Egypt: The hijacked revolution, *Al Jazeera*, 29 March, http://www.aljazeera.com/indepth/opinion/2012/03/201232784226830522.html.
Hillsong Church (2012) Welcome home, http://hillsong.com/.
Hladky, K. (2012) I double-dog dare you in Jesus' name! Claiming Christian wealth and the American prosperity gospel, *Religion Compass*, 6(1), pp. 82–96.
Houston, B. (2002) *How to Live a Blessed Life* (Sydney: Maximised Leadership Inc).
Houtart, F. (2010) The multiple crisis and beyond, *Globalizations*, 7(1), pp. 9–15.
Hulme, M. (2009) *Why We Disagree About Climate Change* (Cambridge: Cambridge University Press).
Hulme, M. (2010) Problems with making and governing global kinds of knowledge, *Global Environmental Change*, 20, pp. 558–564.
Hurd, E. S. (2008) *The Politics of Secularism in International Relations* (Princeton, NJ: Princeton University Press).

Hussein, S. A. (1998) On neoliberalism and culturalism: A view from the South, *International Review of Sociology*, 8(2), pp. 299–311.
Juergensmeyer, M. (2000) *Terror in the Mind of God: The Global Rise of Religious Violence* (Berkeley: University of California Press).
Juergensmeyer, M. (2008) *Global Rebellion: Religious Challenges to the Secular State, from Christian Militias to al Qaeda* (Berkeley: University of California Press).
Karam, A. (ed.) (2004) *Transnational Political Islam: Religion, Ideology and Power* (London: Pluto Press).
Kassab, E. S. (2010) *Contemporary Arab Thought: Cultural Critique in Comparative Perspective* (New York: Columbia University Press).
Kepel, G. (2004) *The War for Muslim Minds: Islam and the West* (Cambridge, MA: Harvard University Press).
Knibbe, K. (2011) Nigerian missionaries in Europe: History repeating itself or a meeting of multiple modernities?, *Journal of Religion in Europe*, 4, pp. 471–487.
Laustsen, C. B. & Waever, O. (2000) In defence of religion: Sacred referent objects for securitization, *Millennium*, 29(3), pp. 705–739.
Leustean, L. N. & Madeley, John, T. S. (2009) Religion, politics and law in the European Union: An introduction, *Religion, State and Society*, 37(1), pp. 3–18.
Lioy, D. (2007) The heart of the prosperity gospel: Self or Savior? *Conspectus*, 4, pp. 41–64, http://www.satsonline.org/userfiles/Lioy,Theheartoftheprosperitygospel.pdf.
Lynch, C. (2011) Religious humanitarianism and the global politics of secularism, in C. Calhoun, M. Juergensmeyer & J. Van Antwerpen (eds) *Rethinking Secularism* (Oxford: Oxford University Press), pp. 204–224.
Mandaville, P. (2007) *Global Political Islam* (London and New York: Routledge).
Marx, K. & Friedrich, E. (1992 [1848]) *The Communist Manifesto* (Oxford: Oxford University Press).
Mavelli, L. (2012a) *Europe's Encounter with Islam: The Secular and the Post-Secular* (London: Routledge).
Mavelli, L. (2012b) Postsecular resistance, the body and the 2011 Egyptian revolution, *Review of International Studies*, 38(5), pp. 1057–1078.
Mavelli, L. & Petito, F. (2012) The postsecular in international relations: An overview, *Review of International Studies*, 38(5), pp. 931–942.
Maxwell, D. (1998) 'Delivered from the spirit of poverty?' Pentecostalism, prosperity and modernity in Zimbabwe, *Journal of Religion in Africa*, 28(3), pp. 350–373.
Mendieta, E. & Vanantwerpen, J. (eds) (2011) Introduction, in *The Power of Religion in the Public Sphere* (New York: Columbia University Press), pp. 1–14.
Mepschen, P., Duyvendak, J. W., Tonkens, E. H. (2010) Sexual politics, Orientalism and multicultural citizenship in the Netherlands, *Sociology*, 44(5), pp. 962–979.
Neumann, I. (2011) 'Religion in sort of a global sense': The relevance of religious practices for political community in Battlestar Galactica and beyond, *Journal of Contemporary Religion*, 26(3), pp. 387–401.
Pabst, A. (2012) The secularism of post-secularity: Religion, realism and the revival of grand theory in IR, *Review of International Studies*, 38(5), pp. 995–1017.
Patomäki, H. (2009) The global financial crisis: causes and consequences, *Local Global*, 6(1), pp. 4–27.
Petito, F. & Hatzopoulos, P. (eds) (2003) *Religion in International Relations: The Return from Exile* (New York: Palgrave Macmillan).
Philpott, D. (2002) The challenge of September 11 to secularism in international relations, *World Politics*, 55(1), pp. 66–95.
Philpott, D. (2009) Has the study of global politics found religion? *Annual Review of Political Science*, 12, pp. 183–202.
Pidd, H. (2012) Anders Behring Breivik spent years training and plotting for massacre, *The Guardian*, 24 August, http://www.guardian.co.uk/world/2012/aug/24/anders-behring-breivik-profile-oslo/print.
Price, C. (2011) Australian idolatry: Evangelical Christians resurrecting the music industry, *The Huffington Post*, 15 September, http://www.huffingtonpost.co.uk/christopher-price/hillsong-music-resurrect-australian-charts_b_960602.html.
Rao, K. S. S. (1998) Hinduism and the new economic policy, *International Review of Sociology*, 8(2), pp. 233–238.
Rawls, J. (1999) *The Law of the Peoples and The Idea of Public Reason Revisited* (Cambridge, MA: Harvard University Press).
Rorty, R. (2003) Religion in the public square: A reconsideration, *Journal of Religious Ethics*, 31(1), pp. 141–149.
Rosin, H. (2009) Did Christianity cause the crash? *The Atlantic*, December, http://www.theatlantic.com/magazine/archive/2009/12/did-christianity-cause-the-crash/307764/.
Sadiki, L. (2009) *Rethinking Arab Democratization: Elections Without Democracy* (Oxford: Oxford University Press).

Saxena, K. & Sharma, P. (1998) Hindutva and economic liberalization, *International Review of Sociology*, 8(2), pp. 239–251.
Schutter, O. (2010) *Food Commodities Speculation and Food Price Crises: Regulation to Reduce the Risks of Price Volatility*. UN Rapporteur on the Right to Food Briefing Note 2, September.
Seul, J. R. (1999) Ours is the way of God: Religion, identity and intergroup conflict, *Journal of Peace Research*, 36(5), pp. 553–569.
Soros, G. (2008) The crisis and what to do about it, *New York Review of Books*, 6 November, http://www.nybooks.com/articles/archives/2008/dec/04/the-crisis-what-to-do-about-it/?page=1.
Spickard, J. V. (2013) Making religion irrelevant: The 'resurgent religion' narrative and the critique of neoliberalism, in F. Gauthier & T. Martikainen (eds) *Religion in the Neoliberal Age* (Farnham, UK: Ashgate), pp. 37–52.
Steger, M. B. (2008) *The Rise of the Global Imaginary* (Oxford: Oxford University Press).
Steger, M. (2009) *Globalisms: The Great Ideological Struggle of the Twenty-First Century*, 3rd ed. (Lanham, MD: Rowman and Littlefield).
Steger, M. B., Goodman, J. & Wilson, E. (2013) *Justice Globalism: Ideology, Crises, Policy* (London: Sage).
Stout, J. (2004) *Democracy and Tradition* (Princeton: Princeton University Press).
Strenski, I. (2010) *Why Politics Can't Be Freed from Religion* (Chichester: Wiley-Blackwell).
Taylor, C. (2007) *A Secular Age* (Cambridge, MA and London: Belknap Press).
Thomas, S. M. (2005) *The Global Resurgence of Religion and the Transformation of International Relations* (Basingstoke, UK: Palgrave Macmillan).
Toft, M. D., Philpott, D. & Shah, T. S. (2011) *God's Century: Resurgent Religion and Global Politics* (New York: W.W. Norton).
Uitermark, J. & Gielen, A.-J. (2010) Islam in the spotlight: The mediatisation of politics in an Amsterdam neighbourhood, *Urban Studies*, 47(6), pp. 1325–1342.
Vasquez, M. (2008) Studying religion in motion: A networks approach, *Method and Theory in the Study of Religion*, 20(2), pp. 151–184.
Weber, M. (1918) Science as vocation, in H.H. Gerth and C. Wright Mills (eds) (1948) *From Max Weber: Essays in Sociology* (New York: Oxford University Press), pp. 129–157.
Wiegele, K. (2005) *Investing in Miracles: El Shaddai and the Transformation of Popular Catholicism in the Philippines* (Honolulu: University of Hawaii Press).
Wilkinson, B. (2000) *The Prayer of Jabez* (Oregon: Multnomah Publishers).
Wilson, E. K. (2011) Much to be proud of, much to be done: Faith-based organisations and the politics of asylum in Australia, *Journal of Refugee Studies*, 24(3), pp. 548–564.
Wilson, E. K. (2012) *After Secularism: Rethinking Religion in Global Politics* (Basingstoke: Palgrave Macmillan).
Wolf, M. (2009) Seeds of its own destruction, *Financial Times*, 8 March, http://www.ft.com/intl/cms/s/0/c6c5bd36-0c0c-11de-b87d-0000779fd2ac.html#axzz1uP9chBvW.
World Council of Churches (2005) *Alternative Globalization Addressing Peoples and the Earth* (Geneva: World Council of Churches), http://www.oikoumene.org/fileadmin/files/wcc-main/documents/p3/agape-new.pdf.
World Council of Churches (2009) Will the global financial crisis mark the end of "moneytheism"?, Press release on the global financial crisis, http://www.oikoumene.org/en/news/news-management/eng/a/browse/7/article/1634/will-the-global-financial.html.

Erin Wilson is Director of the Centre for Religion, Conflict and the Public Domain at the University of Groningen. She is the author of *After Secularism: Rethinking Religion in Global Politics* (Palgrave Macmillan, 2012) and co-author, with Manfred B. Steger and James Goodman, of *Justice Globalism: Ideology, Crises, Policy* (Sage, 2013).

Manfred B. Steger is Professor of Political Science at the University of Hawai'i at Manoa and Research Leader in the Global Cities Research Institute at RMIT University. He is the author or editor of over 20 books, including author of the best-selling *Globalization: A Very Short Introduction*, 2nd ed. (Oxford University Press, 2009) and co-author, with Erin Wilson and James Goodman, of *Justice Globalism: Ideology, Crises, Policy* (Sage, 2013).

Index

9/11 109–20; decline of protest movement 113; decline of size of public demonstration 113; difficulty in maintaining networks after 114; key event, as 120; strengths becoming problems 117; trigger of dichotomous framework of civilisation/terrorism 115; *A Paradise Built in Hell* 103–4

American Society for Industrial Security 46
Another Future is Possible 70, 76–8, 79
Anthropocene 97–106; definition 98; environmental crisis 99' "anticipatory history" 100, 106; interconnections of 101
Appdadurai 57
applied disaster resilience 43–4
Arab Spring 76, 92, 119,148
Arrighi, G. 2
Arundhati, Roy 59–60
Ashforth, B.E.56–7
Asia-Pacific summit 110
Australia 109–20; Global Justice Movement, and 109–20

Bangalore Call Centres 3, 55–66; alienation of 61;demand of 60; ambivalence of families 63; complexities of 65; culture, and 65–6; economic liberalisation, and 57; function of 56; gender, and 60–2; global linkages, and 57; *jugaar* 58; local culture of 58–9; managerial techniques 56; marriage, and 62–5; "passing" as British or American 59–60; personality responsibility, and 61–2; pornography, and 64; skills over qualifications 60–1; sociality at work 59
Bankoff, G. 18 -19
Basi, J. Tina 62
Bayoumi, Mustafa 56
Bhabha,Homi 56
Biel, Robert 5
Bramble, T. 110
Breivik, Anders 149

Carroll,W. 3–5, 72

Carson, Rachel 100
chaos theory 17–18
Charkabarty, Dipesh 100
Christian identity 149
CitiBank 30
CitiFinancial 30
citizen journalism 123–34: anti-WTO 131–2; definition of 127; emotional responses of 126–7; evolution of 131–132; genesis of 131; historical tendencies of 132; Hong Kong In-Media 126; instrumental mobilisation forces, and 131; Local Action, and 128; Po, Leung, and 126; similarities to Occupy movement 134
Clark, Nigel 101
class antagonism 70–72; contemporary global crisis 72; Marxism, and 71; reproduction, and 71–72
Cold War 119
communication failure 25–37; bloggers 31–4; "Chinese Whisper" 33; class sensibility, and 34–5; complexity 37; corporate life 37; correlations, and 32; crashes 33–4; data 36–7; disruptive events, and 29; ethnographic observation 26; Financial Crisis, and 27; information society, and 26; Information Workspace 26; insecurity at work, and 30–1; models, and 29–30; models as reality 31; mortgage market 34; pressures of 36; quant 32; remedies 35; risks 31, 36; software, and 28–9
conferences; Kobe 22; Rio Earth Summit 22 (ADD), 69–70; Yokohama 22
Conservative-Liberal coalition 42
Cook,N. 88
Cooper, M. 49
counter hegemony 75–8
crisis 1–2; conflicts 2; manifestation of contradiction 2
Crutzen, Paul 34,97

Da Rimini, Francesca 9–10 123–34
Davis, Mike 3–4

INDEX

Definition 2–4; agency 4; managerialism 3; political change, and 3–4
Derman, Emmanuel 32–3, 36
DeSilvey, Caitlin 99–100
Dollard, M. 56–7
Dooling, R. 26–8

Eberle, Christopher 142–4
English Defence League 149
environmental justice 97–106; "anticipatory history" 100; broader eco-social relationships, and 102; central concerns of 101; class bias 101; context of 98; disasters, and 102; enormity of environmental problems, and 105–6; facilitating committee 75–6; Hurricane Katrina, and 102–4; imaginaries of injustice 98–99; interconnections of 101; vulnerabilities, and 104; Yucca Mountain 104–5

Factory Act of 1948 60
Fritz, Charles 21
Fukushima accident 16–17

Gabriel, Y. 15
Garcia-Acosta 16
Gender 60–2
Ghosh, Devleena 3, 7, 55–66
Gilkes, Kai 31
global financial crisis 91–3; asymmetries revealed by 92; contrasts due to 93; links between state and corporate capitalism 91; turning point, as 91–3
Global Justice Movement 93, 109–20; anti-war protests, and 118; Australia 109–20; cancellation of CHOGM 115–16; decline of movement 112–14; Europe, and 112; evidence for collapse of movement 114–19; factors from outside movement 114; Forbes Global CEO Conference protests; global elites, and 116; Gramscian-Marxist framework, and 110; interviews with activists 110–11; lack of existing spaces 117; movement identity 111; Nike superstore protest, and 111–12; pre-existing weakness of 117–19; reawakening of 119–20; "reflexive activists" 111; United States, and 118–19
Global North 92
Global South 92
globalization; definition of 143
Goodman, James 2,3, 8, 69–79
green economy 69–79; *Another Future is Possible* 76–8; "bio-civilisation" 75, 76; "business as usual" 72; class antagonism 70–2; dynamic potentials 78–9; exploitation, and 79; Gramscian theory, and 70; governmental spheres 74; reports 73–4; social movements, and 76; static outcomes 78–9; UN Rio 20+, and 69–70, 73–4; UNEP, and 79
Gurbaxani, Prakash 60

Habermas, Jurgen 144–5
Hadden, Jennifer 112, 118 -19
Hansell, Saul 26,28
Hardt, M. 71, 133
Harvey, David 5, 72, 92
hegemony 69–79; forging of 73–5
Hewitt, K. 20
Ho, Karen 32
Hochschild, Arlie 56
Hodge, Bob 3, 6–7, 13–23
Holloway, John 132
Homer-Dixon, Thomas 19
Hong Kong 9–10,123–34; changing mediascape of 130–1; destruction of piers 123–4; gentrification, and 124–5; Hong Kong Administrative Region 125–6; mass demonstrations 130; metropolis of 132–3; Piers Preservation Movement 123, 125–30; spatial reordering 125; urban development 133
Hong Kong In-Media 126; platform as 127
Houston, Donna 2,9, 97–106
Humphrys, Elizabeth 9, 109–20
Hurricane Ike 28
Hurricane Katrina 7, 19–20, 99, 102–4; media images of 102; social inequalities of 103
Hydra Paradox 6–7. 13–23; CEO opinions 14; ; chaos theory, and 17–18; disaster management, and 20–1; definition 7; globalisation, and 21–2; Google hits of 13; management fantasy, and 15; meanings of 15–16; "mindset" 17; nature of myth 15; paradox, as 14; recent manifestations of myth 16
Hyogo Declaration and Framework for Action 22

IBM 14
India Today 57
Indignados 119
Information Workspace 26
Ingham, I. 20
International Council for Science 74
International Standards Organisation 46–7; institutionalisation of practices 47
Interventionism 83–94; *glocal* imaginaries 93
Iraq War 19–20; trajectory of 84–5

Kalantzis, Mary 115
Katz, Cindy 99, 103

INDEX

Kliman, A. 25
Klein. N. 2, 19
Knee, Jonathan 26

Latin America Disaster Resilience network 20
Lewig, K. 56
Liboiron, M. 93

Mann, Geoff 101
marriage 62–5; opposition of families 63–4; toll on 64
Marshall, Jonathan Paul 3, 7, 25–37
Michaelson, A. 32
Mies, M. 61
Mirchandani, Kiran 57
Minns, J. 110
Misztal, B. 22
Mugabe, Robert 116
Munck, R. 3
My Life as A Quant 32

Nadeem, Shahzad 57
Negri, A. 71
neoliberalism 41–51, 142–3; 9/11 security drivers 44; applying resilience 42–3; Hong Kong, and 124; learning from 50–1; New Orleans 103, 106; operationalising policy context 44–5; organisational characteristic, as 43; preparedness 45 ; professional network 45–6; religion and, 145–7; resilience, and 41–2, 44–50; roots of 42–3; secularism, and 142–3; wealth creation 147; "zombie neoliberalism" 42
New York Times 26

O'Connor, J. 2
Obama, Barack 145–146
Ohmae, K. 65
The Occupied Wall Street Journal 90
Occupy cosmopolitanism 85–91; connection to local activist networks and unions 87; consensus, difficulty of 90; contrasts between 93–4; critical reflections of 89; globalist views of movement 87; inconsistencies of 89; inequality, and 92; process of 86; racial and communal divisions 89; resistance within the resistance 89; studies on 85; trends of 88; views of 85
Occupy NYC Declaration Flowchart 90–1

Per Bak 17–18
piers preservation movement 123, 125–30; democracy of 134; diverse modes of protest, and 127–8; emotional responses of 126–7; events 129–30; new social subject, creation of 133; social impact of 125; symbolism of 125–6; symbols of colonialism, and 128
Piowachue 16
Po, Leung 126
Poster, Mark 56

Reitan, Ruth 119
religion 139–50; academic literature of 141; crisis of secularism 139–40; globalism, and 145–8; globalization, effect of 140; growing influence of 140; justice-globalist values 148; neoliberalism 142–7; neotraditionalism, and 149; new-ageism 150; processes of globalization, and 141; religious language 147; religious movements 146; resistance to dogmatic approach 141; response to global crisis 143–4; violence ,and 149
resilience 44–50; contradiction of 45; disasters, and 48; future research 49; measure of 49–50; policies and standards 45; rigidity trap 47–50; UK and 49
rigidity trap 47–50
Rio +20 69–70, 73–77
Rio de Janeiro 22
Risk Management Standard 47
Robertson, R.T. 22, 86
Rodriguez, Clemencia 127
Rogers, Peter 7, 41–51
Romney, Mitt 145–6

Salleh, Ariel 8, 69–79
Salmon, F. 26, 28, 31
Seattle protests 109–10
Sau-chong, So 127
secularism 139–50; crisis of 139; Enlightenment, and 144
Smith, Adam 18–19
Smith, Nigel 101
Solnit, Rebecca 7, 19, 102–4
Special Issue 5
Silent Spring 100, 106
Spickard, J. 149
Steger, Manfred B. 10, 139
Stockholm Resilience Centre 43
Synthesis Report 73

Taleb, Nassim Nicholas 28–9
Tarrow Sidney 112, 118–19
Temporary Autonomous Zone 128, 129; definition of 129
Times of India 59
Toft, M. 149–50
transformation 4–6; crisis, and 6; *laissez-faire* capitalism, and 5

INDEX

transversalization 83–94; Occupy Cosmopolitanism, and 86; definition of 86–8; *ideological*
Trivedi, Harish 59–60

Uggla, F. 88
UK Cabinet Office 44
United Nations 8, 46–7
Upside of Down 19
Urry, J. 14, 17

Van de Pijl, K. 70

Wainwright, Joel 101
Ward, Vicki 32
Wilson, Erin K. 10, 139

World Bank 57
World Business Council for Sustainable Development 74
World Economic Forum 5
World Social Forum 5
World Trade Organization 109

Yang, P.H. 129
Yucca Mountain 104–5; burial of radioactive waste, and 105; demise of project 105

Zadeh, Lofti 18
Zoque 16